Knowledge Organization and Classification in International Information Retrieval

Knowledge Organization and Classification in International Information Retrieval has been co-published simultaneously as *Cataloging & Classification Quarterly*, Volume 37, Numbers 1/2 2003.

Knowledge Organization and Classification in International Information Retrieval

Nancy J. Williamson, PhD
Clare Beghtol, PhD
Editors

Knowledge Organization and Classification in International Information Retrieval has been co-published simultaneously as *Cataloging & Classification Quarterly,* Volume 37, Numbers 1/2 2003.

Routledge
Taylor & Francis Group
NEW YORK AND LONDON

First published by
The Haworth Press, Inc., 10 Alice Street, Binghamton, NY 13904-1580

This edition published 2013 by Routledge

Routledge
Taylor & Francis Group
711 Third Avenue
New York, NY 10017

Routledge
Taylor & Francis Group
2 Park Square, Milton Park
Abingdon, Oxon OX14 4RN

Knowledge Organization and Classification in International Information Retrieval has been co-published simultaneously as *Cataloging & Classification Quarterly*, Volume 37, Numbers 1/2 2003.

Cover design by Jennifer M. Gaska.

Library of Congress Cataloging-in-Publication Data

Knowledge organization and classification in international information retrieval / Nancy J. Williamson, Clare Beghtol, editors.
p. cm.
"Co-published simultaneously as Cataloging & classification quarterly, volume 37, numbers 1/2, 2003."
Includes bibliographical references and index.
ISBN 0-7890-2354-7 (alk. paper) – ISBN 0-7890-2355-5 (pbk. : alk. paper)
1. Information organization. 2. Classification. 3. Information retrieval. I. Williamson, Nancy Joyce. II. Beghtol, Clare, 1942-
Z666.5.K59 2003
025–dc22

2003027498

Knowledge Organization and Classification in International Information Retrieval

CONTENTS

ABOUT THE EDITORS

Nancy J. Williamson, PhD, is Professor Emeritus, Faculty of Information Studies, University of Toronto, Toronto, Canada, where she taught courses in organization of information for 30 years. Now retired, Dr. Williamson continues to teach a course in the Subject Approach to Information. She is a member of the Editorial Board of *CCQ*, a member of ASISt and of the American Library Association. In the case of ALA, she has served as chair of the Subject Analysis Committee, chair of the Cataloging and Classification Section, and Director-at-Large of ALCTS. In addition, Dr. Williamson has been active in a number of international organizations, including the IFLA, Standing Committee on Classification and Indexing, and Chair of the FID Committee on Classification Research (FID/CR). Currently she is a member of the Executive Board of the International Society for Knowledge Organization (ISKO), and is working with the Editor of UDC on research into the "feasibility of the conversion of UDC into a fully faceted classification system."

Clare Beghtol, PhD, is Associate Professor, Associate Dean and Graduate Coordinator, Faculty of Information Studies, University of Toronto, Toronto, Canada. She is former President of the International Society for Knowledge Organization (ISKO) and serves as a Consulting Editor for its journal *Knowledge Organization*. Dr. Beghtol is active in the American Society for Information Science and Technology (ASISt) and in its Special Interest Group for Classification Research (SIC/CR), of which she is a former Chair. She teaches courses on bibliographic control, theories of classification and knowledge organization, and the practice of major bibliographic classification and subject heading systems. In addition, Dr. Beghtol is Faculty Liaison for the Iter Gateway to the Middle Ages and Renaissance web portal project (http://www.itergateway.org/) and advises on subject systems for its Iter Bibliography for Middle Ages and Renaissance Materials, which uses the Library of Congress Subject Headings (LCSH) and the Dewey Decimal Classification (DDC). Her current research concerns ethical questions for knowledge organization in light of issues resulting from the globalization of information and knowledge.

Introduction

The field of knowledge organization and classification occupies a particularly essential place in our efforts to deal with the increasing globalization of information and knowledge. The technical ability to connect the world to all kinds of information resources and services via the Internet, multinational intranets, and domain portals and gateways has outpaced our ability to address the problems of information retrieval for specific linguistic, cultural, and domain communities of discourse. Articles in this volume address these closely related issues from the vantage points of a number of areas of research and practice in knowledge organization and classification. Authors from Canada, France, India, Rumania, Spain and the United States address the issues from much broader perspectives than those of their own linguistic, cultural and domain preferences. In this way, we have attempted to provide issues that span the boundaries of nationality, of language, of kinds of knowledge organization and classification systems, of information and knowledge domains, of information and knowledge resources, and of different approaches to the cultural semantics of the globalization of information and knowledge.

Specifically, this volume is divided into four sections that address major themes for internationalized information and knowledge. Papers in the first section, "General Bibliographic Systems," concern the future of general bibliographic classification systems–how they can be adapted for the requirements of specific subject contexts, how their conceptual constructs can be compared and possibly modified, and how the problems that arise from the specificity of concepts expressed in different languages can be exposed and addressed. Papers in the second section, "Information Organization in Knowledge Resources," look at knowledge organization and classification as one of the vital components within specific kinds of information and knowledge re-

---

[Haworth co-indexing entry note]: "Introduction." Williamson, Nancy J., and Clare Beghtol. Co-published simultaneously in *Cataloging & Classification Quarterly* (The Haworth Information Press, an imprint of The Haworth Press, Inc.) Vol. 37, No. 1/2, 2003, pp. 1-2; and: *Knowledge Organization and Classification in International Information Retrieval* (ed: Nancy J. Williamson, and Clare Beghtol) The Haworth Information Press, an imprint of The Haworth Press, Inc., 2003, pp. 1-2. Single or multiple copies of this article are available for a fee from The Haworth Document Delivery Service [1-800-HAWORTH, 9:00 a.m. - 5:00 p.m. (EST). E-mail address: docdelivery@haworthpress.com].

http://www.haworthpress.com/store/product.asp?sku=J104

Digital Object Identifier: 10.1300/J104v37n01_01

sources: the interrelationships of knowledge organization and classification in libraries and on the Web; classificatory structures in web resources for education; the creation of knowledge-based products using knowledge organization and classification techniques; and as knowledge discovery tools that can operate across domains. "Linguistics, Terminology, and Natural Language Processing" includes analyses of the state-of-the-art in natural human language processing, the potential of terminological theory and research for the design of information retrieval tools and resources, and the linguistic issues that arise in the creation of metadata crosswalks and tagging for large-scale knowledge repositories. Finally, the section "Knowledge in the World and the World of Knowledge" addresses the ontological foundations of knowledge organization and classification, views of knowledge management in organizations from different cultural perspectives, and the effect of differing purposes on knowledge organization and classification systems for the same domain.

We hope that you will find these papers as stimulating as we have and that engagement with these issues and perspectives will prove rewarding and challenging for both the theory and practice of knowledge organization and classification systems.

Nancy J. Williamson
Clare Beghtol

The Future of General Classification

Jens-Erik Mai

SUMMARY. Discusses problems related to accessing multiple collections using a single retrieval language. Surveys the concepts of interoperability and switching language. Finds that mapping between more indexing languages always will be an approximation. Surveys the issues related to general classification and contrasts that to special classifications. Argues for the use of general classifications to provide access to collections nationally and internationally. *[Article copies available for a fee from The Haworth Document Delivery Service: 1-800-HAWORTH. E-mail address: <docdelivery@haworthpress.com> Website: <http://www.HaworthPress.com> © 2003 by The Haworth Press, Inc. All rights reserved.]*

KEYWORDS. Interoperability, switching languages, general classification, special classification

Jens-Erik Mai, PhD, is Assistant Professor, Information School, University of Washington, Mary Gates Hall, Suite 370, Box 352840, Seattle, WA 98195-2840 USA (E-mail: jemai@u.washington.edu).

[Haworth co-indexing entry note]: "The Future of General Classification." Mai, Jens-Erik. Co-published simultaneously in *Cataloging & Classification Quarterly* (The Haworth Information Press, an imprint of The Haworth Press, Inc.) Vol. 37, No. 1/2, 2003, pp. 3-12; and: *Knowledge Organization and Classification in International Information Retrieval* (ed: Nancy J. Williamson, and Clare Beghtol) The Haworth Information Press, an imprint of The Haworth Press, Inc., 2003, pp. 3-12. Single or multiple copies of this article are available for a fee from The Haworth Document Delivery Service [1-800-HAWORTH, 9:00 a.m. - 5:00 p.m. (EST). E-mail address: docdelivery@haworthpress.com].

http://www.haworthpress.com/store/product.asp?sku=J104

Digital Object Identifier: 10.1300/J104v37n01_02

INTRODUCTION

The exchange of bibliographic records is common and the interest in interoperability is growing. The latter is the notion that users from one interface and using one search language will be able to search multiple databases and collections at the same time. Exchange of bibliographic records and interoperability is of interest, not only because of economic advantages, but also because of the possibilities of increasing the exchange of ideas across domains and the possibilities of more exhaustive search results.

For the purpose of analyzing the issues related to the development of such future information systems it might be sensible to separate the issues related to descriptive cataloging from the issues related to subject representation. This paper will treat the issues related to subject representation and will furthermore focus on the use of general classification schemes for accessing documents across domains and collections.

The core idea explored here is that if documents in different collections were organized and represented with a common classification system, then access to the material would be enhanced since the documents on the same subject matter would be classified under the same entry across all collections. This idea is far from new. In fact, this is the core of Dewey's "invention" of the decimal classification system by which he envisioned that all knowledge could be classified. Francis Miksa[1] explains:

> There can be little doubt that Dewey fully intended to make an extensive, hierarchically arranged scheme, which covered all knowledge, a scheme that could be used in libraries to organize books according to the knowledge the books contained.

The real benefit of Dewey's invention was that the same books at different libraries would have the same call numbers and that it would be easier to navigate different libraries since they would be organized in the same way. This ensured that a person searching for books about a particular subject could be sure that the books would be classified under the same entries in any library.

If those libraries were connected in a network a user could, in fact, retrieve the bibliographic records for books on a particular topic even though only a fraction of the books were included in a particular library's collection and the rest were scattered in a number of libraries around the country–or even around the world.

This is not a novel idea. Dorothy May Norris[2] explains how English Franciscan monks in the late 13th century created a shared catalog, *Registrum Librorum Angliae*, of collections in 183 English monastery libraries. The monks traveled from monastery to monastery and used the shared catalog to keep informed about what works were available at the different libraries that they planned to visit.

The traditional suggestion to solve the problem of interoperability has been to create a switching language to translate back and forth between different classification systems. Although this has generally been considered a very difficult task, the idea is gaining new attention, especially since the Internet has provided opportunities to search in more information retrieval systems simultaneously.

This paper reviews the applicability of subject interoperability and evaluates the purpose of special and general classification schemes, and suggests that the purpose of general classification schemes is to facilitate interoperability among different information retrieval systems and that the purpose of special classification schemes, on the other hand, is to give access to the material at a greater level of exhaustivity and specificity.

INTEROPERABILITY

There is a sense in the information science community that, with the advent of the World Wide Web (WWW), the previous models for information use have become obsolete. William Moen[3] states that "The convergence of computer and communications technologies of the late 20th century has profoundly affected information creation, distribution, access, and use," and this has caused a change in how people access information; he continues: "Few would deny that the Internet, primarily through the World Wide Web, has increased users' expectations for access to information."[4] Reflecting on personal experience, it is correct that many of us have changed our information behavior lately. In researching for this paper, for instance, I frequently searched different catalogs and databases for relevant literature right here at my desk and I printed the articles on the printer right next to me, and there is no doubt that I tend to expect that this is possible today. In that sense, one could say that the access to the material has changed significantly with the advent of these technologies. However, the meaning of the term access is crucial here. The way I have used access above has been to talk about how I gained access to the physical documents via a network connection and printed on a local printer. Nevertheless, the real question for the information profession is how these technologies have changed the way we provide access to the documents in terms of search facilities. That is, how has the advent of network technologies changed the way we build and use search mechanisms? In this sense, access refers to the knowledge organization and information retrieval tools that are used.

The creation of the WWW and networks has brought forth the idea of *interoperability*. This concept is used and referred to in many places in the literature and in current practice, but the exact definition of the term is still discussed. Arms et al.[5] offer this definition:

> The goal of interoperability is to build coherent services for users, from components that are technically different and managed by different organizations. This requires agreements to cooperate at three levels: technical, content, and organizational.

Of these three levels, the content level is of special interest here. This level covers "data and metadata, and includes semantic agreements on the interpretation of the information."[6] The descriptive representation of documents has received much attention among interoperability researchers, whereas subject representation is neglected, overviewed, or regarded as unproblematic.

Traditionally, there have been two avenues to ensure some degree of subject interoperability across different collections, as indicated by Lancaster[7] (citing Neelameghan):

1. To use an intermediate language or switching language through, or by, which one moves from one information system to another.
2. To use the same or very nearly the same information storage and retrieval language in all the information systems.

There has been much research into the problems related to switching languages and compatibility of different indexing language systems. Dahlberg[8] has produced an annotated bibliography that covers 450 entities and 40 years of work in the area. Switching language is the idea that a user could use the same indexing language to search in information systems that are indexed with different indexing languages. Lancaster explains, "A user could sit at a terminal in center A and enter terms from A's vocabulary. The terms would be converted to the codes of X and switched to the appropriate terms in, say, D's vocabulary."[9]

The basic idea of a switching language is that the user would only have to learn one retrieval system and one controlled vocabulary and that the user would be able to use that one system to search a range of different systems simultaneously. For this to be possible, each of the indexing languages would have to be mapped against the common switching language (denoted as X in Figure 1). It would be rather simple to add another indexing language to the list of indexing languages that can be switched between them, and there is no limit to the number of indexing languages that could be attached to the switching language.

It must, however, be expected that "a reasonable level of commonality in subject matter . . . exist among centers; otherwise there would be little point in the activity."[10] It would be very difficult to switch between a thesaurus on

FIGURE 1. A Switching Language

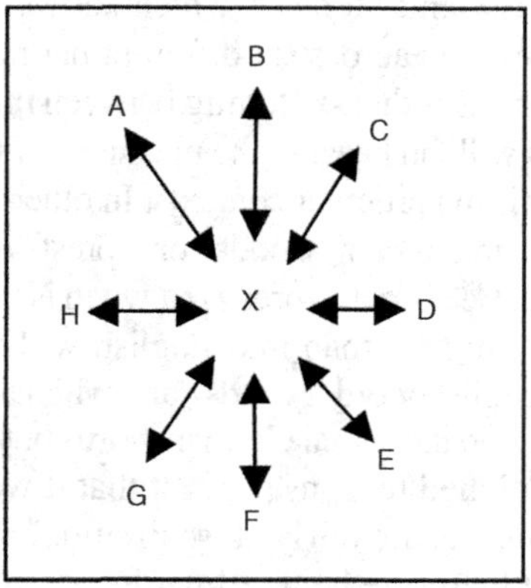

physics and a thesaurus on sociology, whereas it would be easier to switch between a number of thesauri on either of the subjects fields.

With modern information technologies the work involved in mapping between the indexing languages and the switching language is reasonable. However, the main problem related to switching languages goes beyond technology and labor and is really a problem that is buried in language and meaning. The main problem can be summed up to that fact that there very seldom exists an indexing term *Q* in an indexing language *A* that has the exact same meaning as an indexing term *Q'* in indexing language *B*, even for indexing languages that cover the same subject field. In other words, the mapping will always be an approximation.

There are three main reasons for this:

1. Pre-coordination. The levels and kinds of pre-coordination vary from indexing language to indexing language, so a concept might not be expressed using the exact same coordination of terms in two indexing languages.
2. Hierarchical structure. The meaning of any indexing term in an indexing language is determined by the term's place in the hierarchical structure, so even if the same term exists in two indexing languages the meaning of the terms might not be the same.
3. Absence of concepts. The level of specificity might vary from indexing language to indexing language, so concepts that are expressed in one indexing language are not expressed in the other indexing language.

In an international environment, where more natural languages are involved, the absence of concepts takes another twist. It is only seldom that there exist one-to-one relationships between words in different natural languages. Birger Hjørland,[11] following Hjelmslev, gives the example in Figure 2 of the words "tree," "wood," "woods," and "forest," which shows that these words do not have one-to-one counterparts across six different natural languages.

The consequence for this is that switching between indexing languages in different natural languages will fail because the meanings of the words are determined from the use of the words in particular contexts. In other words, the German word "wald" can be translated into either "woods" or "forest" depending on the context. It is obvious that a single tree is not a forest, but when is a woods large enough be a forest? A person translating German into English will have to make a decision about when to use the English word "woods" and when to use the word "forest"; a decision that is not based on the actual German words but on the use and context.

The three aforementioned reasons suggest that it would only be possible to switch between systems that are fairly close in subject coverage and classificatory structure. It might therefore be worthwhile to consider the second avenue to ensuring interoperability between different collections, namely that of using the same indexing language for multiple collections. This takes us back to Dewey's idea about the classification of the universe of knowledge that I refer to in the introduction.

GENERAL AND SPECIAL CLASSIFICATION

The basic idea behind general classification is that a single classification covers the entire universe of knowledge, that is, all subject fields. There are today a number of such systems in use across the world. Some of these are common and used in many libraries, some are widely known but not used in many (or any) libraries, and some are constructed specifically for one particular library. There exist, furthermore, a number of special classification systems that only cover a part of the universe of knowledge, in the sense that these systems focus on specific subject fields.

FIGURE 2. Cultural Relativity in Word Meanings

<table>
<tr><th>English</th><th>German</th><th>Danish</th><th>French</th><th>Italian</th><th>Spanish</th></tr>
<tr><td></td><td>Baum</td><td rowspan="2">Træ</td><td>Arbre</td><td>Albero</td><td>Arbol</td></tr>
<tr><td rowspan="2">Wood</td><td rowspan="2">Holz</td><td rowspan="3">Bois</td><td rowspan="2">Legno</td><td>Lena</td></tr>
<tr><td rowspan="3">Skov</td><td>Madera</td></tr>
<tr><td>Woods</td><td rowspan="2">Wald</td><td>Basco</td><td>Basque</td></tr>
<tr><td>Forest</td><td>Foret</td><td>Foresta</td><td>Selva</td></tr>
</table>

The distinction between general and special classification is generally taken to be that, "A general classification covers the whole of being; a special classification some parts of it."[12] However, this distinction is not the most helpful because any "special" classification scheme will, in reality, provide for a broad range in subject matter. As Derek Langridge explains: "There is no such thing as a special library in this sense: all special libraries contain a range of subjects in addition to their central interest."[13] It might be more helpful to think of any classification scheme as a classification scheme that has a special purpose.

In spite of the fact that there exist a number of general classification systems, the nature and status of general classification systems have been discussed in the literature and it has often been concluded that the construction and use of such general systems is unattainable. Brian Vickery[14] lists five reasons why existing general classification systems are unsatisfactory:

1. Most of them do not give adequate detail for accurate specification of the highly complex subjects in papers and reports that documentation must handle today.
2. Despite the comprehensiveness and variety of certain general schemes, they do not fully cater to the special viewpoints of each particular library and information center.
3. Even if they are varied in viewpoint, they do not sufficiently provide for the flexible combination of terms which highly specific subject headings demand.
4. Even if flexible, they achieve such flexibility only by unnecessarily lengthy or complicated notational means.
5. They fail to give optimum helpfulness in filing order.

The general criticism here is that the general classification system fails to represent the documents at a level of specificity that is required or desired by the users. This is related to the notion of "the force of discrimination" (as David Blair[15] has recently named it), which dictates that the intellectual content of a document should be represented and described in as much detail as possible for any given information retrieval system. The idea is that if documents in a particular information retrieval system are described and represented as fully and specifically as possible, then the users of the system would be able to query the system for exactly those documents that are relevant to the user at that particular time.

It is a classic recommendation in the classification and indexing literature that documents should be represented as specifically as possible; it dates back to Cutter's recommendation of the *specific entry*.[16] Jack Mills[17] stated very clearly that "a classification should provide maximum detail in specification, both in the enumeration of isolates within categories and in facilities for combing these to indicate compounds." All leading textbooks and guidelines on indexing and classification follow this recommendation and advocate that the intellectual content of documents should be represented as specifically as possible.

However, the specificity of any particular document is relative to the context and use of that document. In other words, for any document it would only be possible to identify the specificity of that document relative to a particular user group, time and place, i.e., the purpose of the classification system will determine the interpretation and representation of the documents for that system.

A general classification will not have a single purpose, since the classification is not serving a particular domain or particular interests, and will therefore, in effect, not serve any purpose. As Broadfield[18] says, "a general purpose classification is likely to display no purpose at all." He continues by saying that classification for general purposes is impossible:

> While it is possible to classify the parts of medical science as specific ways in which the general medical purpose is advanced, and to classify the parts of mathematics, economics, or anthology on the same principle, to arrange these four sciences so that they all contribute to one purpose is impossible without knowing to what purpose they do contribute.[19]

A few pages later, Broadfield[20] calls on the advocates of general classification schemes to set forth the purposes that the general classifications serve,

> On those, therefore, who wish to find a theory of general classification the onus is placed of showing that there is a general purpose, that it takes various forms related as the species to the genus, and that "characteristics" essential to the working out of such a purpose throughout the system can be found.

Although special classifications only treat parts of the universe of knowledge, that treatment is relative to a specific understanding of the whole universe of knowledge. A general classification, on the other hand, assumes no special understanding or treatment of the universe of knowledge and de facto claims a neutral and objective representation of the universe of knowledge. It has been shown in numerous papers that any classification is, in fact, biased and it is generally accepted that classifications cannot be neutral and objective.[21]

The distinction between special and general classifications is that special classifications serve a specific purpose and will explicitly incorporate that specific purpose in their structure and in their representation of documents using the systems. The systems and the representation of documents will aim at being as specific as possible since this will enhance and ease the retrieval of documents. General classifications, on the other hand, have as their purposes to structure and represent potentially all subjects, and the problem in using these systems is that any document could potentially be represented in a number of ways using the system depending on context and potential use.

CONCLUSIONS, DISCUSSION AND IMPLICATIONS

There is no doubt that the future of libraries includes providing access to collections that are remote–physically, culturally, and subject wise. Also, there is no doubt that there is a pressure to facilitate access to these remote collections using modern information technology. The real question for the classification and indexing community is how these demands will and should be met.

This paper has reviewed some of the core problems related to two possible solutions to the demands, namely, that of creating switching languages and providing access to documents using a range of indexing languages and providing a mechanism to search across a number of collections simultaneously, and that of using a general classification scheme to provide access to the whole universe of knowledge via one single classification. I have shown that both of these solutions are theoretically problematic and in practice unattainable.

Subject representation is tied to the purposes, cultural, and contextual circumstances in which the representation is produced. This creates problems when the subject representation is exported from one country to another, especially if the subject representation is exhaustive and specific.

However, the international exchange of bibliographic records and the interoperability across information retrieval systems will be possible if general classification systems are used in conjunction with special indexing systems. The general classification systems will then serve as the broad organization of knowledge and the sciences, and the special systems will serve as the domain oriented organization and presentation of documents.

The purpose of general classifications will then not be to represent the documents as specifically as possible but to represent the documents for the purpose of stating which domain and sub-domains that the documents potentially could be used in. Such systems will not be useable for retrieving documents on specific subjects but will be very helpful in navigating the international production of knowledge. The upshot of this suggestion is that the documents need to be represented for two quite different purposes, namely, for a potential worldwide audience and for the local users. The global users are served best if the material is represented using two different classification systems–a general and a special.

The future task for classification research is to explore the theoretical foundations and principles for the construction and use of general classification systems that serve a worldwide audience for the purpose of organizing knowledge and the sciences.

REFERENCES

1. Francis L. Miksa, *The DDC, the Universe of Knowledge, and the Post-Modern Library*. Albany, NY: Forest Press, 1998.

2. Dorothy May Norris, *A History of Cataloguing and Cataloguing Methods*. London: Grafton, 1939. pp. 30-34.

3. William E. Moen, "Interoperability for information access: Technical standards and policy considerations," *Journal of Academic Librarianship*, 26: 2 (2000): 129.

4. *Ibid.*

5. William Y. Arms, Diane Hillmann; Carl Lagoze, Dean Krafft, Marisa Richard, John Saylor, Carol Terrizzi, and Herbert Van de Sompel, "A Spectrum of interoperability: the site for science prototype for the NSDL," *D-Lib Magazine*, 8: 1 (2002). http://www.dlib.org.

6. *Ibid.*

7. F. W. Lancaster, *Vocabulary Control for Information Retrieval*, 2nd edition. Arlington, VA: Information Resources Press, 1986. p. 80.

8. Ingetraut Dahlberg, "The compatibility guidelines–a re-evaluation" in *Compatibility and Integration of Order Systems: Research Seminar Proceedings of the TIP/ISKO Meeting, Warsaw, 13-15 September 1995*. Warsaw: Wydawnictwo, 1996. pp. 32-45.

9. as 7, p. 189.

10. as 7, p. 190.

11. Birger Hjørland, "Principia informatica: foundational theory of information and principles of information services," in *Emerging Frameworks and Methods: Proceedings of the Fourth International Conference on Conceptions of Library and Information Science*. Greenwood Village, CO: Libraries Unlimited, 2002. p. 113.

12. W.C. Berwick Sayers, *An Introduction to Library Classification, Theoretical, Historical and Practical, with Readings, Exercises and Examination Papers*. London: Grafton, 1944. §118.

13. Derek W. Langridge, "Alternative starting points in classification," *Cataloging & Classification Quarterly* 19: 3/4 (1995): 7.

14. Brian C. Vickery, *Faceted Classification: A Guide to Construction and Use of Special Schemes*. London: Aslib, 1960. p. 7.

15. David C. Blair, "The Challenge of commercial document retrieval, Part I: Major issues, and a framework based on search exhaustivity, determinacy of representation and document collection size," *Information Processing and Management* 38 (2001): 273-291.

16. Charles A. Cutter, *Rules for a Printed Dictionary Catalog: US Bureau of Education, Special Report on Public Libraries*. Washington DC: US Government Printing Office, 1876.

17. Jack Mills, "Inadequacies of existing general classification schemes," in *Some Problems of a General Classification Scheme: Report of a Conference Held in London, June 1963*. London: Library Association, 1964. p. 33.

18. A. Broadfield, *The Philosophy of Classification*. London: Grafton, 1946. p. 87.

19. *Ibid.*

20. as 18, p. 89.

21. Hope Olson, "Mapping beyond Dewey's boundaries: Constructing classificatory space for marginalized knowledge domains," *Library Trends* 47: 2 (1998): 233:254.

22. Paul Miller, "Interoperability: What is it and why should I want it?" *Ariadne* 24 (2000), http://www.ariadne.ac.uk/.

Adapting Dominant Classifications to Particular Contexts

Angela Kublik
Virginia Clevette
Dennis Ward
Hope A. Olson

SUMMARY. This paper addresses the process of adapting to a particular culture or context a classification that has grown out of western culture to become a global standard. The authors use a project that adapts *DDC* for use in a feminist/women's issues context to demonstrate an approach that works. The project is particularly useful as an interdisciplinary example. Discussion consists of four parts: (1) definition of the problem indicating the need for adaptation and efforts to date; (2) description of the methodology developed for creating an expansion; (3) description of the interface developed for actually doing the work, with its potential for a distributed group to work on it together (could even be internationally distributed); and

Angela Kublik, Virginia Clevette, Dennis Ward and Hope A. Olson are all affiliated with the School of Library & Information Studies, University of Alberta.

Address correspondence to: Professor Hope A. Olson, PhD, School of Library and Information Studies, University of Alberta, 3-20 Rutherford South, Edmonton, Alberta T6G 2J4, Canada (E-mail: hope.olson@ualberta.ca).

This research was funded by the Social Sciences and Humanities Research Council of Canada Research Grant 410-98-1588.

[Haworth co-indexing entry note]: "Adapting Dominant Classifications to Particular Contexts." Kublik, Angela et al. Co-published simultaneously in *Cataloging & Classification Quarterly* (The Haworth Information Press, an imprint of The Haworth Press, Inc.) Vol. 37, No. 1/2, 2003, pp. 13-31; and: *Knowledge Organization and Classification in International Information Retrieval* (ed: Nancy J. Williamson, and Clare Beghtol) The Haworth Information Press, an imprint of The Haworth Press, Inc., 2003, pp. 13-31. Single or multiple copies of this article are available for a fee from The Haworth Document Delivery Service [1-800-HAWORTH, 9:00 a.m. - 5:00 p.m. (EST). E-mail address: docdelivery@haworthpress.com].

http://www.haworthpress.com/store/product.asp?sku=J104

Digital Object Identifier: 10.1300/J104v37n01_03

(4) generalization of how the methodology could be used for particular contexts by country, ethnicity, perspective or other defining factors.

KEYWORDS. *Dewey Decimal Classification*, feminism, women's issues, adaptation of classification systems

INTRODUCTION

Critiques of the representation of marginalized groups and cultures and related topics in standard subject access vocabularies abound. Hope A. Olson and Rose Schlegl (2001) found, in an extensive analysis of these critiques, that most of these critiques focus on the widely used standards: *Dewey Decimal Classification* (*DDC*), *Library of Congress Classification* (*LCC*), and *Library of Congress Subject Headings* (p. 67). Many are concerned with the representation of women or feminist topics. Most critiques are analyses of problems. Some of the critiques also offer solutions, in particular, discussions of classification schemes that describe supplements (or, in *DDC* parlance, expansions). Tamara Lincoln (1987) describes a supplement to *LCC* for Alaskan Native languages. Poori Soltani (1996) describes the need for expansions in Iran and Arabic countries. Others have suggested revisions such as Fraiser McConnell's (1984, 1985, 1985a) proposed changes to *DDC* for peoples, languages and geography of Melanesia.

Most interesting in relation to this article is the work by Oh Dong-Guen and Yeo Ji-Suk (2001) to adapt *DDC*'s religion schedules for use in countries characterized by religious diversity (having no single dominant religion) with Korea as the exemplar. Oh and Yeo present one of the few conceptually grounded discussions of the process of addressing the cultural limitations of mainstream classification. Our research project develops a model for this process and tests it by creating a women's studies supplement (or expansion) to *DDC*. We believe that our model is potentially transferable to other cultural contexts marginalized in mainstream classifications.

METHODOLOGY

To develop a supplement to a standard classification scheme requires four steps:

1. identification of gaps and instances of bias in relation to the marginalized group or culture of interest

2. development of a plan for addressing these problems
3. implementation of the plan
4. testing the efficacy of the result.

To identify the gaps and instances of bias in *DDC* in relation to women's studies, we used a specialized vocabulary, *A Women's Thesaurus* (Capek 1987), developed by a diverse group of librarians and subject specialists, drawing on 35 earlier feminist vocabularies and tested at a wide range of U.S. and international sites. We endeavoured to link each of its approximately 5,000 descriptors to one or more *DDC* numbers. Some topics had no corresponding *DDC* number and so suggested a gap for potential expansion. Other topics were linked to *DDC* numbers of varying appropriateness. We assessed each of these links for goodness of fit using three variables: coextensiveness, reflection of gender, and rhetorical space (for details see http://www.ualberta.ca/~holson/femclass/variables.htm). Coextensiveness is how well the number accommodates the topic. Results fell into four categories: a close match, a number broader than the descriptor, partial coverage of the descriptor topic, or no match. The second variable, reflection of gender, assessed whether and by what means a gendered treatment of the topic could be indicated in the *DDC* number. The most common means is adding the notation for "women" from the *DDC* standard subdivisions (Table 1). The third variable, rhetorical space, looks beyond the number itself to its context. How comfortably will a topic sit in a particular number. What else is classified in the same number? What topics sit on either side of it? Where is it in the hierarchy?

Assessment of the links helped us to identify nine *DDC* ranges of particular importance for feminist expansion and revision:

133.4 Demonology and witchcraft

155.3 Sex psychology and psychology of the sexes

170 Ethics (Moral philosophy)

305.42 Social role and status of women

306.7 Institutions pertaining to relations of the sexes

331.4 Women workers

360 Social problems and services

390 Customs, etiquette, folklore

610 Medicine

Other individual numbers were also identified as problematic. Perhaps most dramatic was the need to accommodate feminist theory as a topic in itself and as an aspect of other topics.

The process of building the expansion has two aspects: the development of content and its enablement through use of information technology. This process will be discussed in some detail in the next two sections.

The final step in this project was to test the expansion for its applicability. Two tests were used. The first test involved finding terms in the *Canadian Women's Thesaurus/Le thesaurus feministe du Canada* (1990) that do not appear in *A Women's Thesaurus* and verifying that the combination of *DDC* and our expansion could accommodate these additional topics. The second test classified a sample of new print publications and web pages in a wide range of feminist and women's studies topics to ensure that newer topics had not been missed. Both of these tests were largely successful and the few topics not covered were duly integrated into the expansion.

Our project was executed as a research study to test a method as well as produce an expansion. It was made possible by a grant from the Social Sciences and Humanities Research Council of Canada. Over the course of three years two library school faculty and two or three master's students each summer implemented this work and a related project (for details see http://lily.slis.ualberta.ca/nodewey/). The description of our project will be followed by a discussion of its generalizability.

PLAN FOR ADDRESSING BIAS AND OMISSION

Our plan includes three approaches or contexts for change: "global," "regional," and "local." "Global" revisions are intended to remedy the clearest marginalizations and exclusions. "Regional" changes (regional in the sense of feminist or women's studies as an area of study) are intended to offer greater specificity. "Local" adaptations are suggested options that can be used to contextualize *DDC* to an individual situation–changes that allow for different emphasis and interpretation in particular libraries.

These three contexts are informed by specifications particular to the standard–in this project the five "kinds of development," as described in the *DDC Editorial Rules* manual:

1. Major revision (New schedule): "The schedule has been completely reworked and has been removed to a new location so that there is no conflict with the old schedule" (1).

2. Major revision (Complete revision): "The base number remains the same as in the previous edition, but virtually all of the subdivisions are changed" (1).
3. Major revision (Extensive revision): "The base number and main outline of the schedule remains intact, but many of the subdivisions are reworked" (1).
4. Moderate revision: "The schedule undergoes revision with expansions, reductions, regularization of structure, and new terminology and wording" (2).
5. Minor revision: "The old text is edited to conform to current rules" (2).

While making changes within the three contexts–global, regional, and local–all five kinds of revision were used. By working within these five "kinds of development," we were able to develop techniques compatible, for the most part, with the current schedules.

IMPLEMENTATION

Within the "global" context we have made suggestions for revisions that create rhetorical spaces within the existing schedules to allow feminist voices to be heard. Typically, global changes are minor or moderate revisions, in terms of the *DDC* editorial policy. For example, in the 21st edition of *DDC* (*DDC21*, current at the time of writing), nursing personnel are not classed as a subdivision of 610.695 "Specific kinds of medical personnel," but are instead assigned the number 610.73069, which is a subdivision of education and research. By classifying the topic of "nursing personnel" under education and research, it has been effectively ghettoized. Library users browsing the shelves for books about the medical professions may not find books about nursing, since they would be shelved some distance away from the materials about physicians and technicians. To solve this problem, we have simply moved nurses to a number now vacant in the health personnel section, thus classing it in an open rhetorical space:

610	Medical Sciences Medicine
610.6	Organizations, management, professions
610.69	Medical personnel
610.695	Specific kinds of medical personnel
610.6952	Physicians
610.6953	Medical technicians and assistants
610.6954	**Nursing personnel (proposed number)**

610.7	Education, research, nursing, ...
610.71	Education
610.72	Research; statistical methodology
610.73	Nursing and services of medical techs...
[610.73069	**Nursing personnel (DDC21 number)]**

This revision is minor in terms of the *DDC* editorial policy.

Some of the global changes we proposed were, however, more extensive. For example, the proposed changes to 360 "Social problems and services; associations" would be considered a moderate revision, since we have changed much of the terminology within the schedule in order to shift the emphasis from "social *problems*" to "social *issues*," thus alleviating the problem of marginalized groups being represented as "problems." In the current schedule, social services to "unmarried mothers" are classed under 362.8392. The heading "unmarried mothers" is benign in and of itself, and would appear to create an open rhetorical space in which to class materials that provide information about social services to unmarried mothers. However, the context within which the heading exists is more problematic because the prominence of the word "problems" in the hierarchy implies, through hierarchical force, that unmarried mothers are considered to be a "problem." By changing the terminology throughout the 360s schedule, to emphasize "social issues" and "social services" rather than "social problems," a more positive rhetorical space has been created. Table 1 compares the current and proposed schedules.

The regional changes that have been suggested are compatible with *DDC*, even while they allow for the classification of concepts previously excluded or marginalized by being subsumed within a broader number. One example of a regional change is the provision for feminism as a theoretical viewpoint in the 140s, and the creation of a parallel "Table X," which allows for numbers to be built to represent specific schools of feminist theory.

When the terms from *A Women's Thesaurus* were mapped to *DDC*, the term "feminism" was assigned the number 305.42:

300	Social sciences
305	Social groups
305.4	Women
305.42	Social role and status of women

Although this seems like an appropriate place for discussions of feminism, since the purpose of many feminist works is to examine the social role and sta-

TABLE 1. Comparison of Current and Proposed 360 Schedule

	Current DDC21 Heading	**Proposed Heading**
360	Social problems and services; associations	Social issues and services; associations
362	Social welfare problems and services	Social services to marginalized groups of persons
362.8	Problems of and services to other groups	Services to other marginalized groups
362.83	Women	Services to specific classes of women *Add to base number 362.839 notation 08 from Table 1 to indicate specific classes of women, e.g., 362.83908697 services to unmarried mothers*
362.839	Unmarried mothers	Do not use, class in 362.83908697

tus of women, 305.42 has become a catch-all number that is used to lump all discussions of women and feminism together, thus ghettoizing them. A total of 130 terms from *A Women's Thesaurus* were assigned the number 305.42 during the mapping stage of the research, including: Black women's studies, cleavage, courtesans, cross cultural feminism, debutantes, feminist ethics, first wave feminism, supermom, and women's art. Indeed, even this small number of terms clearly illustrates the need for greater specificity, as well as the need for a space in which to class discussions of feminist theory as separate from discussions of women as a social group.

As a result, a space was created for feminism and feminist theory in the 140s. This change would likely be considered a major revision (new schedule) according to the *DDC* editorial guidelines. A general idea of this development can be seen in the following summary:

140 Specific philosophical schools and view points

Including the concept of ideology, of a world view, of a system of beliefs

140.17 Feminism

140.172 Historical feminisms

140.173 General approaches

140.174 Cultural feminisms

140.175 Conceptual feminisms

140.176 Spiritual feminisms

140.177 Psychological approaches

140.178 Ecofeminism

Although the subdivisions have been omitted here (for example, General approaches has the subdivision 140.1731 Mainstream feminism, which is further subdivided to 140.17312 Liberal feminism), even this basic outline of the schedule demonstrates the increased specificity available for discussions of feminist theory. Furthermore, an additional table (nicknamed "Table X") has been created, based on this new 140.17 schedule, to allow for numbers to be built to indicate that a work in another discipline makes use of a particular feminist viewpoint.

Other changes include significant departures from standard *DDC*. One example of an extensive revision, that will likely be most useful for very specialized collections, is the schedule suggested to replace 616.8 Diseases of nervous system and mental disorders. This *DDC21* schedule was problematic because it used outdated terminology, and also because several illnesses that are associated primarily with women are ghettoized within it:

616.8 Diseases of nervous system and mental disorder

616.85 Miscellaneous diseases of nervous system and mental disorders

616.852 Neuroses

Subdivisions of 616.852 Neuroses include: Anxiety neuroses (including panic disorder), obsessive compulsive neurosis, hysterical neuroses, eating disorders (including subdivisions for anorexia nervosa and bulimia), and depressive neuroses (with the note "class here works on depression"). Thus, all of these medical conditions have been ghettoized by lumping them together, under the headings of "miscellaneous" and "neuroses." As we examined previous editions of *DDC*, it became obvious that this schedule was the result of new numbers being created as these conditions came to be recognized by the medical community. Indeed, a ghettoized number is better than no number at all. But we decided that it would be useful to have an alternative to this schedule, which has been patched and repaired many times.

The schedule we propose is based on the *Diagnostic and Statistical Manual of Mental Disorders, Fourth Edition* (*DSM-IV*). Although the *DSM-IV* has been criticized, it provides a more up-to-date basis for a new schedule that uses terminology and a classification of disorders that are the accepted standard within the medical community. The main subdivisions for the proposed schedule, which represents a major revision (complete revision) in terms of the *DDC* editorial policies, are:

616.85-616.86 Mental Disorders

616.852 Disorders usually first diagnosed in infancy, childhood, or adolescence

616.853 Delirium, dementia, and amnestic and other cognitive disorders

616.854 Schizophrenia and other psychotic disorders

616.855 Mood disorders

616.856 Anxiety disorders

616.857 Somatoform disorders

616.858 Factitious disorders

616.859 Dissociative disorders

616.861 Substance-related disorders

616.862 Sexual and gender identity disorders

616.863 Eating disorders

Much of the terminology within the schedule has changed: for instance, the word "neuroses" does not appear in this schedule, nor does the word "hysterical." Even more significant, the hierarchy no longer lumps together the wide range of disorders that were previously classified together under the heading "Neuroses," but instead distributes them throughout the schedule in appropriate places. The proposed schedule treats sleep disorders, schizophrenia and other psychotic disorders, and eating disorders equally by assigning them to equivalent levels within the hierarchy. Because this schedule completely revises an existing schedule, and would require the reclassification of materials in order to be implemented, it would be most useful within particular local contexts where specialized collections call for an alternative to the existing schedule.

We have outlined the three contexts–global, regional, and local–within which we have proposed changes, and have provided examples of the types of changes suggested within each context. We have also described how those changes fit into existing *DDC* editorial policies. It is important to note, however, that these three contexts are not mutually exclusive. Indeed, many of the global and regional changes we have proposed will be useful within a variety of local contexts. Furthermore, changes suggested for the regional and local context can be adapted for the global context. One example of this kind of adaptation would be the 140.17 Feminism schedule. While only specialized collections may require all of the subdivisions, more general collections could make use of the base number 140.17 to provide a place for theoretical discussions of feminism, thus freeing 305.42 to be used for its original purpose, for materials that discuss the social role and status of women. Indeed, it was our intention that the proposed changes be compatible with *DDC* and allow for individual institutions to determine the degree of specificity required.

A Reflection of Women's Studies Culture

Development of the expansion reflected the culture of women's studies as the basis for revision and expansion. Examining changes to 390 Customs, etiquette, folklore in some depth illustrates this approach.

It is widely acknowledged that, while the male social construct is fashioned in the public realm, the lot of women has typically been to develop their meaning and mythology within the private sphere. It is women and women's culture that informs the intimate gestures of relationship, home, family, community and tradition. As primary caregivers, women become the guardians and transmitters of custom and culture (Dawit and Busia, 1995, 2). Within *DDC*, 300 Social Sciences offers the best rhetorical space for issues defining women, their role, their understanding, their experience. The expansion applied to 390-393, broadens the scope of the existing classification to provide a refuge for the expansive vocabulary describing the world of women and their involvement with custom and culture.

Within *DDC21*, the 390s examine custom, etiquette and folklore in broad strokes and apply several assumptions about human society. For example, 390.1-390.4 "Customs of people by specific economic, social, occupational classes," clearly demonstrates a Western European bias founded in the social hierarachy still in place during the early 21st century. Within the expansion, 390.4 has been broadened in an attempt to define occupational groups, and the addition of 390.5 "Customs of lower, alienated, excluded classes," offers a less ghettoizing space for those often excluded from society's mainstream.

The development of expansions for 392 "Customs of life cycle and domestic life" and 393 "Death customs," took their impetus from the vocabulary offered by *A Women's Thesaurus* and the *Canadian Feminist Thesaurus*. Many of the terms in these volumes described the cultural phenomena of women, their roles, their experience and the assumptions made about those roles and that experience. While the majority of concepts could be classified within the existing schedules, the results were often less than satisfactory due to the rhetoric implied by the hierarchical structure of that classification. Clitoridectomy (often referred to as female circumcision) was such an example. Within the *DDC21* index, circumcision for both male and female are given a medical and a cultural space. The number 618.1059 speaks to the surgical nature of the procedure within the discipline of gynecology, yet gynecology is itself a ghettoized concept, being relegated to 618 "Other branches of medicine." As a cultural activity, clitoridectomy falls within the broad classification of 392.1 "Customs of birth, puberty, majority." This classification is, again, very broad in its scope, including both male and female circumcision. The number 392.1 is also demonstrative of a closed rhetorical space in that it is an all inclusive number that does not provide for discussion of gender specific aspects of the experience, including the question of society's right to control female sexuality. Within the expansion of 392.1 there are both "Customs relating to attainment of puberty" and "Customs relating to the attainment of majority" with relevant subdivisions for female (392.142 or 392.152) and male experience (392.143 or 392.153). Clitoridectomy (392.1424) now finds refuge in a gendered rhetorical space that follows from "Attainment of puberty" or rites associated with sexual awakening.

There are many examples throughout the 390 classification for which developed expansions provide a better rhetorical space for the female experience. From traditions of dress, which are intimately entwined with the image of women, to kinship ties and values in marriage, the 390 expansion endeavours to answer the fundamental feminist question of how women create and experience their culture.

DATABASE CONSTRUCTION AND ACCESS TOOLS

Development of the expansion and its potential accessibility is made possible by the software created specifically for the purpose. As with the development of the expansion schedule, these tools are models with potential transferability to projects in other cultural contexts.

Design Philosophy and Purpose

The database construction and access tools were developed to meet the needs of the *DDC* project, and in particular to:

- Store feminist vocabularies
- Store new classification records
- Provide linkages between the vocabularies and the classification records
- Facilitate construction of new classification records and linkages
- Provide a search interface to support development and testing.

The aim was to provide a set of tools that allowed the researchers to concentrate on the intellectual problems of the project in as efficient a manner as possible. To achieve this goal, it was important that:

- Familiar software interfaces should be used wherever possible
- Keystrokes should be minimized
- Cooperation and collaboration should be facilitated.

A further goal from the outset was that our project should act as a prototype for similar projects in the future. Hence we focused on the use of software (Linux, Apache, PHP, MySQL) that was widely available and inexpensive, and thus easily accessible to others. The database is maintained on a web server, and could in principle be searched and updated from any computer on the Internet, facilitating collaborations between geographically distributed researchers.

The System: Database Design

The database structure is shown schematically in Figure 1, with the *Canadian Feminist Thesaurus* tables omitted for brevity.

The database includes three main types of information:

- Vocabularies, which in this figure are represented by the Dewey Index Terms and *A Women's Thesaurus*
- Dewey numbers, which are linked to thesaurus terms
- New Dewey (or expansion) numbers, which are linked to thesaurus terms and also to Dewey Index Terms.

The data tables at the top of the figure contain terms, Dewey numbers, keywords, etc., while the "link" tables at the bottom provide information about the linkages between the data tables. Thus the Links table for the thesaurus provides the relationships information for the terms of the thesaurus, indicating which terms are related and the type of relationship (e.g., broader term, narrower term, etc.) that is present. The DewFields table is an exception, as it contains the data fields for the New Dewey expansion numbers.

The arrows indicate the paths taken when a query is executed on the database. For example, to find out what thesaurus terms were linked to a given New Dewey number, the software would determine the key value for that New Dewey number from the NewDewey table, find the linked key values for thesaurus terms in the NewLinks table, and finally use those thesaurus key values to identify (and display) the thesaurus terms from the Terms table.

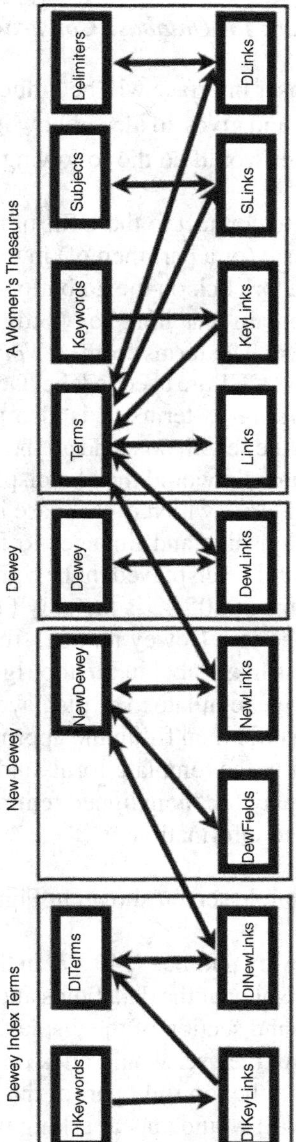

FIGURE 1. Database Structure

The System: User Interface for Database Construction

The discussion of the user interface will be limited to an example that illustrates some of its features and gives an idea of how it works. To get the display shown in Figure 2, the user would do the following:

- Use a web browser to connect to the URL of the database update page.
- Enter a thesaurus term (or a part thereof) in the box at the top left of the screen and hit **Enter** or click on the **go** button. All of the terms from the vocabularies that contain matching keywords would be displayed in the left column as shown. The terms from *A Women's Thesaurus* are unlabelled, while DIT and CFT are used to label Dewey Index Terms and *Canadian Feminist Thesaurus* terms. It is also possible to enter part of a Dewey number into the search box, and all the matching Dewey numbers and New Dewey numbers would then be displayed.
- Click on the desired term, which in this case is "nonaligned feminism." The thesaurus relationships and linkages to Dewey numbers and New Dewey numbers would be displayed in the right hand side of the window as shown. The linkage to 305.42 is the only link to a Dewey number.
- To add a new linkage to a Dewey number, the user would click on the **Add** link beside the Links: label in the top right hand part of the screen. This causes the linkage template to be displayed in the middle part of the window. The user would then fill in the appropriate Dewey number and linkage information in the template form, and click on the **Save** button when done. The display for "nonaligned feminism" would be updated to show the new linkage information.

To produce the second sample screen shown in Figure 3, the user would:

- Click on the new Dewey number "140.17" in the sample screen in Figure 2. This produces a display of the data fields and linked thesaurus terms as shown in the right hand section of the display.
- To update this record, the user would click on the **Chge** link to the right of the **Dewey** label in the top right part of the screen.
- A window (not shown) would appear asking what Dewey record should be updated, and the user would type in (or, more usually, cut and paste) the chosen Dewey number and click a submit button.
- A form showing the fields for that New Dewey record would then appear in the central section of the window as shown. The user could modify any of the information and then scroll down to a submit button at the bottom of that frame.

FIGURE 2. Entry of Links

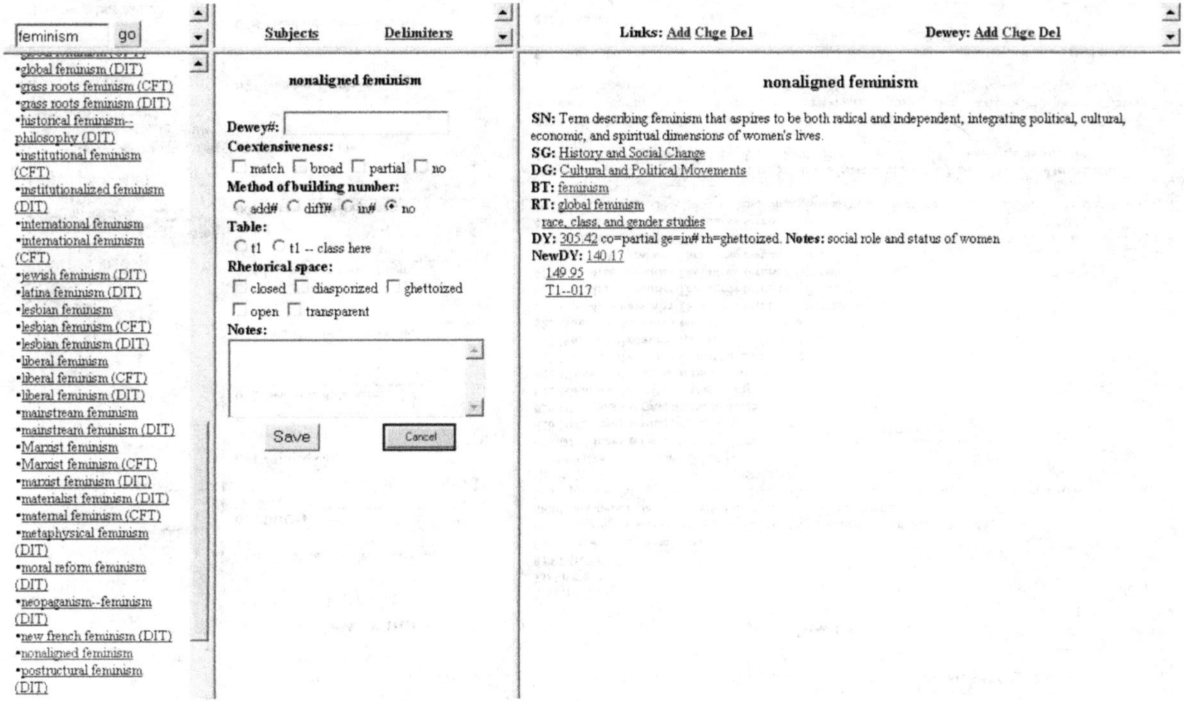

FIGURE 3. Changing Classification Numbers

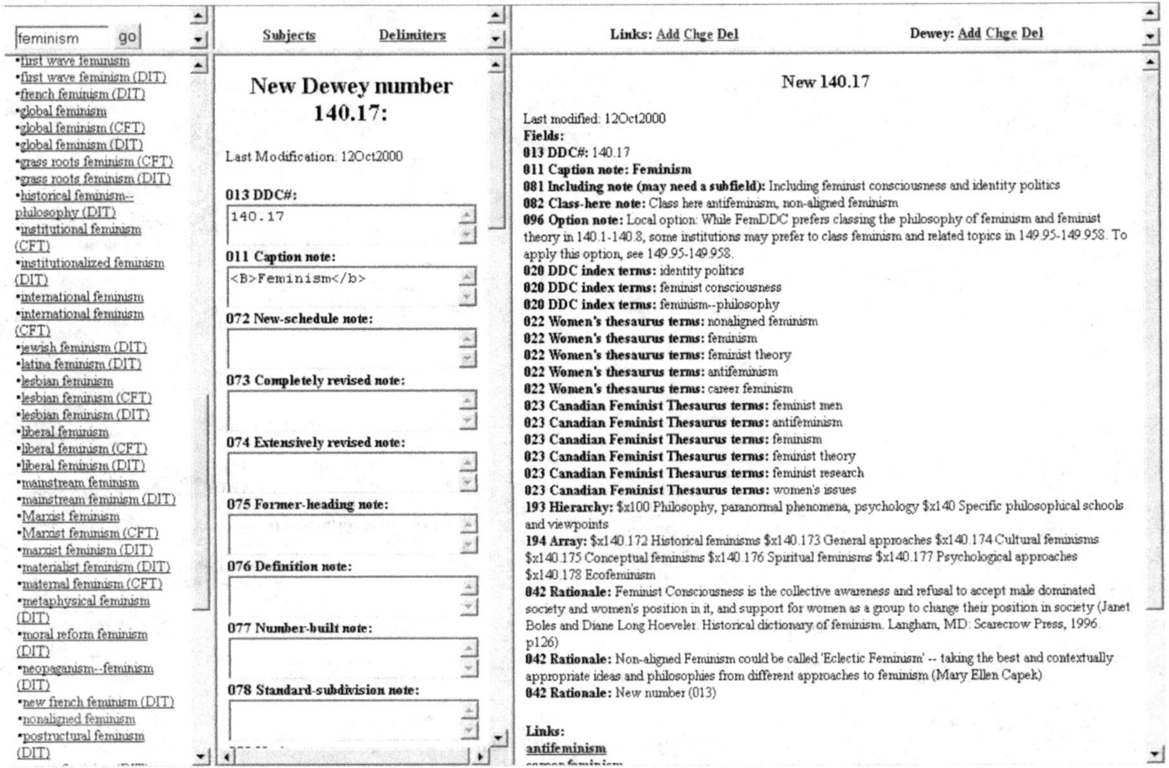

A number of other facilities are provided which are not shown here. These include:

- A more streamlined search interface that allows Dewey numbers to be plugged into web catalogues–a similar interface with the Dewey content excised may be accessed via http://lily.slis.ualberta.ca/nodewey/.
- A web form and database for collecting feedback from expert users during the testing phase of the project.

CONCLUSION

The result of this project is two-fold. On a concrete level we have developed a tool, an expansion for use with *DDC* for the organization of collections with an emphasis on women's studies or related areas. On a methodological level we have developed, applied and tested a process for developing specialized supplements for mainstream classification.

The expansion is successful for several reasons. First, it is grounded in the culture of women's studies and feminism through use of *A Women's Thesaurus*, reading in the subject area and consultation with subject specialists. Second, in any particular context, the expansion can be implemented as a whole or in part. The nine subclasses are largely independent of each other, so a particular library or agency might choose to use the changes to 610 Medicine, but not those in 390 Culture, etiquette, folklore. Third, local options and the introduction of a new table for perspectives allow tailoring for particular instances. Fourth, the expansion generally follows the practices of *DDC* so it is highly compatible with the full classification and further enhancement or combination with other expansions is reasonably easy. Fifth, changes to existing *DDC* numbers were made only after consulting a selection of online library catalogues to ensure that topics moved were those with the fewest holdings whenever feasible. Finally, the database is capable of distributed development and use.

The expansion project was undertaken with the knowledge of the publishers of *DDC*, however they now object to its publication. As a result of this legal impasse, the expansion is not publicly available.

The method developed in this research is a simple one and success in this instance suggests its possible generalizability. As noted earlier, it consists of four basic steps to achieve success similar to ours:

1. Identification of gaps and instances of bias in relation to the marginalized group or culture of interest
2. Development of a plan for addressing these problems
3. Implementation of the plan
4. Testing the efficacy of the result.

The first step is to identify areas of the mainstream classification that require expansion or revision. Use of a credible specialized subject access tool ensures a comprehensive assessment. We used a thesaurus, but subject headings, an ontology, or a specialized classification would also be viable. It is important to assess not only the existence of topics within the mainstream classification, but also the friendliness of the "neighbourhood" for each topic.

The second step is to create a plan for developing the expansion. The three major factors to consider are compatibility with the mainstream classification, credibility of the new developments, and ease of application. In our project, compatibility with *DDC* was maintained by following the main principles set out in the introduction to *DDC* and in the *DDC Editorial Rules*. Credibility refers here to the intellectual content, which must reflect the marginalized group or culture as well as possible. The choice of a subject vocabulary in step one, along with reference to a range of published sources and consultation with experts, can address this concern. Finally, it is vital that the expansion be easy to apply. Real life examples, such as consideration of appropriate libraries' holdings, can guide choices, especially where drastic changes are needed. Creation of the expansion in sections allows for application of parts of it when not all is required, also making application less labour-intensive.

The third and fourth steps, implementation and testing, can be readily combined into an iterative process. Consultation of other specialized vocabularies and preliminary application to the literature with which the expansion will be used can inform the effective development of the expansion. The development and even the plan should be subject to revision as the process proceeds.

The expansion that we have created reveals development of other expansions as a potential approach to ameliorating the omissions and biases of mainstream classifications. This approach has the advantage that an established classification can still handle the majority of materials and specialized treatment can be focused where most needed for a particular group or culture. For some situations, this arrangement makes manageable the development of culturally appropriate classification in a world that is increasingly homogenized. We hope that our experience can serve as a prototype for others.

REFERENCES

1. Olson, Hope A. and Rose Schlegl. 2001. "Standardization, Objectivity, and user focus: A meta-analysis of subject access critiques," *Cataloging & Classification Quarterly*, 32: no. 2: 61-80. See also database available at: http://www.ualberta.ca/~holson/marginal/bias in subject access standards.htm.

2. Lincoln, Tamara. 1987. "Ethno-linguistic misrepresentations of the Alaskan native languages as mirrored in the Library of Congress system of cataloging and classification," *Cataloging & Classification Quarterly* 7 no. 3: 69-90.

3. Soltani, Poori. 1996. "Translation and expansion of classification systems in the Arab countries and Iran," *International Cataloguing and Bibliographic Control* 25, no.1: 13-15.

4. McConnell, Fraiser. 1984. "Classification of Melanesia: Proposals for revision of DDC, Table 2," *Cataloging & Classification Quarterly* 5, no.1: 53-60.

5. McConnell, Fraiser. 1985. "Languages of Melanesia: Problems and proposals in classification," *Cataloging & Classification Quarterly* 5, no. 3: 57-66.

6. McConnell, Fraiser. 1985. "Peoples of Melanesia: Proposals for revision of DDC 19, Table 5," *Cataloging & Classification Quarterly* 5, no. 4: 47-51.

7. Oh Dong-Guen and Yeo Ji-Suk. 2001. "Suggesting an option for DDC Class Religion (200) for nations in which religious diversity predominates," *Knowledge Organization* 28, no. 3: 75-84.

8. Capek, M.E.S. (Ed.). 1987. *A Women's Thesaurus*. New York: Harper & Row.

9. Canadian Women's Indexing Group. 1990. *The Canadian feminist thesaurus/Le thesaurus feministe du Canada*. Toronto: OISE Press.

10. *DDC Editorial Rules*.

11. *Diagnostic and Statistical Manual of Mental Disorders*. 2000. 4th Edition. Washington, DC: American Psychiatric Association.

12. Dawit, Sebia and Abena Busia. 1995. "Thinking about 'culture': Some programme pointers," Caroline Sweetman, ed. *Women and Culture*. Oxford: Oxfam Focus on Gender: 2.

Stretching Conceptual Structures in Classifications Across Languages and Cultures

Barbara H. Kwaśnik
Victoria L. Rubin

SUMMARY. The authors describe the difficulties of translating classifications from a source language and culture to another language and culture. To demonstrate these problems, kinship terms and concepts from native speakers of fourteen languages were collected and analyzed to find differences between their terms and structures and those used in English. Using the representations of kinship terms in the *Library of Congress Classification* (LCC) and the *Dewey Decimal Classification* (DDC) as examples, the authors identified the source of possible lack of mapping between the domain of kinship in the fourteen languages studied and the LCC and DDC. Finally, some preliminary suggestions for how to make translated classifications more linguistically and culturally hospitable are offered. *[Article copies available for a fee from The Haworth Document Delivery Service: 1-800-HAWORTH. E-mail address: <docdelivery@haworthpress.com> Website: <http://www.HaworthPress.com> © 2003 by The Haworth Press, Inc. All rights reserved.]*

Barbara H. Kwaśnik, PhD, is Associate Professor, School of Information Studies, Syracuse University, Syracuse, NY 13244 USA (E-mail: bkwasnik@syr.edu). Victoria L. Rubin is a Doctoral Student in Information Transfer, School of Information Studies, Syracuse University, and Research Analyst, Center for Natural Language Processing, Syracuse University, 4-206 Center for Science and Technology, Syracuse, NY 13244 USA (E-mail: vlrubin@mailbox.syr.edu).

[Haworth co-indexing entry note]: "Stretching Conceptual Structures in Classifications Across Languages and Cultures." Kwaśnik, Barbara H., and Victoria L. Rubin. Co-published simultaneously in *Cataloging & Classification Quarterly* (The Haworth Information Press, an imprint of The Haworth Press, Inc.) Vol. 37, No. 1/2, 2003, pp. 33-47; and: *Knowledge Organization and Classification in International Information Retrieval* (ed: Nancy J. Williamson, and Clare Beghtol) The Haworth Information Press, an imprint of The Haworth Press, Inc., 2003, pp. 33-47. Single or multiple copies of this article are available for a fee from The Haworth Document Delivery Service [1-800-HAWORTH, 9:00 a.m. - 5:00 p.m. (EST). E-mail address: docdelivery@haworthpress.com].

http://www.haworthpress.com/store/product.asp?sku=J104

Digital Object Identifier: 10.1300/J104v37n01_04

KEYWORDS. Classification, translation, cultural hospitality, *Dewey Decimal Classification* (DDC), *Library of Congress Classification* (LCC)

INTRODUCTION

Michèle Hudon points out that one of the problems traditionally associated with the construction of multilingual thesauri is that of stretching the language of the component vocabularies to make them fit a foreign conceptual structure to the point where they become barely recognizable to their own speakers.[1] In this paper we extend this problem to classification schemes in general.

Over the last few decades we have seen a move towards unification and standardization of bibliographic systems, not just in the United States, but also globally. This means that traditional classifications, originally designed in a particular country (such as the *Dewey Decimal Classification*), or even for a particular collection (such as the *Library of Congress Classification*), are now being stretched, in Hudon's words, to cover cultural and linguistic artefacts and concepts quite different from those originally intended.

As classification schemes are being expanded and translated to "go global," we are faced with many of the same problems encountered in translation in general: issues of vocabulary, syntax, and semantics. In addition to these concerns, however, when dealing with classifications it is also necessary to consider the differences in knowledge structures–that is, the way in which the classification scheme represents a set of terms and concepts, but also how it comprises a pattern of relationships among those concepts. These relationships reflect an overall view of how the concepts are construed by a given discourse community in a given context. Thus, in harmonizing classification schemes across languages and cultures, we must address not only the issues of the terms, but also the way in which these terms are bound up in knowledge representations.

Why is this important? First of all, we might consider the basic purpose of classification schemes, which is to provide pointers and access to a body of works, as well as to the ideas and knowledge recorded in those works. To do this effectively, a classification must reflect concepts in such a way that a searcher can make use of several strategies:

1. The first strategy is that of finding what one already knows is there. This is called a *known-item search*. For example: "I'm looking for a recipe for flan." I hope, therefore, that the classification incorporates a concept for flan, and by using the term *flan*, I will find a recipe for it.

2. The second strategy is to be able to find what one hopes or suspects is there, but which one is perhaps unable to articulate. For this, a classification is helpful by grouping similar things together so that a searcher can locate a promising "neighborhood" and explore it. So, I might look under *desserts* and find a recipe for flan.

For both of these strategies to work it is necessary that searchers know what the ideas and concepts are to begin with, and then how they might be grouped.

Beyond these basic functions, classifications have a third very useful role in knowledge organization and retrieval, and that is to represent a field of knowledge in such a way that a great deal of information becomes evident through the classification structure itself.[2] For instance, if we learn from a classification of desserts that a *flan* is a type of *custard*, then we have gained a quick and efficient way of knowing quite a bit about flans (providing, of course, that we know what a custard is). In this way classifications are tools for learning and discovery, and not just for storage and retrieval of documents. For a classification to fulfill this particular role adequately, it must be a reflection of some sort of consensual meaning. That is, it must be reasonable and "true" for a user that a *flan* is a kind of *custard*. The problem arises, however, when we realize that we cannot take for granted that such a relationship of *flan* to *custard* is universally held, or that this will be the first or preferred way of construing the notion of *flan*.

Clare Beghtol[3] argues that making classifications culturally hospitable by including provisions for specific aspects of different cultures will enhance their appropriateness and utility for the purposes of worldwide information flow. For a classification designed from one perspective and for one culture to be hospitable to a different culture and language, it must take into account other possible relationships and other possible ways of identifying and labeling.

In this paper we provide one example of the differences in knowledge structures from language to language, culture to culture, and then suggest ways in which these differences can be accommodated in culturally hospitable translations. For our example we have chosen the culturally bound domain of kinship terms because notions of kinship are basic and universal (in that we all have relatives), but also unique to specific cultures (in that each culture integrates the concept of family differently). We explore the differences in kinship terms and relationships in fourteen languages and compare this to the representation of kinship terms and relationships in the *Dewey Decimal Classification* (DDC)[4] and the *Library of Congress Classification* (LCC).[5] The purpose of this inquiry is to demonstrate and describe the various kinds of problems that arise if one tries to extend, or stretch, the DDC and LCC for use in these languages, and the cultures in which they are embedded.

STUDY DESIGN

Our Informants

We interviewed fourteen informants (eight women and six men) of diverse language and cultural backgrounds. All but one are graduate students studying in the United States. We included four major Asian languages, two Slavic languages, and a single representative each from the following language groups: Indian, Dravidian, Negro-African, Oceanic Indonesian, Semitic, Turkic Altaic, Germanic, and Romance. See Table 1 for a summary of the informants' languages, language families, and countries of origin.

Data Collection Challenges

Our greatest challenge in designing the data-collection procedures was to be able to discover what terms and relationships are used in our informants' own languages. Since all of them are fairly proficient English speakers and familiar with U.S. culture, we did not want them to respond by anticipating our own understanding of kinship. We needed a technique that would elicit responses without overly influencing these responses to suit us, the interviewers. This was not to be an exercise in one-to-one translation. For example, we did want to start with the English term *uncle*, and ask what the equivalent is in their

TABLE 1. Our Informants

Informant's Country of Origin	Language Family	Language
China	Asian	Mandarin
Japan	Asian	Japanese
Korea	Asian	Korean
Thailand	Asian	Thai
Poland	Slavic	Polish
Ukraine	Slavic	Russian
The Netherlands	Germanic	Dutch
Malaysia	Oceanic / Indonesian	Malay
Sri Lanka	Indian	Sinhalese
Zimbabwe	Negro-African	Shona
India	Dravidian	Malayalam
Turkey	Turkic / Altaic	Turkish
Jordan	Semitic	Arabic
France	Romance	French

language. Doing so would assume that there is in fact a term for *uncle* in their language, that the notion of *uncle* is more or less the same as ours, and that the term *uncle* extends to the same sorts of people as it does in our culture.

Thus, we adapted a form of ethnographic interview suggested by Spradley,[6] in which the interviewer and informant are co-researchers–that is, they explore the question together, but as much as possible from the informant's point of view. The researcher tries not to impose his or her own conceptual structures, but instead seeks to elicit terms and the meaning of the terms from the informants' narratives. It is an iterative process in which the researcher attempts to use and reuse the informant's terminology in consequent questions and clarifies the meaning of relevant terms, again using the informant's own vocabulary. Put another way, the challenge was to avoid "putting words into our informants' mouths." We also wanted to collect information about the contextual nuances of the various terms and relationships.

The Interviews

The interviews were conducted as informal conversations, and did not follow a set format. We followed these general steps, with some minor differences from respondent to respondent:

1. To get things started and to provide a conceptual anchor, we asked the informants to imagine an important family gathering, e.g., a holiday dinner or a wedding, and to tell us who would typically be there.
2. As the informant described the family gathering, he (or she) identified terms used for various kin, both their personal name and then the generic name for that relative. For instance, he or she might mention that Aunt Theresa would be there, and then tell us the term for *aunt*. Each generic term was written in the informant's language on a sticky note and placed on a large sheet of newsprint. (Languages using other alphabets were transliterated.) In the center of the page the informant placed himself or herself. The various relatives were arranged around the "self" in whatever way the informant found useful. The purpose of physically laying things out was to provide the informant with a visual display, thus triggering other terms that should be included for completeness.
3. The terms generated by the initial question eventually suggested other ones, and gradually the informant filled in gaps in the structure. As prompts, we asked for other similar relationships and terms, and also for differences and distinctions.
4. As we went along, the informant sometimes drew lines between the terms to show special connections, or modified the structures as new terms came to mind.

5. Besides the terms themselves, and the relationships among them, the informants also offered many examples of language in use, as well as cultural background to explain the various terminology.
6. We also asked for extended uses of the terms.

All interviews were audiotaped for later reference. Several informants mentioned that exploring their own culture and language and laying the structure out on paper was quite revealing to them, which indicates to us that the process did in fact tap implicit knowledge.

The interviews yielded rich and informative descriptions of the domain of family and kinship in the fourteen languages we studied. Some languages, such as Dutch, seem compact, making relatively few distinctions between various types of kinfolk. Others, for example Chinese and Malay, have elaborate schemes with distinctions made among relatives along several dimensions: age, birth order, gender, mother's or father's side, and so on, with a separate term for each. Informants produced inventories of terms ranging from a low of about twenty terms to a high of over fifty.

Since the purpose of the study is to demonstrate certain issues, we did not attempt to be comprehensive in gathering the data. Respondents continued reporting terms more or less to the level of five generations, with themselves as the middle level, and to one or two layers of cousins and aunts and uncles. The extent of reporting was often determined by what the informant meant by *family*. Some cultures emphasize closeness in large, extended families. Others consider *family* to be only the very nearest of relatives.

ANALYSIS

The results of each of the interviews were compared to English kinship terminology and structures. In particular we looked for the following:

- differences in the scope of each term. Did it cover the same entities?
- empty lexical or conceptual categories, where the informant's language has no term for an English term or *vice versa.*
- differences in criteria for distinction.
- extended uses of terms.
- differences in how terms are used in practice.

This comparative analysis allowed us to identify patterns of issues, which we describe generically in the following section.

Insufficient Specificity

Some languages make distinctions that we do not make in English. For instance, we do not distinguish an *aunt* who is a *mother's sister*, from an aunt who is a *father's sister*, or from an aunt who is an *uncle's wife*. All are called "aunt." Such a distinction is made, however, in many other languages. Put another way, some languages have terms for concepts that we do not bother to name separately. A user would not be able to search using these more specific subject terms because they do not exist in English. Here is a partial list of such distinctions made by other cultures:

- uncles and aunts on mother's and father's side
- grandparents on mother's and father's side
- wives of uncles and husbands of aunts
- wives and husbands of siblings distinguished by siblings' age relationship to speaker
- siblings, cousins, aunts, uncles, distinguished by age, relative to the speaker, or based on birth order (e.g., [my] younger sister, mother's oldest brother, first-born son)

Terms Too Specific

Conversely, we make distinctions in English that are not made in some languages. For instance, we distinguish *siblings* and *cousins*, while in some languages, *siblings* and *cousins* are covered by the same word, but may be distinguished along some other criterion, such as age. Here are typical examples of English terms that are not always distinguished in other languages, and thus will have the same term in that language to cover both of them:

- *cousins* and *siblings* (cousins are called *brothers* and *sisters*)
- *children* and *grandchildren* (all are called *children*)
- *grandparents* and *great-grandparents* (all called *grandparents*)
- *mothers* and *mothers-in-law*; *fathers* and *fathers-in-law* (all called *mothers* and *fathers*)
- *parents* and *step-parents* (both called *parents*)
- *brothers-in-law* and *uncles; sisters-in-law* and *aunts* (called by name given to uncle or aunt)
- *sons* and *daughters* (both called *child*)
- *granddaughters* and *grandsons* (both called *grandchild*)
- *mothers* and *aunts* (aunts, and sometimes older sisters are called *mother*)

Sometimes this lack of distinction is prompted by cultural attitudes. For instance, in cultures where divorce is rare, or is perhaps glossed over, there are no special terms for stepchildren and stepparents.

Missing Terms

A lexical hole occurs when there is no term in one language for a term that exists in another language. For example, in many cultures, the role of the godparents is very important, and there are terms not only for the godparents themselves, but also for the relationship between them. There is no term for this relationship in English, not because there is no notion of godparents, but rather because there is no notion of a unique kinship relationship between them. Conversely, there are terms in English that are so specific to our culture that they may be irrelevant, and therefore not named, in other cultures. An example of this is "gay marriage."

Misclassifications

A misclassification occurs when a concept in one language is classified in another language in a way that does not conform to how that concept is construed. For example, DDC places the notion of *mistress* under 306.736 (extramarital relations). Of the languages and cultures we studied there are several in which the mistress lives in the same home as the family and is considered part of it. The legitimacy of her place in the family is shown by names such as *little mother*. In yet other cultures, the mistress is considered "extramarital" but is considered legitimate for tax-deduction purposes, and thus falls somewhere between *little mother* and *other woman*.

Differing Classification Criteria

A common reason for a lack of mapping from one classification to another is the fact that entities are classed based on different criteria. For example, we classify our kin by generation (forbears and children), by marriage (in-laws) and by sex (daughters, sons, aunts, uncles). We do not distinguish siblings by birth order; we do not use father's and mother's side as criteria of distinction, and yet these are typical in other languages. Some languages distinguish by sex where we do not (cousins, for instance), or by marriage (uncles' wives being distinct from parents' sisters).

Extensions: The Case of "Aunties"

In almost all languages, kinship terms have a way of being extended to individuals who are not related by blood or marriage. What is interesting is that the term in one language can be affectionately extended (such as calling all close women friends of your mother's age *auntie*), or it can be rude in another language (such as insulting a woman by implying she is old by calling her *auntie*). The purpose of most of the extended meanings is to give kinship status to those not technically related, and is meant as a way of showing closeness. Sometimes, though, the extended meanings are used to smooth over disruptions in family life, for example extending the term *mother* to your *stepmother*, or the term *father* to the older brother of a deceased father (in Shona).

Language in Use

Each culture experiences shifts in kinship norms and values, and the classification and terminology eventually reflect this. Where once distinctions were made for political or social reasons such as royal inheritance, they may no longer be relevant. On the other hand, new social forms emerge requiring new labels. For instance, many Dutch couples do not marry, and yet there is no universally accepted term for the man and woman who live together and have children but are not married. There is a gap in the classification, or a shift. Thus, in The Netherlands, the term *illegitimate child* has very little meaning if a large proportion of children technically fall into this category, and yet are considered "legitimate" in every other way: legally and socially.

COMPARISON WITH LCC AND DDC

Once the basic differences were identified we wanted to see how the issue played out in the LCC and the DDC. We looked for the samples of representations of kinship terms in the schedules of each of these schemes and found a number of ways in which the classifications provided by our informants did not map well to LCC and DDC.

The Library of Congress Classification

This is the most widely used classification in academic and research libraries. It was originally a scheme devised to accommodate the collection of the United States Congress, hence its disproportionate coverage of certain topics, such as the military and political sciences. It is thus a document-centered (rather than subject-centered) classification. Since its inception, however, the LCC has grown to reflect much wider collections than those of the Congress of the United States, making it in many ways a *de facto* national classification. If a subject category does not already exist, it gets added as works get published; thus we can assume that there is at least one work for each subject category in the LCC. In this way we can say that LCC emerges from a strong cultural and literary warrant.

Kinship and family are covered mainly in the H schedules (the Social Sciences), as well as scattered throughout other schedules for various special topics such as psychological, legal, mythical, and religious aspects. For the sake of simplicity, we cover only the Hs in this discussion, since these sections provide the most straightforward treatment of family and will serve to show up the various issues.

We see in Figure 1 that the LCC representation of kinship and family contains a blend of straightforward kinship terms, terms representing social phenomena, as well as a few terms that seem out of place (e.g., HQ759.2: *Mother's Day*). Many of the problems discussed above are evident in this classification:

- insufficient specificity to describe, for instance, different terms for aunts and uncles on mother's and father's side;
- overly specific terms that may not be used in other languages, such as *cousins*;
- culturally significant terms that may not map accurately to all languages, such as *working mothers*;
- different criteria of distinction, in that there is no provision for distinguishing by age or birth order, which is critical in some languages (for instance, *first son, little sister*, and so on).

All in all, the LCC does not seem culturally hospitable. Because it is an enumerative system (that is, the main goal is to find a place for each subject, rather than to build a coherent structure), it is difficult to see how it could be altered easily to accommodate concepts and conceptual structures from other languages, except to add them here and there in the same arbitrary way the English terms seem to be added. In other words, the LCC's classification does not seem to do a particularly good job of describing our own kinship terms and structures. This might add to the problems of translating it into other languages.

Dewey Decimal Classification

This classification, developed by Melvil Dewey over a century ago, is based on a model of knowledge that reflects nineteenth-century academic disciplines in the United States. Even though it has undergone over twenty revisions, it still shows this bias in the distribution of classes and the relative difficulty of using it for non-Christian, non-Western works. The DDC is a deductive classification, which means that categories exist (or can be built) even if there is no work published on a given topic.

FIGURE 1. Library of Congress Classification. HQ756-HQ759.97: The Family. Marriage. Home

HQ	756	Husbands. Fathers.
	756.5	Father's Day
	756.6	Househusbands
	756.7	Adolescent fathers
	759	Wives. Mothers.
	759.2	Mother's Day
	759.25	Mothers-in-law
	759.3	Absentee mothers
	759.4	Adolescent mothers
	759.43	Middle-aged mothers
	759.45	Unmarried mothers
	759.48	Working mothers
	759.5	Surrogate mothers
	759.6	Executives' wives
	759.64	Teenage parents. Adolescent parents.
	759.7	Foster parents
	759.8	Parents-in-law
	759.9	Grandparents
	759.912	Handicapped parents
	759.913	Parents of handicapped children
	759.914	Parents of sexually abused children
	759.915	Single parents
	759.92	Stepparents. Stepfamilies.
	759.94	Aunts. Uncles.
	759.96	Brothers. Sisters.
	759.97	Cousins

The main concepts of family and kinship are represented in two ways in the DDC. The first is in the main schedules in the 300's (Social Sciences). This deals with family as a social institution, and focuses on family relationships (see Figure 2).

This section of the DDC does not really represent kinship *per se*, but rather relationships among kin, as well as the various ways in which families might be configured. It is a list of subjects, however, that is clearly embedded in our own culture. Various key relationships from other cultures are not included. For instance, the DDC does not include the notion of relationships with aunts and uncles as well as with cousins, which is critical in many cultures. As in the LCC, there are terms that might be perplexing or irrelevant to other cultures (e.g., *suburban family*). The conceptual structure, though, is generic and open, and thus, it is possible to add subjects without too much confusion. For instance, one could add the Chinese notion of "reverse marriage" where the husband joins the wife's family, and becomes part of it, rather than the other way around. Under *grandparent-child relationships* (306.8744), one could add the specific types of grandparents, such as those on one side of the family or the other.

FIGURE 2. Dewey Decimal Classification. 306.8: Marriage and Family (Excerpts)

300	Social Sciences
306	Culture and Institutions
306.8	Marriage and family
306.85	Family (Including nonconsanguinal family)
306.852	Rural family
306.853	Suburban family
306.854	Urban family
306.855	Nuclear family
306.856	Single-parent family
306.857	Extended family
306.858	Patriarchal family
306.859	Matriarchal family
306.87	Intrafamily relationships
306.872	Husband-wife relationship
306.874	Parent-child relationship
306.8742	Father-child relationship
306.8743	Mother-child relationship
306.8744	Grandparent-child relationship
306.875	Sibling relationships
306.8752	Brother-brother relationship
306.8753	Brother-sister relationship
306.8754	Sister-sister relationship

The other way in which the DDC represents concepts of family is through *Table 7, Groups of Persons* (see Figure 3). The subject categories from the tables are not used alone, but rather are added as suffixes to subject categories from the main schedules in order to make them more specific. For example: 306.8 is the number for "Marriage and Family." We can add a suffix from Table 2, the geographic tables, –095, for instance, which would yield 306.8095, meaning "Marriage and family in Asia."

Table 7 in the DDC is interesting because instead of classifying kinship relationships by using our own English terms (and therefore our criteria for distinction), the categories are described generically. So, instead of calling the category *Sons and Daughters* (our term for this concept), it is called *Direct Descendants*. It would be relatively easy to add the various specific names for *first son, oldest daughter*, even if a language did not have exactly equivalent terms for and undifferentiated *son* or *daughter*. It would also be relatively simple to add categories for "inside" and "outside" families, which differentiates by the mother's and father's sides of the family.

Another interesting feature of Table 7 is that it does address the issue of "age" in individuals, but age is construed as a phase in a person's life, such as being a teenager, rather than a permanent condition. In other languages, age is important as well, but it stays static. That is, once you are the first-born son,

FIGURE 3. Dewey Decimal Classification. Table 7: Groups of Persons (Excerpts)

Notation	Caption
--04	Persons by sex and kinship characteristics
	<Persons by sex>
--041	Males
--042	Females
	<Persons by kinship characteristics>
--043	Direct ancestors and their surrogates
--0431	Parents (adoptive and foster parents, stepparents)
--0432	Grandparents (direct forbears other than parents)
--044	Direct descendants and their counterparts
--0441	Sons and daughters (adopted, foster children, stepchildren)
--0442	Grandchildren (direct descendants other than 1st generation)
--045	Siblings (brothers and sisters by blood, adoption, foster care, remarriage of parents)
--046	Collateral kinsmen (uncles, aunts, nephews, nieces, cousins)
--05	Persons by age
--054	Young people (children)
--0542	Infants
--0543	Children three to five
--0544	Children six to eleven
--055	Young people twelve to twenty (adolescents, teenagers, young adults, youth)
--056	Adults
--0562	Young adults
--0564	Persons in middle adulthood
--0565	Persons in late adulthood

you are *older brother* to your younger siblings, and you remain in this category forever. You do not grow out of it, and even death does not alter your seniority in terms of labeling.

A FRAMEWORK FOR CULTURALLY HOSPITABLE CLASSIFICATION TRANSLATION

Having demonstrated the various errors of classification mapping and difficulties of translation, in this section we present some preliminary suggestions for how a classification can more successfully be translated or extended to other cultures and languages.

- For errors of insufficiently precise terminology in the target language, add the appropriate terms.
- For errors of extraneous categories, prune the classification of terms that make no sense in the target language, or leave them "fallow" to be unused.
- In the case of one term in the target language being used for two or more terms in English, make sure to make cross references (see also). This is to ensure that the notion of *cousins* will not be lost to a person who searches

only for *brothers and sisters*, because there is no separate term for *cousins* in his or her language.

- For errors of conceptual structure, such as the misclassification of *mistress*, add modifiers or scope notes to clarify the terms and treat them each as a separate entity. Then classify each in its appropriate place in the scheme: Mistress (illicit extramarital relationship); Mistress (legitimate extramarital relationship).
- Describe categories as generically as possible so that a variety of terms can be logically classed in them.

This does not solve all of the problems, of course. An ideal translation that is 100 percent culturally and linguistically sensitive is probably not achievable because the criteria we would have to use are extremely complex, dynamic, and subjective. If we adopt culturally and linguistically hospitable practices, however, we will improve our classification-translation results in terms of making them more useful to their constituencies. Even if we are successful in this endeavor, though, we will still have to address problems that might arise from trying to be everything to everyone: these might include lack of clarity and cohesiveness or inability to incorporate diverse structures due to fundamental differences.

CONCLUSION

Many problems arise in the process of translation of a classification system from the source to another language and culture. Among these are finding corresponding terminology and being able to reflect the relationship between terms in the target language correctly. We presented evidence that in the process of translating classification structures there may be structural shifts. Some terms have broader definitions; others, narrower ones. There may be differences in how similar terms are construed. There may be additional criteria of distinction (such as birth-order).

We suggest that not only terms themselves but also inter-term relationships need to be preserved in cross-cultural cross-lingual classification translations. It is important to avoid merely translating the source classification word for word, structure by structure. Instead, it is necessary to understand the key classificatory dimensions in any given language. The domain of kinship terms provides a good example because even though it is universal in some ways, there are large differences in how people view family and kinship. In translating a classification scheme of kinship terms what is important to know? If the classification is translated, will it truly reflect the notions of kinship in that language?

Our study is limited by the fact that we had only one informant representing each language, and that person was well aware of English cultural terms. Furthermore, this was not a comprehensive sample of languages. Thus our results can only be suggestive. Nevertheless, we believe that our comparative inventory of cross-classification issues covers a wide range of problems and serves to demonstrate quite vividly that in order to make classifications useful and understandable to their constituencies, we must take steps to ensure that they are able to view them from their own cultural and linguistic perspectives.

BIBLIOGRAPHY

1. Hudon, Michèle. Multilingual thesaurus construction: Integrating the views of different cultures in one gateway to knowledge and concepts. *Knowledge Organization* 24(2):84-91 (1997).

2. Kwaśnik, Barbara H. The role of classification in knowledge representation and discovery. *Library Trends* 48(1):22-47 (1999).

3. Beghtol, Clare. Universal concepts, cultural warrant, and cultural hospitality. In: Maria J. Lopez-Huertas (ed.). Proceedings of the 7th International ISKO Conference, 2002, p. 45-53. *Challenges in Knowledge Representation and Organization for the 21st Century: Integration of Knowledge across Boundaries*. Wurzberg: Ergon, 2002.

4. Dewey, Melvil. *Dewey Decimal Classification and Relative Index. Ed. 21*. Albany, N.Y.: Forest Press, 1996.

5. Droste, Kathleen, and Rita Runchock. *Super LCCS: Gale's Library of Congress Classification Schedules: Combined with Additions and Changes through 1998. Class H: Social Sciences*. Detroit: The Gale Group, 1999.

6. Spradley, James P. *The Ethnographic Interview*. N.Y.: Harcourt Brace Jovanovich, 1979.

The Impact of Specificity on the Retrieval Power of a UDC-Based Multilingual Thesaurus

Victoria Francu

SUMMARY. The article describes the research done over a bibliographic database in order to show the impact the specificity of the knowledge organising tools may have on information retrieval (IR). For this purpose two multilingual Universal Decimal Classification (UDC) based thesauri having different degrees of specificity are considered. Issues of harmonising a classificatory structure with a thesaurus structure are introduced, and significant aspects of information retrieval in a multilingual environment are examined in an extensive manner. Aspects of complementarity are discussed with particular emphasis on the real impact produced on IR by alternative search facilities. Finally, a number of conclusions are formulated as they arise from the study.

Victoria Francu is Librarian, Central University Library of Bucharest (Romania). She is completing her PhD in Library and Information Science at the University of Antwerpen (Belgium) (E-mail: francu@bcub.ro).

The author wishes to acknowledge Dr. Gerhard J. A. Riesthuis, University of Amsterdam, for his assistance in preparing the database to make the automated indexing possible.

The database used in this study contains bibliographic records from the catalogue of the Central University Library of Bucharest (Romania).

[Haworth co-indexing entry note]: "The Impact of Specificity on the Retrieval Power of a UDC-Based Multilingual Thesaurus." Francu, Victoria. Co-published simultaneously in *Cataloging & Classification Quarterly* (The Haworth Information Press, an imprint of The Haworth Press, Inc.) Vol. 37, No. 1/2, 2003, pp. 49-64; and: *Knowledge Organization and Classification in International Information Retrieval* (ed: Nancy J. Williamson, and Clare Beghtol) The Haworth Information Press, an imprint of The Haworth Press, Inc., 2003, pp. 49-64. Single or multiple copies of this article are available for a fee from The Haworth Document Delivery Service [1-800-HAWORTH, 9:00 a.m. - 5:00 p.m. (EST). E-mail address: docdelivery@haworthpress.com].

http://www.haworthpress.com/store/product.asp?sku=J104

Digital Object Identifier: 10.1300/J104v37n01_05

KEYWORDS. Information languages, intermediate languages, Universal Decimal Classification, UDC, compatibility of information languages, multilingual thesauri, information retrieval

INTRODUCTION

The challenge of easier access to information contained in bibliographic databases in which the subjects of documents are represented by unfamiliar (to average users) classification codes–in our case the UDC notations–is the key issue of our study. Our purpose is to demonstrate that multilingual access to information contained in bibliographic databases is possible via multilingual descriptors mapped onto the UDC numbers. This can be automatically done while subjects of the documents are indexed with UDC notations alone.

More specifically, this study is intended to discuss problems of compatibility and integration of information languages and to emphasise major aspects of multilingual access to information through an intermediate language. In our case this intermediate position is undertaken by the UDC. Compatibility of information languages being important to our study, particular importance will be given to aspects of full and partial compatibility along with a few problems regarding the complementarity of the indexing languages involved.

A multilingual thesaurus based on the UDC Pocket Edition,[1] built according to the existing international standards ISO 2788[2] and ISO 5964,[3] will be compared with a smaller one in size, characterised by some particular features generated by its wide coverage on the one hand and its lack of specificity on the other. Going from a lower level of specificity to a higher one affects the building process of the indexing language. At the same time, the use of this thesaurus, wider in coverage than the previous one, has some impact on information retrieval.

CONFIGURATION OF THE EXPERIMENTAL DATABASE AND OBJECTIVES OF THE RESEARCH

In order to accomplish our objectives an experimental database was built from a number of bibliographic records in a real-life classified catalogue. To this bibliographic database four other databases were added so that in the end the experimental database as such has five sections according to our requirements: (1) Bibliographic records–97,918; (2) Records in the Master Reference File (MRF)–61,457; (3) Records in the short MRF–174; (4) Records in the abridged (little) UDC-based thesaurus (LTHES)–1,254; (5) Records in the Pocket Edition UDC-based thesaurus (PTHES)–2,033.

Our objectives are the following:

1. The logical structure of the UDC can be successfully converted into a thesaurus structure;
2. There are difficulties in building UDC-based multilingual thesauri connected with the relational structure, given that the classification system is discipline-oriented and in many parts enumerative; likewise, hierarchies are not always present (for example Class 2 Religion, before revision);
3. Once the thesaurus is implemented in the bibliographic database, the use of UDC-based thesaurus terms gives better search results than the manually assigned descriptors;
4. There are commonalties and particularities in using the two different thesauri in searching according to their specificity level;
5. What the UDC can do and the thesauri cannot, or the importance of keeping separate fields for unique entities;
6. The alternative search methods are complementary to each other;
7. Recall and precision rates and the way they are generated in keeping with the specificity of the search method used in IR.

METHODOLOGY

The experimental database described in the foregoing has in its bibliographic section documents indexed with UDC class numbers in all records, part of them having also manually assigned Romanian descriptors given by the indexers at the time of indexing.[4] Given the application of several successive programs to the UDC notations in order to decompose them into their separate parts and add the corresponding captions to them, the text of the UDC MRF for each UDC notation is also found in the bibliographic database.[5] With these pre-existing elements we started our approach according to the following methodology:

- A UDC-based multilingual thesaurus based on an abridged version of the UDC was built according to the existing international standards: ISO 2788[6] and ISO 5964.[7] The selection of UDC numbers became a list of 1,254 Romanian descriptors that was further developed into a trilingual thesaurus in Romanian, English and French. The resulting thesaurus eventually had about 3,000 terms (descriptors and non-descriptors) in each contributing language and a total of 4,827 terms.[8] This thesaurus has some particular characteristics given its wide coverage on the one hand and its lack of specificity on the other.
- Apart from this, a multilingual thesaurus in the same three languages was built, this time based on the UDC Pocket Edition. Not all the classes of the

UDC are covered by the newly built thesaurus. This thesaurus has a total number of 7,554 terms of which 2,033 are descriptors, the ratio between preferred and non-preferred terms amounting at 3.7. The number of terms in each of the contributing languages is 4,033 for English, 3,735 for French and 3,849 for Romanian. The thesaurus covers all the auxiliary tables, Classes 0, 1, 2, 3, 61 and 8 of the UDC Pocket Edition. Therefore, a more specific information retrieval tool was created to be used in parallel with the initial one and, by comparison, to enable a better perception of the difference specificity makes in information retrieval. Aspects of information retrieval are going to be examined comparatively for documents in the database for which multilingual descriptors in both thesauri have been automatically assigned by programs specially created for this purpose.

- Since the bibliographic records in the database had the subjects of documents initially represented by UDC notations and, through subsequent processing, also by the textual counterpart of these, the ultimate goal of our research is to emphasise the difference in search results generated by the difference in specificity of the two multilingual UDC-based thesauri and additionally to compare the three ways of accessing the information: UDC notations and their textual counterpart, the automatically assigned multilingual descriptors, and the manually assigned descriptors given by the indexers.

The first two in our list of objectives having been extensively dealt with in previous articles,[9] in the current paper we try to explore our goals beginning with the third: the use of UDC-based thesaurus terms in information retrieval and the search results of those compared with the manually assigned descriptors.

AUTOMATICALLY vs. MANUALLY ASSIGNED DESCRIPTORS

In order to test the retrieval power of the multilingual descriptors in the experimental database we made several searches and compared the results. We give here a few examples of these searches.

Search query No. 1: 3 different UDC numbers of which the second is a subdivision of the first: 159.923, 159.923.3, 159.925.

Along with the UDC numbers, as previously said, the subject matter of documents in the database is also represented by Romanian subject headings assigned to bibliographic records at the moment of indexing. Since our intention is to illustrate the overlaps and inconsistencies likely to occur in the case of manual indexing, we give below the correspondence between the captions of the selected UDC numbers and the Romanian descriptors as far as they were used to represent subjects relating to their meanings (Table 1).

Discussion

At first glance the descriptors have very much in common. If we look at 'Caracter (Psihologie)' we see it mentioned in all three sets of Romanian descriptors. A closer look will reveal that the texts of all three UDC numbers also include the word 'Character' and, furthermore, the second UDC number is a subdivision of the first. Therefore, the need was felt for the presence of other two descriptors as counterparts of the first two UDC numbers: 'Tipologie (Psihologie)' and 'Psihologie individuala.' Additionally, a differentiating element was introduced accounting for the higher level of specificity in the second case, i.e., the term 'Personalitate (Psihologie),' which is the exact meaning of the second UDC number. In such cases the consequences for information retrieval will be an increased recall rate but a lower precision rate. Many of the documents retrieved in response to such queries will have other collateral subjects apart from the intended search formulation. As far as we see it, the solution here is to have *one-to-one correspondence between the UDC numbers and the descriptors used in searching*. In other words, a UDC-based thesaurus will alleviate this kind of shortcoming. If such a thesaurus is imbedded in the bibliographic database (as in our experiment), the descriptors will automatically be assigned to the bibliographic records in keeping with the UDC numbers formerly assigned.

TABLE 1. Sample of UDC Numbers and Captions from the Master Reference File and Corresponding Descriptors

UDC numbers	**UDC Captions**	**Manually assigned descriptors**
159.923	Type psychology. Individual psychology. Psychology of individualities. Individuality. Personality. Character psychology. Characterology. Idiosyncrasies. Personal equation. Personality types.	*Tipologie (Psihologie)* *Psihologie individuala* *Caracter (Psihologie)*
159.923.3	Composition of the personality. Character traits. Psychogram.	*Tipologie (Psihologie)* *Caracter (Psihologie)* *Caracterologie* *Personalitate (Psihologie) Psihologie individuala*
159.925	Study of expression. Physical manifestation of mentality. Bodily expression of character.	*Caracter (Psihologie)* *Morfopsihologie* *Fizionomie*

Each time a UDC number is ascribed to a bibliographic record, its corresponding descriptor and only that will be attached to it. In such a way consistency, but also control on the indexing terms, is ensured.

Search query No. 2: acoustics. In Figure 1 we give the results of different searches conducted in the database to illustrate the advantage of automatically assigned descriptors over the manual ones, starting from a descriptor in our multilingual thesaurus this time.

Discussion

As previously argued, this example demonstrates the improved result in terms of precision and lack of ambiguities when automatically assigned descriptors are used as search elements. The number of retrieved records stands as proof for our statements. And indeed, if we compare the number of hits that resulted after the first search, using as query element the term 'Acoustics,' an English descriptor from LTHES, the number of retrieved records is very close to those resulting from a key term from the UDC caption 'Acoustics.' The next three are combined searches in which one of the elements is 'Acoustics' and the other represents the discipline acting as context for the initial term such as: 'Physics,' 'Music' and 'Linguistics.'

The relatively small difference between the UDC caption search mode (second query element) and UDC-based thesaurus term mode (first query element) on the one hand compared with the big difference between the former and the manual descriptor mode (sixth query element) pleads in favour of our approach. In addition to that, the third, fourth and fifth queries, which differentiate instances in the use of our query statement compared with the use of various combinations in manual descriptors (the sixth query), point out in an

FIGURE 1. Automatically Assigned Descriptors

```
Set Hits    Query element                 Current Data Base name = VFDAT
--  ------  -------------
 1   131    "MDE=ACOUSTICS"

 2   159    ?v709^e : 'acoustics'
 3   148    ?v709^e : 'acoustics' and v709^x : 'physics'
 4    10    ?v709^e : 'acoustics' and v709^x : 'music'
 5     2    ?v709^e : 'acoustics' and v709^x : 'linguistics'

 6    26    "BDE=ACUSTICA" + "BDE=ACUSTICA APLICATA" + "BDE=ACUSTICA
             ARHITECTURALA" + "BDE=ACUSTICA FIZIOLOGICA" + "BDE=ACUSTICA
             MEDICALA" + "BDE=ACUSTICA MUZICALA"
```

even clearer manner that the recall rate is, in the last case, quite low. It is true, though, that one of the objective reasons for this very low number of retrieved records is that the manually assigned descriptors have only been used in indexing from a certain moment on in the history of the catalogue.

COMMONALTIES AND PARTICULARITIES IN USING THE TWO THESAURI

One of the main distinctions between LTHES and PTHES is that the first was built from a pre-established list of selected UDC numbers, whereas the second was based on the UDC Pocket Edition. For all that, many of the rules applied in building these thesauri are shared by both.

In mapping the thesaurus terms onto the classification structural framework, the limitations were mostly imposed by the differences in specificity. A solution suggested in an earlier study to overcome this deficiency[10] is what is called '*upward posting*'[11] or '*generic posting*'[12] for an expanded category of terms as compared with what this method was initially established for. According to this device, we treated narrower terms as sibling terms providing 'see' references to the preferred term. This does not prevent such terms from being access terms, however, but they lose their quality as indexing terms. The control on the thesaurus terms is still maintained and the recall rate is not affected by any means. Precision has a lower rate in such circumstance but, as we shall see later, this inconvenience can be overcome by the use of alternative search facilities that coexist in our experiment. Consider Table 2 which illustrates the way we approached the upward posting.[13]

Another of the differences between the two thesauri under discussion is that the first was created for practical purposes, having in mind the usefulness of the concepts–in other words, their adequacy in indexing and information retrieval. This premise was not true for the second thesaurus that followed strictly the UDC structure it was derived from. While the first has a quite enumerative configuration, the other is both enumerative and faceted. This will have an influence on information retrieval that we shall examine later.

As previously noted, all the auxiliary tables, as far as they exist in the UDC Pocket Edition, have their matching terms in PTHES. This was beneficial for Class 8–Linguistics and Literature–for which the main class numbers are built by means of parallel subdivision using the Auxiliary table for languages (Table 1c). An instruction given in the database is meant to bring together the term 'Literature' (821 for individual literatures in UDC) and terms that correspond to the common auxiliaries of language (having this form: = . . .) to denote the literature of a particular language.

TABLE 2. Examples of Upward Posting

ENGLISH	*FRENCH*	*ROMANIAN*
Field crops UDC 633 UF Aromatic plants UF Beverage plants UF Cereals UF Condiment plants UF Edible roots and tubers UF Forage grasses UF Industrial plants UF Leguminosae UF Medicinal plants UF Oleaginous plants UF Plants yielding stimulants UF Sugar plants UF Tanning plants UF Textile plants BT Agriculture	Plantes de culture CDU 633 EP Céréales EP Leguminosae EP Plantes à boissons EP Plantes à tanin EP Plantes aromatiques EP Plantes fourragères EP Plantes industrielles EP Plantes médicinaux EP Plantes oléagineuses EP Plantes stimulantes EP Plantes sucrières EP Plantes textiles EP Racines comestibles et tubercules TG Agriculture	Plante de câmp CZU 633 UF Cereale UF Leguminosae UF Plante aromatice UF Plante de cultură UF Plante de zahăr UF Plante furajere UF Plante industriale UF Plante medicinale UF Plante oleaginoase UF Plante textile UF Rădăcini comestibile şi tuberculii TG Agricultură

This does not apply in LTHES, where the list of most used literatures was already established at the moment the list of Romanian descriptors was made. This brings about the inconvenience of having only a given number of literatures available for which automatic indexing is possible, the rest of them not being indexed at all. The alternative would be an excessively long list of languages and literatures, enumerating all those that are likely to occur in a library collection, but who can decide that?

WHAT THE UDC CAN DO AND THE UDC-BASED THESAURI CANNOT DO

The flexibility of the UDC permits the user to tailor or accommodate any given concept even though there is no class number provided for it. This can be done through *alphabetical additions* that, in theory, can accompany any class number. In practice, though, there are few numbers that have this indication in the UDC tables. For these numbers always followed by different alphabetical additions, there is no possible way to issue thesaurus terms since they cannot be predicted. Furthermore, they cannot be controlled.

Another way the UDC denotes flexibility is that it allows for expressing the category of time by means of the *common auxiliaries of time*. A prescribed list of such auxiliaries of time is given in Table 1g, but other mentions of this category (such as particular dates and ranges of time) are possible according to the

UDC grammar. These auxiliaries of time, just like the alphabetical additions, cannot be predicted nor controlled. Specificity is very much increased by devices such as these. Both types of concepts discussed above are considered to be so-called 'unique entities'[14] and a way to handle this category of information so that it can be retrievable is to keep it in separate fields. Field 706 in Figure 2 is such an example.

COMPLEMENTARITY OF THE ALTERNATIVE SEARCH METHODS

Let us now explore more closely the search methods we have only introduced in a few words so far. Consider Figure 2 in order to have a clear image of how a bibliographic record in the experimental database looks.

The bibliographic record shows what we have discussed earlier: different kinds of access represented by *PTHES descriptors* (prefixed by P-DES), *UDC notations* (prefixed by UDC) and *700 type fields* (706 and 709) that illustrate the conversion of UDC notations and, if complex ones, of their component parts, into natural language words. There is one more thing to be said here, namely that the *alphabetical addition* (Variboba, G.), which is difficult to manage in a thesaurus as a unique entity, is placed in a separate field and thus made available to the user. We deal here with an example of complementary information adding value to the search methods used. The first search, though, uses one of the PTHES descriptors in English and the search result is rather

FIGURE 2. Example of a Bibliographic Record

```
+ 4 / 8  ------------------------------------------------ Format: VFDAT  -+
|TIT:Grammatica albanese con le poesie rare di Variboba / Vincenzo Librandi. |
|     - 2a ed. -  Milano, Ulrico Hoepli, 1928. -  XV,381p., 16cm. -          |
|P-DES:  ^1709!^eAlbanian language^fLangue albanaisee^rLimba albaneză        |
|P-DES:  ^1709!^eAlbanian literature^fLittérature albanaisee^rLiteratura     |
|         albaneză                                                           |
|P-DES:  ^1709!^eGrammar^fGrammaire^rGramatică                               |
|P-DES:  ^1709!^eLiterary studies^fEtudes littéraires^rStudii literare       |
|P-DES:  ^1709!^ePoetry^fPoésie^rPoezie                                      |
|UDC:   811.18`36                                                            |
|UDC:   821.18.09-1                                                          |
|UDC:   821.18.09Variboba, G.                                                |
|676:   811.18`36                                                            |
|676:   821.18.09-1                                                          |
|676:   821.18.09Variboba, G.                                                |
|706:   ^eVariboba, G.                                                       |
|709:   ^a811.18`36^eAlbanian - Grammar^xLinguistics. Languages              |
|709:   ^a821.18.09^eAlbanian - Literary criticism. Literary                 |
|        studies^xLiterature                                                 |
|709:   ^a821.18-1^eAlbanian - Poetry. Poems. Verse^xLiterature              |
|MFN: 38009                                                                  |
+----------------------------------------------------------------------------+
```

close to the other two. 'Albanian language' that goes together with 'Albanian literature' as query element makes the difference in this case.

The missing piece is the representation of subject by way of LTHES. The absence of this search mode is caused by the low level of specificity that this information retrieval tool has, which did not allow for such relatively seldom met literature to be included among the descriptors existing in the list. This is one of the shortcomings of insufficient tuning between the specificity of the two information languages basically used: UDC notations and the UDC-based thesaurus terms. Manual descriptors are not found here either because the record is in the first half of the database.

The bibliographic record shown earlier belongs to the second set of retrieved records, in which we used field 675 for the UDC notation as query element (see the display of the query formulations in Figure 3). An identical search result was obtained as a response to the third query that was initiated by using field 709 for the text of the UDC notation as the query element. Such searches using fields that were designed for UDC notations are hardly expected to be used by the inexperienced user of the database. The first search, though, uses one of the PTHES (Figure 3).

Consider this example in Figure 4 in which the subject is represented by terms in LTHES and PTHES.

The subject is represented by descriptors in each of the multilingual thesauri along with the UDC notation and its textual meaning. The difference between the terms of the two thesauri is that LTHES does not provide a descriptor for the country code, whereas PTHES does. Furthermore, we can notice here the presence of non-descriptors in both cases (prefixed by LNDES and PNDES).

Another round of searches is meant to compare the manually assigned descriptors with the automatically assigned ones in both variants (Figure 5).

FIGURE 3. PTHES Set

```
Set     Hits   Query element                    Current Data Base name = VFDAT

---     ------ -------------
1          9   "PDE=ALBANIAN LANGUAGE" + "PDE=ALBANIAN LITERATURE"
2          8   "675=821.18(05)" + "675=821.18-1=111(082)" +
               "675=821.18-31=133.1" + "675=821.18-31=135.1" +
               "675=821.18-822=133.1" + "675=821.18.09" +
               "675=821.18.09-1" + "675=821.18.09<14/19>" +
               "675=821.18.09VARIBOBA, G."
3          8   "709=821.18" + "709=821.18-1" + "709=821.18-31" +
               "709=821.18-822" + "709=821.18.09"
```

FIGURE 4. Terms in LTHES and PTHES

```
+   3 / 37 -------------------------------------------- Format: VFDAT --+
|TIT:   Japanese financial markets, deficits, dilemmas, and deregulation /   |
|       Robert Alan Feldman. -  Cambridge. Mass, The MIT Press, 1986. -      |
|L-DES:  ^1709:^eFinance^fFinances^rFinanţe                                  |
|LNDES:  ^1709;^eFinancial policy^fPolitique fiscale^rPolitică fiscală       |
|P-DES:  ^1703-^eJapan^fJapon^rJaponia                                       |
|P-DES:  ^1709-^eFinance^fFinances^rFinanţe                                  |
|PNDES:  ^1703>^eNippon^rNippon                                              |
|UDC:   336(520)                                                             |
|676:   336(520)                                                             |
|703:   ^a(520)^eJapan. Nippon (Nihon Koku)                                  |
|709:   ^a336^eFinance. Public finance. Banking. Money^xEconomics. Economic  |
|        sciences                                                            |
|MFN: 14403                                                                  |
+----------------------------------------------------------------------------+
```

The most comprehensive results are given by the LTHES searches and by the 709 field for textual meaning of the UDC notation (101 hits). The high recall rate does not give any guarantee about the precision of the retrieved records. An analysis of this set of search results will reveal that we have here bibliographic records classed not only with 616.1 for 'Cardiovascular complaints' but also with subdivisions of this: ranges with '/' in which this number is included, colon relations in which this number can be the first or the second member, plus multiple common auxiliaries and special auxiliaries accompanying the basic UDC number. A lower result is given by the PTHES search (60 hits). Although restricted numerically, this search has the advantage of the highest precision rate.

The Romanian manual descriptor corresponding to our search topic was found in only 36 records but this number does not say much because Romanian descriptors were assigned to bibliographic records from a certain moment on and not from the beginning of the database (the first record that has Romanian manual descriptors–other than proper nouns like country names and personal names–is record no. 45,695 out of a total of 97,918). In addition to that, it is not certain that this descriptor was consistently assigned to all documents dealing with 'cardiology' or 'cardiovascular complaints' as the counterpart of 616.1 as UDC number.

Summing up, the bibliographic records in the experimental database have subjects represented by different indexing tools with different coverage degrees, and therefore with different degrees of specificity. In the forthcoming part of the study we shall point out the impact the various information languages, and particularly the terms from the two thesauri, have on information retrieval in terms of recall and precision.

FIGURE 5. Comparison of Manually and Automatically Assigned Descriptors

```
Set     Hits    Query element            Current Data Base name = VFDAT
---    ------   -------------
1        36     "BDE=CARDIOLOGIE"
2       101     "MDE=CARDIOVASCULAR COMPLAINTS"
3       101     ? v709 : 'cardiovascular complaints'
4        60     "PDE=CARDIOVASCULAR DISEASES"
```

RECALL AND PRECISION RATES AND SPECIFICITY

Most definitions of thesauri underline one commonly agreed on characteristic, i.e., they are indexing languages that contain controlled vocabularies used in post-coordinated search of information. An equally important characteristic of thesauri is that terms within their structure are related to each other both hierarchically and associatively in a way that may be helpful for their users.

One of the most accurate definitions of a thesaurus is given by the MDA Archaeological Objects Thesaurus:[15]

> A thesaurus is a tool which helps indexers and searchers to choose words consistently to describe things or concepts. The thesaurus is structured in such a way that related words are grouped together and cross-referenced to other groups of words which may be relevant to the subject. Where there is a choice of words with the same or similar meanings, the thesaurus provides a single preferred word and, by arranging terms in a hierarchy, allows the selection of more general or specific words. The purpose of the thesaurus is to standardise the use of terminology, which not only helps in indexing information but also in retrieval. Furthermore, it is a dynamic tool, one which can be developed through the addition or amendment of hierarchies, terms and relationships according to need.

To what extent does this complex definition apply to our study? The experimental database has subjects of the documents in the bibliographic records represented by:

- one or more UDC notations in every one of them–field 675;
- text corresponding to the UDC notations or their broken up parts, if those are correctly assigned from the UDC grammar point of view and they are found in the UDC MRF included in the database–fields 701-709;
- one or more Romanian descriptors manually assigned, beginning with record no. 45,695 out of a total of 97,918 bibliographic records–field 610, access prefix BDE=;

- zero or more UDC-based multilingual descriptors automatically assigned from a thesaurus based on a selection of 1,254 UDC numbers from the whole UDC schedule (LTHES)–field 620, access prefix MDE= for English, MDR= for French and MDR= for Romanian. Additionally there are also non-descriptors accompanying them in field 625, prefixed by MNE=, MNF= and MNR=;
- zero or more UDC-based multilingual descriptors automatically assigned from a thesaurus based on a selection of classes of the UDC having 2,033 descriptors (PTHES)–field 630, access prefix PDE= for English, PDR= for French and PDR= for Romanian. These too have non-descriptors in field 635 prefixed by PNE=, PNF= and PNR=.

The two different thesauri imbedded in the database do not keep all the relations among their terms, but only the non-descriptors, which can be used as access points to the information in the bibliographic records. Therefore, one of the two major characteristics of the thesauri mentioned above does not function here unless the printed versions of LTHES and PTHES go together with the database thus constituted and are used as search guiding tools by the users of the database.

Our findings about the experiments and tests that have been conducted over the database–some of which were shown earlier–are the following:

- the highest recall rate in all of the searches conducted belongs to searches in the 700 fields for broken up UDC notations and their textual meaning;
- the highest precision rate is given by searches with PTHES, provided that searches are conducted for classes that exist in PTHES. Precision is estimated here by comparing the number of hits as a result of searches made with manually assigned descriptors and with automatically assigned descriptors in PTHES. Compare the search results in Figure 6.
- given the broad coverage but lack of specificity, the use of LTHES in information retrieval can give 'no hits' as a search result if the UDC numbers in the bibliographic records are too detailed, but gather consistently large number of hits if descriptors in LTHES find the numbers they are based on in the bibliographic records. For example, a search request for 'psychiatry' will give no hits if the query is MDE='psychiatry,' but also these results for query elements such as shown in Figure 7.

But what is specificity, after all? What we mean by specificity in this study is the possibility of indexing the information under a specific subject heading, not under the class that particular subject heading belongs to (see the 'neurology' and 'psychiatry' examples in Figure 7). In his Rule 106, C. A. Cutter[16] argued

FIGURE 6. Precision Rate for Searches with PTHES

Set	Hits	Query element	Current Data Base name = VFDAT
1	8211	"PDE=ROMANIAN LITERATURE"	
2	2955	"BDE=LITERATURA ROMANA"	
3	8731	? v709^e : 'Romanian' and v709^x : 'literature'	

FIGURE 7. LTHES Descriptors

Set	Hits	Query element	Current Data Base name = VFDAT
1	102	"675=616.89"	
2	198	"PDE=PSYCHIATRY"	
3	0	"MDE=PSYCHIATRY"	
3	216	"MDE=NEUROLOGY"	
4	95	"BDE=psihiatrie	

in favor of an entry for the subject heading and not for the class which included the subject. We too, plead for the possibility to be as precise in indexing as possible and as consistent as possible, while avoiding ambiguities and overlapping, for enhanced information retrieval.

CONCLUSIONS

This study shows that the information in a classified library catalogue containing multilingual bibliographic data can be accessed by natural language words existing in multilingual UDC-based thesauri. The recall and precision rates for such search tools vary according to the specificity level of the thesaurus terms used in IR. Ideally, the coverage and specificity of the IR tool should be as close as possible to the level of specificity of the classification notations assigned to the bibliographic records. For a database like the one used in this study the alternative search methods are meant to give improved search results, providing in many cases ways out if 'no hit' responses are given to particular queries. Furthermore, unique entities like alphabetical additions and dates or ranges of time, permitted by the UDC grammar, can be evidenced in separate fields and consequently accessed if needed, in spite of the thesauri being incapable of handling or controlling them.

Eventually, the UDC notations in a classified catalogue can be and are the backbone for a variety of search methods based on the UDC structure. Its language independence allows for switching between languages that translate the UDC codes into thesaurus terms in as many languages as needed or merely into words that represent their own meaning.

REFERENCES

1. UDC Pocket Edition. *Universal Decimal Classification Pocket Edition*, PD 1000. London, British Standards Institution, 1999.

2. International Organisation for Standardisation. ISO 2788: *Guidelines for the establishment and development of monolingual thesauri*. 2nd ed. Geneva: ISO, 1986.

3. International Organisation for Standardisation. ISO 5964: *Guidelines for the establishment and development of multilingual thesauri*. Geneva: ISO, 1985.

4. Frâncu, Victoria. Language-Independent Structures and Multilingual Information Access. In: *Challenges in Knowledge Representation and Organization for the 21st Century. Integration of Knowledge across Boundaries: Proceedings of the Seventh International ISKO Conference, 10-13 July 2002, Granada, Spain*. Edited by Maria J. Lopez-Huertas with the assistance of Francisco J. Munoz-Fernandez. Würzburg: Ergon, 2002.

5. Riesthuis, G.J.A. Searching with Words: Re-use of Subject Indexing. In: *Extensions and Corrections to the UDC*, 21: 24-32 (1999).

6. International Organisation for Standardisation. ISO 2788: *Guidelines for the establishment and development of monolingual thesauri*. 2nd ed. Geneva: ISO, 1986.

7. International Organisation for Standardisation. ISO 5964: *Guidelines for the establishment and development of multilingual thesauri*. Geneva: ISO, 1985.

8. Frâncu, Victoria. Language-Independent Structures and Multilingual Information Access. In: *Challenges in Knowledge Representation and Organization for the 21st Century. Integration of Knowledge across Boundaries: Proceedings of the Seventh International ISKO Conference, 10-13 July 2002, Granada, Spain*. Edited by Maria J. Lopez-Huertas with the assistance of Francisco J. Munoz-Fernandez. Würzburg: Ergon, 2002. p. 406.

9. Frâncu, Victoria (1996). Building a Multilingual Thesaurus based on UDC. In: *Knowledge Organization and Change: proceedings of the 4th International ISKO Conference, 15-18 July, Washington, DC*. Edited by Rebecca Green. Frankfurt/Main: Indeks, pp.144-154. Frâncu, Victoria (1999). A Universal Classification System going through Changes. In: *Advances in Classification Research: Proceedings of the 10th ASIS SIG/CR Classification Research Workshop, October 31, 1999*, held at the 62nd ASIS Annual Meeting, Washington, D.C. Edited by H. Albrechtsen and J.-E. Mai, pp. 55-71. Frâncu, Victoria (2000). Harmonizing a Universal Classification System with an Interdisciplinary Multilingual Thesaurus: Advantages and Limitations. In: *Dynamism and Stability in Knowledge Organization: Proceedings of the Sixth International ISKO Conference, 10-13 July 2000, Toronto, Canada*. Edited by Clare Beghtol, Lynne C. Howarth, Nancy Williamson. Würzburg: Ergon, 2000.

10. Frâncu, Victoria. Harmonizing a Universal Classification System with an Interdisciplinary Multilingual Thesaurus: Advantages and Limitations. In: *Dynamism and Stability in Knowledge Organization: Proceedings of the Sixth International ISKO*

Conference, 10-13 July 2000, Toronto, Canada. Edited by Clare Beghtol, Lynne C. Howarth, Nancy Williamson. Würzburg: Ergon, 2000.

11. Aitchison, J. & Gilchrist, A. *Thesaurus Construction: A Practical Manual*. 2nd ed. London: Aslib, 1987. p. 12.

12. National Information Standards Organization. Guidelines for the Construction, Format, and Management of Monolingual Thesauri. ANSI/NISO Z39.19-1994. New York: NISO,1994.

13. Frâncu, Victoria. Harmonizing a Universal Classification System with an Interdisciplinary Multilingual Thesaurus: Advantages and Limitations. In: *Dynamism and Stability in Knowledge Organization: Proceedings of the Sixth International ISKO Conference, 10-13 July 2000, Toronto, Canada*. Edited by Clare Beghtol, Lynne C. Howarth, Nancy Williamson. Würzburg: Ergon, 2000.

14. National Information Standards Organization. *Guidelines for the Construction, Format, and Management of Monolingual Thesauri*. ANSI/NISO Z39.19-1994. New York: NISO,1994.

15. *MDA Archaeological Objects Thesaurus* (1997). Available at: http://www.mda.org.uk/archobj/archcon.htm.

16. Cutter, Charles A. *Rules for a Dictionary Catalogue*. 4th ed. Washington, D.C., 1904.

INFORMATION ORGANIZATION IN KNOWLEDGE RESOURCES

Knowledge Organization from Libraries to the Web: Strong Demands on the Weakest Side of International Librarianship

Maria Inês Cordeiro

SUMMARY. This paper reflects on some major aspects related to library subject access systems in the era of networked information. The main argument builds on the fact that we nowadays witness the strongest demand and expectation on subject access tools, coming from far beyond the traditional library world, but the field remains the weakest side of international

Maria Inês Cordeiro is Library Information System Manager, Art Library, Calouste Gulbenkian Foundation, Av. Berna 45A–PT 1067-001 Lisbon, Portugal (E-mail: ilopes@gulbenkian.pt).

[Haworth co-indexing entry note]: "Knowledge Organization from Libraries to the Web: Strong Demands on the Weakest Side of International Librarianship." Cordeiro, Maria Inês. Co-published simultaneously in *Cataloging & Classification Quarterly* (The Haworth Information Press, an imprint of The Haworth Press, Inc.) Vol. 37, No. 1/2, 2003, pp. 65-79; and: *Knowledge Organization and Classification in International Information Retrieval* (ed: Nancy J. Williamson, and Clare Beghtol) The Haworth Information Press, an imprint of The Haworth Press, Inc., 2003, pp. 65-79. Single or multiple copies of this article are available for a fee from The Haworth Document Delivery Service [1-800-HAWORTH, 9:00 a.m. - 5:00 p.m. (EST). E-mail address: docdelivery@haworthpress.com].

http://www.haworthpress.com/store/product.asp?sku=J104

Digital Object Identifier: 10.1300/J104v37n01_06

librarianship. While the emergence to cope with the practical challenges of a wider environment is emphasized, the need to reinforce the internationalization of knowledge organization as a professional library matter is stressed, not only at the pragmatic level but also, more importantly, in theoretical terms.

KEYWORDS. Knowledge organization, networked information retrieval, subject access, subject indexing, subject heading languages

INTRODUCTION

Knowledge organization has always been recognized amongst the library's primary functions, and libraries have been the major provider of such a service. The profound changes introduced by the Internet have increased the concerns around *knowledge* and *knowledge organization*, diversifying the perspectives about information management. The field has become more complex and less of a unique and clearly identified professional field. Quite suddenly, knowledge organization finds itself in the multiple crossroads of the overcrowded and distributed information landscape brought about by the WWW. In the new WWW context, neither the good models for best guiding one's way in the information routes, nor the efficient means to embark for safe, purposeful and well-succeeded information retrieval journeys have yet appeared.

The complexity in devising retrieval solutions for a growing diversity of scattered and independently managed information resources can explain why subject access has become central in the network environment. Being more resource-independent and at a higher level when compared to other aspects of resource description and identification, subject access appears as a more powerful common denominator, potentially capable of alleviating or bypassing the countless other heterogeneities that can be found about many other aspects of information resources management. Yet, such a common denominator is amongst the most complex to define, express, manage and use, as it is the less bound to objective characteristics and the more exposed to all sorts of contextual factors.

Subject access increased in importance along with an expanding range of information discovery and retrieval services, among which professional library services are only a small part, but apparently having an augmented and special role. This situation brings as many opportunities as challenges, and the current context and circumstances of library knowledge organization (KO) tools should be regarded not only in the light of novel contexts but also in the perspective of their intrinsic weaknesses and strengths, either concerning their original targets, or the expanded environment they currently face. One aspect that deserves particular attention is how consolidated the subject matter is in the professional scene, especially at the international level.

THE EXPANDED ENVIRONMENT OF KNOWLEDGE ORGANIZATON

The global network is the transforming reality of the information environment. First of all, it is about distributed information resources and distributed computing. Distributed computing has elicited the trend towards higher levels of abstraction and more formalized ontological support for information systems. The concept of *ontology*, so close to the library concept of *knowledge organization*–the space where classification systems, thesauri and other controlled vocabularies for information retrieval have been produced–arose in the information systems field with little relation to the experience held in library and information science.[1] Ontologies "emerged from academic obscurity into mainstream business and practice on the Web,"[2] expanding from the research level of *knowledge representation*, to applied fields such as knowledge bases, new methods of software engineering,[3] or information brokering based on metadata for knowledge domains. Simultaneously, interoperability became a more and more crucial aspect of information systems, and evolved by concentrating the core issues in the semantic axis of information structures and services. Such evolution from simple syntax and structure to semantics is well illustrated by the Semantic Web movement[4] and all the developments around it.

All of these trends are leading to changes with impacts wider than the field of information retrieval (IR), normally the one where knowledge organization issues have been discussed. They convey changes in systems paradigms, raising new base concepts, such as the concept of "composability," in which components tend to be system independent, adaptable, extendable and reusable. KO tools are only one among the various kinds of information components envisaged by distributed, interoperable systems. But they are of a fundamental kind, because the use of common, shared or otherwise imparted *formal languages* (i.e., controlled vocabularies) is of utmost importance to convey explicit and shareable knowledge representations in the distributed environment. Yet, most of them have not been developed, or modified, having practical solutions for wide shareability, adaptability, extensibility and reusability in mind. This is generally the case for the data structure and content of library authority files and for the solutions to manage and convey KO tools.[5]

Besides structure and content, the conceptual basis of KO tools is often not explicit or well documented, because they have been mostly developed in a pragmatic way and for the needs of a confined reality–a library information system or a community of libraries. In this respect, what can be learned from the above trends in technology is the need for higher levels of abstraction in such tools, providing key common conceptualisations, in order to support semantic interoperability solutions that require cross-domain and interdisciplinary expertise. This is as important nowadays as, in the words of Doerr, "the problems computer scientists and system implementers have to comprehend the logic of cultural concepts seems to be equally notorious as the inability of the cultural professionals to communicate those to computer scientists."[6] All these are novel or currently highlighted aspects that make the future of KO tools more complex and demanding.

SUBJECT ACCESS IN A TURMOIL: WIDER TARGETS, MORE COMPLEXITY, UNCLEAR DIRECTIONS

Now in company with more diversified information service providers, libraries populate the new and turbulent network landscape with a difficult threefold purpose: to maintain and improve the quality of the subject access service concerning the kind of resources they have long been focused on; to extend and develop the same level of service to every new kind of information resource; and to provide support for subject access interoperability across different domains and services, encompassing not only the distributed library world, but also non-library information stakeholders, service providers and users. Libraries cannot–and do not–ignore these drivers of change, but future directions are far from clear. The field of library KO is going through a transitional state that is composed simultaneously of uncertainty and of expectation–uncertainty about the future of library subject indexing practices, both in terms of sustainability and theoretical approaches (a situation that the profession has felt since the '80s without major evolution), and expectation about the role and contribution of traditional library KO tools as ingredients for IR solutions for newly emerged network services.

On the one hand, the central challenge in extending bibliographic control to the WWW content is mostly a matter of scale, requiring feasible and sustainable solutions. Therefore, for the sake of efficacy, a useful balance between scale and practicability should be reflected in the adoption of technical solutions. This balance is managerial by nature and it is not new in terms of subject access management, as we can read in Fugmann.[7] But the fact is that significant and visible experience in true managerial approaches cannot be drawn from the practical field of subject access in libraries, while scale and practicability have been better addressed by other IR service providers, relying more on technological solutions than on intellectually based mechanisms, as is notable, the case of Web search engines.

On the other hand, we cannot say that the field has renewed or endured its theoretical basis. In between the pragmatic approaches, ongoing long existing practices, and the recurrent technical discussions around the same kind of questions and issues for almost twenty years, the profession has been breathing a sense of failure,[8] of much of the same,[9] of obsolete philosophy,[10] or even of being a neglected and poorly understood field.[11]

While this is not easily perceived from outside the profession, feasible and sustainable solutions for WWW coverage have been mostly based on pure technological devices with a very low level of semantic processing. Misunderstandings about their virtues and limitations, and also about what knowledge organization is really about–namely the difference between *indexing* and *structuring*[12]–are major aspects in need of clarification in the still naïve stage of the WWW. Naïveté about subject retrieval in the networked environment can appear from different sides: from many of the producers of Web search services (notably subject directories) arguably more intuitive than traditional KO tools which ignore basic qualities of knowledge organization schemes,[13] to traditionalistic approaches where the solution appears to be in simply transferring existing practices and tools to the networked environment. In between these, the need for further research comes into view, either because of indications about different user behaviour in the hypertext environment[14] or because traditional tools may not be scalable and widely applicable enough.[15] Besides, as pointed out by Jansen and Pooch,[16] simple comparisons between traditional library services and the performance of Web search services can be misleading and of little use because the Web is a new search environment requiring its own metrics and methodologies, independent from traditional information retrieval and OPACs.

From this turmoil of different targets and understandings, the clearest idea shared by all parties interested in these matters is that library subject access tools are needed and useful beyond the traditional scope of library services. While this idea is positive and stimulating, it is less clear how such professional tools can be directly re-used by other professional communities with different professional backgrounds and concerns, or even by non-professionals, as is the case of anyone publishing resources with subject access metadata taken from a given classification, subject heading list or thesaurus using, for example, the Dublin Core element set. Without further analysis, it may seem that creating subject access is only about KO tools, that both the tools and the results of their application are intended for the same audiences and, therefore, that they are good enough if they can be understood and used by anyone. The matter is not so simple, for several reasons: first, because library KO tools are not only vocabularies, and they have been prepared to be used mostly by library and information professionals, but the results of their application have had other users in mind; second, because subject IR products and services that appear simple to use can often hide a degree of complexity which is proportionate to the sophistication needed to support the functionalities they provide, and this is not evident from the user side.

Reflecting on these aspects–and this reflection can hardly come from outside the library profession–is important in order to overcome misconceptions and to help devise solutions to extend the library KO tools' applicability, without having necessarily to downgrade them in their application in library services. Besides, these aspects are only little branches stemming from another main trunk of the matter, right in the heart of the profession: despite its core importance, subject access remains the weakest side of international librarianship. Recognizing this is important in order to clearly devise the place and state of library subject access systems in face of the current challenging environment, and such a reality should not to be clouded by the many changes, new pressures and different understandings that come with it.

LIBRARY SUBJECT ACCESS: A BRIEF INTROSPECTION

The knowledge organization function in libraries is built upon formalized information structures–subject indexing languages as surrogates of natural language–aimed at some kind of *unification* regarding both the conceptual reference framework in which concepts/subjects can be understood and the diversity of their possible forms of representation and communication. In this perspective the library function is primarily one of communication, but implying at its core a large spectrum of issues related to *conceptual structures* and *language*. Subject indexing languages encompass both these fields and are assumed as abstractions and reductions aiming at producing *knowledge representations* with a level of validity and stability that overcomes the individual's level,[17] in order to provide for efficient *communication with* a given community of users, *about* the content of a given pool of information resources and/or on a given subject area. In this sense, subject heading languages are more or less complex *sets of conventions* intended to supersede the endless idiosyncrasies in knowledge representations that may appear in the natural world of externalized information. Unification, disambiguation and structuring are then the aims of such conventions. They can be attained in different degrees, by different means and devices, not all equally suitable, or sustainable, for all purposes and situations.

The multiple aspects to cope with, and the imprecise boundaries of the goals in setting up such conventions, have always placed knowledge organization as the most challenging side of librarianship. Being the most appealing in intellectual terms, it is also the most difficult one in terms of practical achievements of general acceptance. Not only is it the most demanding in scientific and interdisciplinary skills, the most costly for the library operation, and one of the most influential aspects of the evaluation of library information retrieval systems by the public, but it is also the most affected by the proliferation of local methods, policies and standards. All of these aspects make subject indexing activities especially vulnerable in face of budget, technical and policy constraints. In the history of library catalogues, subject access changes leading to disruptions are more frequent than changes made at the bibliographic description level;[18] they can be motivated by many different reasons, but are not usually alien to the high costs of human indexing versus the hard-to-measure benefits. Furthermore, on this ground it is very easy to spread the disbelief of the possibility of improving the intellectual process itself, as is, for example, the case about indexer consistency studies.[19]

Although subject access has always been the focus of a significant amount of professional literature, the practical fact is that the subject indexing and retrieval area remains the one where less professional consensus has been achieved and where the need for comprehensive research toward sounder theoretical foundations has been felt.[20] Therefore, the field remains one where education and training, and professional experience, can show more aspects, on the basis of academic traditions or of other practical reasons.

This is fairly true if we compare the levels of common understanding and standardization achieved at the international level in subject indexing and in descriptive cataloguing. The existing normative tools with international scope (such as the ISO guidelines (5963, 5964 and 2788) and, more recently, the IFLA *Guidelines for Subject Authority and Reference Entries*) are mostly intended for very general guidance in operations or for procedures that are only part of the whole process of subject indexing. The ISO documents especially remain without major improvement[21] long after their shortcomings have been noted. In this context, the place of conceptual standards has been taken by certain KO tools that can be viewed as *de facto* standards, mostly those that are universal in scope or of international use, like UDC and Dewey, or alphabetical systems used by a wide group of different bibliographic agencies pertaining to the same linguistic group, as has happened with LCSH, or those dealing with the same subject area, such as MeSH or AAT.

Nevertheless, this *de facto* standardization does not follow the same reasons and mechanisms for achieving consensus that usually feed the making and maintenance of a standard, *i.e.*, responding to common needs by developing first a common conceptual basis. Rather, such an adoption is motivated mostly by economic factors and, when applied far from the context of their production, such tools are often unilaterally modified and adapted to local needs, not without consequences for compatibility. This happens more with subject heading languages which, for all the previously mentioned reasons, have been the object of co-operative initiatives that have flourished in the last decade. Rather than simply adopting a common solution, these kinds of initiatives (such as SACO (Library of Congress) and RAMEAU (Bibliothèque nationale de France)) bring a new work strategy that openly shares efforts, resources and responsibilities and provides for wider compatibility of subject retrieval in different catalogues available in the network environment. This trend, led by cataloguing distribution cooperative services, union catalogues, library networks, etc., is indubitably important and has brought advantages and useful experiences, but such initiatives address the pragmatic aspects of the problem mostly. The same is true, more recently, about the emergence of work to find inexpensive and quick solutions for cross-sectoral subject search, *e.g.,* encompassing libraries, museums, archives and other electronic services communities. Although contributing to bring them together around the problem of multiple KO tools, the initiatives addressing cross-sectoral information spaces are, again, principally fueled by pragmatic concerns (see, for example, Nicholson *et al.*[22]).

ALPHABETIC SUBJECT ACCESS SYSTEMS: ALPHABETIC APPROACHES ARE NOT ENOUGH

We may say that, in general, alphabetical subject indexing systems suffer from more types of barriers and constraints than classifications, either in the stage of conception and building or at the application level. This is mainly because classification schemes are usually authored and managed centrally by organizations independent of library services, and also because they can be conceived and used without having to deal intensively with linguistic issues. Besides, classifications are mostly built *a priori*, meaning the prior establishment of at least general principles, structures and devices; *i.e.*, a minimal theoretical basis that has to be explicit and is required as a pre-condition for putting the systems to work. Therefore, they are usually better documented than subject heading systems, which are more often developed in a pragmatic and *a posteriori* way, in many cases lacking or postponing the reflection on or consolidation of a theoretical basis until a later stage. LCSH is a paradigmatic example in this respect (see Stone[23]). The lack of a coherent set of principles, rules and long term strategy for LCSH led to the so called "subject code movement" in the eighties, an important expression of such theoretical gaps.[24]

Making use of subsets of the natural language, subject heading systems are therefore usable in some ways even if the underlying principles and rules are not clarified, explicitly formalized or clearly understood. The diversity among alphabetical subject indexing systems comes from aspects internal or local to each system, affecting the types of criteria, options, conventions and devices used in the control of terminology, in the building of semantic structures and in the control of representation forms. They have evolved in different historical, linguistic and technical contexts, with different backgrounds, bearing different practices, which also have generated differences in technical concepts/terminology, sometimes affecting professional communication and understanding. This can be illustrated, in extreme levels, by two very common examples.

One, at the level of particular professional terminology, is the very simple case of the term/concept of *subject heading* versus *descriptor*, where the first is still closely associated with pre-coordinated systems and all of their historical issues and characteristics, in a way that appears for many to have little convergence with the more recent thesaurus terminology. This example is the paradox of a field where the control of terminology is paramount. The term "subject heading" seems to emphasize better the "access function," and in theory does not convey any assumptions about the level of representation, namely if pre-coordinated or not, or about the quality of its vocabulary control and semantic (paradigmatic) structure. Yet, it is more connoted with subject description, because it is used mostly in pre-coordinated, *i.e.*, subject co-extensive systems. Conversely, the term "descriptor," which seems more bound to description, has a stronger connotation with facilitating access, as it comes from the era of thesaurus development, where the granularity of concepts and the primacy of lexicon, using controlled representations, was a response to the constraints of the unidirectional retrieval of descriptive phrases (conventional pre-coordinated subject headings).

In a more encompassing perspective at the level where the field is defined are the terms/concepts of "aboutness," "subject," "topic," etc. (see Hjørland[25]). The difficulties here show how the very concept of subject analysis, or subject indexing, holds a large share of the fuzziness and dispersion that affects the understanding of library and information science, notably in its invisible substrate.[26]

In between these two distant points, another significant case can be made for the syntagmatic aspects of a subject indexing language; *i.e.*, the most discussed, yet still far from being clarified, issue of pre-coordination. For many years it has been one of the most controversial topics in subject indexing in several aspects: its value and usefulness for users, its practicability in economic terms, its technical difficulties . . . and, above all, its relevance in automated retrieval systems. In the professional debate, it has been hard to find answers as the matter is "elusive, interesting and difficult" as concluded by E. Svenonius, who presents not less than 20 different criteria (most of them coming from M. Taube) to discuss the subject.[27] Despite the importance of syntagmatic relationships for the communicative function of subject heading languages, they have always received much less attention than paradigmatic relationships, and this imbalance, noted by Green,[28] is still in place. A wealth of literature has been produced showing very different approaches and positions about pre-coordination, concerning either traditional catalogues or Internet retrieval issues (see, for example, Mann[29] *versus* Chan[30]). Besides, it seems that technological advances have not been helping consensus on the matter, as networked resources expand and when low cost solutions may appear not only as the most practicable ones but also, in spite of the lower quality, satisfactory enough. Again, it is the ground on which this controversy still develops that is often not clarified, namely about the levels and goals of professional and non-professional solutions, and the reasons why, where and how different options can be more or less appropriate and feasible.

Most of the above mentioned issues arise from the complexity, dynamics and plasticity of *language*, the foreground of all these problems, whether it is about natural language, controlled languages or the language that expresses professional concerns and concepts. The complexity of language issues and, therefore, of controlled and professional languages, is nowadays increased with the *multilingual requirements* of the networked environment[31] which particularly affect the reach of alphabetical subject systems. Although the usefulness and power of structured terminological languages within the network environment is largely recognized, it is clear that the language-independence nature of classifications is among the factors that contribute to highlight their network applicability.[32]

Also, the growing *interdisciplinarity* of knowledge domains, now more exposed in the network environment, is bringing new complexities with implications for information retrieval languages, which influence some traditional qualities and features of subject representation systems, such as *stability* and *enumeration*. Therefore, new conceptual trends are subtly changing the underlying philosophy of subject systems, adding to the difficulty in finding common ground among them. It is the trend towards non-enumerative systems, through the growing importance of faceted analysis in classifications[33] and the trend to compromise between *precision and specificity* and *flexibility and scalability* in alphabetical subject headings, through facet decomposition and syntax simplification (see O'Neill *et al.*[34]); or towards alternative design of syntax expressions, such as in USE–*Universal Subject Environment*–in order to cope with multinational, multilingual and multicultural usability of complex subject headings.[35]

SEEKING COMMON GROUND

This very brief characterization of what is in the air in the professional field stresses the need for strengthening its conceptual basis at a level higher than that of particular systems or solutions. Notably the need exists to pursue better consensus and understanding at an international level about subject alphabetical retrieval systems. But how can this be achieved in our current complex and fast-changing environment? There are no easy answers, all the more since nowadays the meaning of *standard* and *standardization* is becoming diffuse. Nevertheless, some paths can be devised and these begin by getting a deeper knowledge about what is in our current library subject systems.

A first step in this direction was already taken within IFLA, with the study *Principles Underlying Subject Heading Languages.*[36] Developed with wide international participation, the study provides a framework of agreed definitions and principles according to which 11 subject indexing systems, pertaining to ten different countries and 9 languages, were analyzed. Each reviewed system is represented with quite comprehensive information, taken from the systems' materials (manuals or other introductory or guidance tools, subject heading lists, etc.). A very useful aspect is that all texts from sources published in languages other than English were translated, only the examples of subject headings remaining in their original languages. What was achieved with this first step? Not much that can provide future solutions, but a lot in terms of starting potential.

Some aspects were immediately revealed. Subject systems are currently more advanced and concordant with each other in the kinds of technical devices for terminological control and semantic (paradigmatic) linking, although they show differences in the depth of the linguistic analysis behind their structures. On the other hand, while they all consider rules for subject heading syntax in some way, they are less structured and similar in respect to syntagmatic aspects of subject headings. Here we can identify an area where some kind of standardization would be very useful, making it easier for the user to understand headings' structure in different systems, and facilitating the mapping of data structures between systems. Another general aspect that the study shows is that the definition of systematic and comprehensive subject indexing policies is still a weak aspect, deserving to be emphasized and supported by sharing experiences and producing recommendations. Finally, it is worth noting that in most of the cases–especially European–the systems' manuals or guidelines are quite recent (six were prepared or published in their first version since 1985, most of them having updated editions before 1990).[37] This fairly recent editorial activity concerning manuals and guidelines for subject heading systems shows that the concern with the theoretical framework is currently higher than in the past. It also demonstrates a renewed vitality that contradicts the (not uncommon) view about alphabetical systems, namely those that use pre-coordination, as 'legacy' systems maintained by mere tradition. These are just some general points raised in a brief overview of the study, as it lends itself to a multitude of analysis, that can serve different purposes.

What the study best consubstantiates is the goal of promoting *understanding of different SHLs by identifying commonalities underlying them and providing a structure for their comparative study.* All the other goals defined for the *Principles* are more open and have a prospective nature: *to facilitate subject access to information on an international level; to assist in developing SHLs . . . ; to provide a theoretical rationale for particular standards or guidelines for SHL construction and application.* These goals reveal the place of *Principles Underlying Subject Heading Languages (SHLs)* as a starting point. Therefore, the study is not intended, as it may seem at first sight (*e.g.*, in Hoerman & Furniss[38]) as an evaluation and it does not predict future agendas, but leaves an ineffaceable mark about the need and potential of future developments in subject heading languages at the international level. It seeks *unity in diversity* which is, in the words of Elaine Svenonius in the *Foreword* of her recent book, "one of the grander aims of science, by reducing surface phenomena to simpler underlying regularities."[39] Understanding such regularities is not to offer immediate solutions. Yet it is fundamental to begin with, if questions, problems and particular issues requiring solutions are not exclusive to one system and have no benefit in being addressed regarding others.

Furthering what is already achieved, or promoting other international initiatives related to the same scope and aims would greatly benefit the theoretical background of the subject indexing field, while fostering a much needed consolidation of both conceptual and pragmatic frameworks for subject indexing tools at an international level.

CONCLUSION

The perspective we have tried to convey is that any efforts to improve the conceptual basis and the capabilities of already existing subject access services and tools (no matter how small their coverage now may appear in the face of the massive Web search engines) can apply to all of the expanded library purposes mentioned in the beginning. This may not seem clear for many of those nowadays engaged mostly with the technological side of search and retrieval systems, namely with the Internet search industry, for whom there may be no big attraction in the so-called "library technicalities" because they are not novel, or carry with them a hard to understand luggage of rules and procedures. It is, however, irrefutable that library culture in the KO field should be refined and reinforced at the conceptual and standard levels, if the aim is to support effective KO tools with a wider target.

The new major difficulty that has been added to the field is the "open-endedness" of the network environment, making it difficult to understand–and to define–what the objectives are. "Where limits are not set, objectives cannot be measured, and if they cannot be measured, they are unrealistic. It is at the level of formulating objectives that coping with open-endedness and formulating minimal sets of data elements need to be addressed."[40] In our view, such "minimal sets" are not only about data elements, but also about a minimum of more profound, although general, ontological commitments. For realistic commitments, *i.e.*, sustainable in the long term and of wide impact, such a minimum is to be drawn from a professional ground better consolidated at the international level.

REFERENCES*

1. Soergel, D. The rise of ontologies or the reinvention of classification. *Journal of The American Society of Information Science*, 50 (12): 1119-1120 (1999).

2. Mcguiness, D.L. *Ontologies come of age* (2001) [online]. http://www.ksl.stanford.edu/people/dlm/papers/ontologies-come-of-age-mit-press-(with-citation).htm.

3. Gruber, T.R. *Towards principles for the design of ontologies used for knowledge sharing* [online] (1993). http://ksl-web.stanford.edu/KSL_Abstracts/KSL-93-04.html. Guarino, N. Formal ontology and information systems. In *Formal Ontology in Information Systems*. Proc. of FOIS'98, Trento, Italy, 1998, p. 3-15. IOS Press, Amsterdam, 1998. Also available online at: http://www.ladseb.pd.cnr.it/infor/Ontology/Papers/FOIS98.pdf.

4. Berners-Lee, T.; Hendler, J.; Lassila, O. The semantic web. *Scientific American*, May 2001 [online]. http://www.sciam.com/2001/0501issue/0501berners-lee.html.

5. Cordeiro, M.I. From Library Authority Control to Network Authoritative Metadata Sources. Paper presented to the IFLA Satellite Meeting *Subject Retrieval in a Networked Environment*, Dublin, Ohio, Aug. 14-16, 2001. Cordeiro, M.I.; Slavic, A. Data models for knowledge organization tools: evolution and perspectives. In *Challenges in knowledge representation and organization for the 21st century: integration of knowledge across boundaries. Proc. of the Seventh International ISKO Conference, 10-13 July 2002, Granada, Spain*, 127-134. Edited by Maria Lopez-Huertas. Würzburg: Ergon Verlag, 2002.

6. Doerr, M. The CIDOC CRM–An ontological approach to semantic interoperability of metadata (2001), p. 5 [online]. http://cidoc.ics.forth.gr/crm_documents.html.

7. Fugmann, R. Obstacles to progress in mechanized subject access and the necessity of a paradigm change. In *Saving the time of the library user through subject access innovation: papers in honor of Pauline Atherton Cochrane*, p. 7-45. Champaign, IL: Grad. School of Lib. and Inf. Science, 2000.

8. Weinberg, B.H. Complexity in indexing systems–abandonment and failure: implications for organizing the Internet. *Proc. of the ASIS Annual Conference, 1996* (1996) [online]. http://www.asis.org/annual-96/ElectronicProceedings/weinberg.html.

9. McIlwaine, I.C. and Williamson, N.J. International trends in subject analysis research. *Knowledge Organization*, 26(1):23-29 (1999).

10. as in 7.

11. Bloomfield, M. Indexing: neglected and poorly understood. *Cataloging & Classification Quarterly*, 33 (1):63-75 (2001).

12. Denemberg, R. *Structuring and indexing the Internet* (1996) [online]. http://lcweb.loc.gov/z3950/agency/papers/italy.html.

13. Hudon, M. Innovation and tradition in knowledge organization schemes on the Internet, or, finding one's way in the virtual library. In *Dynamism and stability in knowledge organization. Proc. of the Sixth International ISKO Conference, 2000* p. 35-40. Edited by Clare Beghtol, Lynne C. Howarth and Nancy J. Williamson. Würzburg: Ergon, 2000.

14. Hert, C.A.; Jacob, E.K.; Dawson, P. A usability assessment of online indexing structures in the networked environment. *Journal of the American Society for Information Science and Technology*, 51(11):971-988 (2000).

15. Chan, L.M. Exploiting LCSH, LCC and DDC to retrieve networked resources. *Bicentennial Conference on Bibliographic Control for the New Millenium, Library of Congress, 2000* [online]. http://lcweb.loc.gov/catdir/bibcontrol/chan_paper.html.

16. Jansen, B.J.; Pooch, U. A review of web searching studies and a framework for future research. *Journal of the American Society for Information Science and Technology*, 52(3):235-246 (2001).

17. Gödert, W. Information as a cognitive construction: a communication-theoretic model and consequences for information systems. *Knowledge Organization*, 23(4): 206-212 (1996).

18. Williamson, N.J. Standards and rules for subject access. *Cataloging & Classification Quarterly*, 21(3/4):55-176 (1996).

19. Mann, T. "Cataloguing must change!" and indexer consistency studies: misreading the evidence at our peril. *Cataloging & Classification Quarterly* 23(3/4):3-45 (1997).

20. Milstead, J.L. Needs for research in indexing. *Journal of the American Society for Information Science and Technology*, 45 (8):577-582 (1994).

21. Williamson, N.J. Standards and rules for subject access. *Cataloging & Classification Quarterly*, 21(3/4):55-176 (1996). Williamson, N. J. Thesauri in the digital age: stability and dynamism in their development and use. In *Dynamism and stability in knowledge organization. Proc. of the Sixth International ISKO Conference, 2000* p. 268-274. Edited by Clare Beghtol, Lynne C. Howarth and Nancy J. Williamson. Würzburg: Ergon, 2000: 268-274.

22. Nicholson, D. *et al.* HILT: High-Level Thesaurus Project: Final Report to RSLP & JISC (2001) [online]. http://hilt.cdlr.strath.ac.uk/Reports/Documents/HILTfinalreport.doc.

23. Stone, A. The LCSH century: a brief history of the Library of Congress Subject Headings, and introduction to the centennial essays. *Cataloging & Classification Quarterly* 29(1/2):1-15 (2000).

24. Studwell, W. USE, the Universal Subject Environment: a new subject access approach in the time of the Internet. In *Internet Searching and Indexing*, p. 197-209. New York, London, Oxford: The Haworth Press, Inc., 2000.

25. Hjørland, B. Towards a theory of aboutness, subject, topicality, theme, domain, field, content . . . and relevance. *Journal of the American Society for Information Science and Technology*, 52(9):774-778 (2001).

26. Bates, M. The invisible substrate of information science. *Journal of the American Society for Information Science*, 50 (12):1043-1050 (1999).

27. Svenonius, E. Precordination or not? In *Subject indexing: principles and practices in the 90's. Proc. of the IFLA Satellite Meeting held in Lisbon, Portugal, 17-18 August 1993*, 231-255. München: K.G. Saur, 1995.

28. Green, R. Syntagmatic relationships in index languages: a reassessment. *Library Quarterly*, 65 (4):365-385 (1995).

29. Mann, T. Is precoordination unnecessary in LCSH? Are web sites more important to catalog than books? A reference librarian's thoughts on the future of bibliographic control. *Bicentennial Conference on Bibliographic Control for the New Millenium, Library of Congress, 2000* [online]. http://lcweb.loc.gov/catdir/bibcontrol/mann_paper.html.

30. Chan, L.M. Exploiting LCSH, LCC and DDC to retrieve networked resources. *Bicentennial Conference on Bibliographic Control for the New Millenium, Library of Congress, 2000* [online]. http://lcweb.loc.gov/catdir/bibcontrol/chan_paper.html.

31. Chan, L.M.; Lin, X.; Zeng, M. Structural and multilingual approaches to subject access on the Web. *65th IFLA Council and General Conference, Bangkok, 2000* (1999) [online]. http://www.ifla.org/IV/ifla65/papers/012-117e.htm.

32. Koch, T. *et al.* The role of classification schemes in Internet resource description and discovery. DESIRE Project deliverable D3.2 (3) (1997) [online]. http://www.ukoln.ac.uk/metadata/desire/classification/.

33. McIlwaine, I.C. and Williamson, N.J. International trends in subject analysis research. *Knowledge Organization*, 26(1):23-29 (1999). Hjørland, B.; Albrechtsen, H. An analysis of some trends in classification research. *Knowledge Organization*, 26(3):31-139 (1999).

34. O'Neill, E.T. *et al.* FAST: Faceted Application of Subject Terminology. Paper presented to the IFLA Satellite Meeting *Subject Retrieval in a Networked Environment*, Dublin, Ohio, Aug. 14-16, 2001 (in press).

35. Studwell, W. USE, the Universal Subject Environment: a new subject access approach in the time of the Internet. In *Internet Searching and Indexing*, p. 197-209. New York, London, Oxford: The Haworth Press, Inc., 2000.

36. Lopes; M.I.; Beall, J., *eds. Principles underlying subject heading languages (SHLs).* [Prepared by] the Working Group on Principles Underlying Subject Heading Languages and approved by the IFLA Section on Classification and Indexing. München: Saur, 1999.

37. Lopes, M.I. Principles underlying subject heading languages: an international approach. *61st IFLA Council and General Conference, Istanbul, 1995* (1995) [online]. http://www.ifla.org/IV/ifla61/61-lopm.htm. Also in *International Cataloguing and Bibliographic Control*, 25(1) (Jan.-Mar.):10-12 (1996).

38. Hoerman, H.L.; Furniss, K.A. Turning practice into principles: a comparison of the IFLA principles underlying subject heading languages (SHLs) and the principles underlying the Library of Congress Subject Headings system. *Cataloging & Classification Quarterly*, 29(1/2):31-52 (2000).

39. Svenonius, E. *The intellectual foundation of information organization.* Foreword. Cambridge, MA; London: The MIT Press, 2000.

40. Svenonius, E. *The intellectual foundation of information organization.* p. 23. Cambridge, MA; London: The MIT Press, 2000.

*All URLs accessed 2002.08.26.

Expanding Audiences for Education-Related Information and Resources: Classificatory Structures on the World Wide Web

Michèle Hudon

SUMMARY. Education is a culturally and politically branded domain of knowledge and practice, and education specialists have traditionally remained somewhat isolated, communicating mainly on the general level of "basic educational principles." The expansion of the World Wide Web could change this situation; there exist on the Web a substantial number of education-related resources which have become accessible to international audiences. In this paper, the authors look at how these resources are organized with a view to answering two questions: (1) In a context of global exchanges, are education-related resources available on the Web organized in such a way as to maximize efficiency of identification and retrieval? (2) In virtual libraries with specialized collections on education, do categorization schemes and terminology reflect anything other than local perspectives and systems? *[Article copies available for a fee from The Haworth Document Delivery Service: 1-800-HAWORTH. E-mail address: <docdelivery@haworthpress.com> Website: <http://www.HaworthPress.com> © 2003 by The Haworth Press, Inc. All rights reserved.]*

Michèle Hudon, PhD, is Assistant Professor, École de bibliothéconomie et des sciences de l'information, Université de Montréal, C.P. 6128, Succursale Centre-ville, Montréal, Québec H3C 3J7, Canada (E-mail: michele.hudon@umontreal.ca).

[Haworth co-indexing entry note]: "Expanding Audiences for Education-Related Information and Resources: Classificatory Structures on the World Wide Web." Hudon, Michèle. Co-published simultaneously in *Cataloging & Classification Quarterly* (The Haworth Information Press, an imprint of The Haworth Press, Inc.) Vol. 37, No. 1/2, 2003, pp. 81-96; and: *Knowledge Organization and Classification in International Information Retrieval* (ed: Nancy J. Williamson, and Clare Beghtol) The Haworth Information Press, an imprint of The Haworth Press, Inc., 2003, pp. 81-96. Single or multiple copies of this article are available for a fee from The Haworth Document Delivery Service [1-800-HAWORTH, 9:00 a.m. - 5:00 p.m. (EST). E-mail address: docdelivery@haworthpress.com].

http://www.haworthpress.com/store/product.asp?sku=J104

Digital Object Identifier: 10.1300/J104v37n01_07

KEYWORDS. Virtual libraries, education-related resources, Web directories, subject trees

INTRODUCTION

Education is a culturally and politically branded domain of knowledge and practice. Objectives, methods and systems vary considerably from one country, territory or state to another. This constitutes a significant obstacle to efficient information finding and information sharing, and communities of educators and education specialists have traditionally remained somewhat isolated, communicating mainly on the general level of "basic educational principles."

The expansion of the World Wide Web could change this situation: on the Web, internationally, nationally and regionally dispersed domain specialists can regroup into a localized community where time and space are no longer issues.[1] Educators from around the world now participate in online discussions, converse in real-time, collaborate through e-mail, and share the contents of specialized databases. Furthermore, there exist on the Web a substantial number of education-related resources which bypass national borders and have become accessible to international audiences. There is some evidence, however, that the Web is not used as much as it could be by researchers and practitioners in education.[2]

It seems relatively easy to locate instructional resources on the Web, but much more difficult to uncover resources that have education as their main subject, and that are concerned with theory, philosophy and research rather than with the daily activities and tools of teaching and training. A keyword or free-text search using the word "education" by itself, or even in combination with any other, will retrieve thousands of hits, most of which have nothing or only little to do with education as a field of knowledge. The use of hierarchical structures offered in general directories or in special virtual libraries could thus be productive for the researcher in education, who has a lesser need for localized and personalized information than her/his colleague working in the classroom.

Our current research focuses on two questions: (1) In a context of global exchanges, are education-related resources available on the Web organized in such a way as to maximize efficiency of identification and retrieval? (2) In virtual libraries with specialized collections on education, do categorization schemes and terminology reflect anything other than local perspectives and systems?

In this paper, we submit interesting observations made while comparing, among themselves and with traditional classificatory structures, a sample of subject trees setup manually or semi-automatically on the Web as navigation aids for the information searcher in the field of education. Elements of comparison include: the structure (i.e., main categories and sub-categories), the facets used to partition sets of resources, the level of specificity allowed, and the potential for exhaustivity. Also addressed is the issue of whether the chosen categories and relations may be considered universal, and therefore transferable from one culture to another. Obstacles remaining at the terminological level are discussed briefly. The process of classifying itself, accuracy of resource placement, and the estimated quality and relevance of classified resources are not examined here.

CLASSIFICATORY STRUCTURES AND VIRTUAL LIBRARIES

To facilitate the discovery of Web resources, a large number of subject categorizing schemes have been developed. Variously known as subject guides, subject directories, subject trees and so on, they "manifest the traditional classification principles of hierarchical structure, domain partition, subordination of the specific to the general, and array of related subjects."[3] Web content organizers have been quick to recognize the advantages offered by hierarchical structures: improved browsing facilities, possibility of broadening or narrowing a search as required, logical partitioning of a database, provision of a context, potential for high precision searching, potential for multilingual access, and improved interoperability where the same structures are used. Implementing a concept-based approach with which users are already familiar, subject trees are structured in such a way as to represent the relationships between the different concepts. This is done either through the use of references (e.g., documents *see also* reports) or by grouping similar subjects and documents,[4] allowing users to make their own relevance judgments, as they prefer to do.[5] The classificatory structure is viewed as "a desirable compliment [*sic*] to a search engine type service."[6] Subject trees have yet to go through systematic performance testing, and although there is only loose and indirect evidence that these rather expensive search tools are indeed used by average Web searchers,[7] established structures continue to expand while dozens of new classified sites are launched every day.

On the Web, traditional bibliographic classification schemes coexist with home-grown structures strictly based on literary warrant and built through a bottom-up approach "particularly well suited to the mass of varied and fluctuating material that makes up so much of the Web."[8] Home-grown structures are flexible and easy to modify, unconstrained by the physical demands of shelf arrangement and proprietary collections, and they can very quickly absorb new areas of interest. On the other hand, they amplify the problem of classification subjectivity. Resource classification and scheme development are often synchronous processes, potentially leading to lack of consistency in classification and to low representational predictability in access and retrieval.

Home-grown classificatory structures typically integrate into a single sequence domains or topics (e.g., Distance learning), resource types (e.g., Journals), and audiences (Children's pages). This has much to do with the fact that distinctions that were possible in a physical setting, where journals and children's materials were separated from the rest of the collection for example, cannot be made anymore. While in traditional bibliographic classification a notation representing resource type, location, potential audience, etc., was "appended" to that representing a particular subject, home-grown structures, with no absolute need for notation, tend to be strictly enumerative and put on the same level, for example, topic and form of presentation (Early childhood education and Web directories are examples from *Yahoo!*). This is viewed by some as a retrograde approach to classification, as it does not account for the post coordination facilities afforded by modern information processing technology, and can accommodate little more than a superficial level of subject analysis.[9]

Classificatory structures are at the core of virtual libraries. Virtual libraries are systematically organized collections of selected active links to electronic resources available on the Web. General Web directories act as general virtual libraries, and the scope of their collections compares to that of traditional public or academic libraries. Web directories are where most searchers, novices and specialists alike, will first browse for information. Virtual libraries do not provide direct physical access to their collections, forcing the information searcher through several levels of more or less systematic conceptual organization before allowing her/him to access a Web page, site or document.

To be useful, structured resource organization schemes must be intuitive, logical and easy to navigate. In our context, this calls for an examination of whether it is at the very least possible, and preferably easy, for a searcher to discover previously unknown relevant education-related resources through a process of logical navigation from general categories to precise topics. The logic of the navigation may be linked either to simple instinct or to learned familiarity with traditional ways of presenting education-related information in reference sources and in traditional bibliographic classification schemes.

LOCATING EDUCATION-RELATED RESOURCES IN GENERAL WEB DIRECTORIES

In traditional bibliographic organization schemes, Education is found at the first or second level of the hierarchy. In both the *Dewey Decimal Classification* (DDC) and the *Universal Decimal Classification* (UDC) for example, Education is at the 100 Divisions level, within the Social sciences main class. In the *Library of Congress Classification* (LCC), Education is itself a first-level class, but it belongs to a cluster of classes that include the various social sciences and match the 300/3 class in the DDC and UDC respectively.

Table 1 shows that, in traditional as in home-grown classificatory structures, Education is usually a high-level entry. Even though a few directories give it only sub-category status, and position it in such questionable environments as Library or Reference, among Flags, Museums, and Parliamentary practice, collections of education-related resources remain easy to locate.

A downward move within hierarchies reveals many similarities and important differences in sub-arrangements, both at the conceptual and at the terminological levels. Table 2 lists second-level categories proposed respectively by *Yahoo!* (13 of 39 categories), *Open Directory/Google* (13 of 20 categories), and *Librarian's Index to the Internet* (LII) (13 of 44 categories). For comparison purposes, the internal layouts of DDC 370 and of LCC class L have also been supplied. DDC is already used to structure general virtual collections (see, for example: Canadian Information by Subject at http://www.nlc-bnc.ca/caninfo/ecaninfo.htm and Bubl Link at http://bubl.ac.uk/link/ddc.html). As for LCC, it is very familiar to researchers due to its wide application in North American academic and research libraries.

The expansion to the second hierarchical level in the organization of the discipline shows more of the same lack of discrimination between various types of resources, and want of directions as to what aspect of a complex subject (e.g., a bibliography on bilingual adult basic education in Canada) has been, or should be, given priority in classifying and when searching for resources.

Three universal facets of the domain of education will be recognized easily among the sub-categories. They are: educational level, type of education, and specific population (or targeted audience). An obvious commonality is the use of some or all educational levels as subdividing criteria. Levels are not, how-

TABLE 1. Education in Bibliographic Classification Schemes and General Web Directories

Classificatory structure	Location of Education
DDC (21st ed.)	3 Social sciences > 37 Education
LCC	L Education
Yahoo![17]	Home > Education
AltaVista[18]	Home > Library > Education
Open Directory Project[19]/*Google*[20]	Home > Reference > Education
Librarians' Index to the Internet[21]	Home > Education

TABLE 2. First Level of Subdivision of Education in Bibliographic Classification Schemes and Web Directories

DDC (8/8)	LCC (4/4)	*Yahoo*! (13/39)	*Open Directory/Google* (13/20)	*Librarian's Index to the Internet* (13/44)
370 Education 371 School and their activities; special education 372 Elementary ed. 373 Secondary ed. 374 Adult education 375 Curricula 378 Higher education 379 Public policy issues in education	L Education (general) LA History of education LB Theory and practice of education LC Special aspects of education	Academic competitions Adult and continuing education Bibliographies Chats and Forums Conferences Distance learning Early childhood education Financial aid Higher education Instructional technology K-12 Policy Theory and methods	Alumni directories Colleges and universities Directories Distance learning Early childhood Educators Home schooling How to study Instructional technology K through 12 Methods and theories Special education Subjects	General resources Accreditation Basic education Business schools California Choosing a college Distance education Early childhood Environmental education Internet in education Learning disabilities Literacy School violence and safety

ever, presented in a consistent fashion: Primary and secondary education can be lumped together or split, and designations vary: K-12, K through 12, Elementary education–Secondary education, Primary and secondary school, etc. Higher education and Colleges and universities contain similar resources. Distance education/Distance learning and Instructional technology appear in most structures, but surprisingly the facet Subject (i.e., subject taught) does not. DDC and LCC naturally appear more focused, with fewer sub-categories to choose from; but even there, categories overlap, and this generates ambiguity. In LCC for example, what is considered a special aspect of education that is not already part of its theory or practice? At this level, it is interesting to note that none of the organization schemes presents classes that are mutually exclusive. For the searcher, however, traditional bibliographic schemes continue to offer a definite advantage in that they contain notes, cross-references and explanations, all components that are sorely lacking in home-grown structures.

Flatter and simpler configurations are consistently preferred in subject gateways. The classificatory structures of general Web directories are shallow, varying from three levels (a *de facto* standard in most virtual libraries) to a maximum, rarely reached, of nine levels. Shown below are examples of structural depth provided:

Yahoo!

Home > Education > Theories and methods > Montessori methods > Teacher education

Open Directory/Google

Home > Reference > Education > Methods and theories > Learning theories > Inquiry based learning > Theory > Activity theory

Librarian's Index to the Internet

Home > Education and Libraries > Education topics > Study skills

The logic of the hierarchies thus created is reasonably explicit and quite acceptable, with the occasional mishap such as the listing of both Directories and Alumni directories as coordinate classes in the same sequence of the *Open Directory/Google*, when the second one is a natural sub-class of the first one. Following a tendency toward normal distribution, the bulk of postings is found at the middle levels. The designation of the various categories, however, does not allow the searcher to know in advance whether the latter contain instructional materials, resources on education with background information on the process of teaching and its results, or both. It is unclear as to what will be found in a category labeled Educators.

Home-grown subject trees are entirely dependent on the content of existing collections. Such structures could never become useful reference tools, and one may even question their efficiency as navigation tools since there will always be missing hierarchical levels in the structures and important gaps in the internal arrangement of classes and sub-classes. One may only hope that cross-classification treatments, made possible in a hyperlinked environment, have indeed been implemented.

Associative relations between categories and between sub-categories are few and far between, with the *Open Directory/Google* faring slightly better by offering such useful relationships as, for example, the semantic connection established between Reference > Education > Methods and theories > Learning theories and Society > Philosophy > Philosophy of education.

On the whole, with the exception of the *Librarian's Index to the Internet*, the proposed structures and headings are general and rather conventional. LII, however, offers a list of specific and very pragmatic second-level categories (Business schools, Choosing a college, Environmental education, School violence and safety, etc.) that are obviously intended for an American audience rather than for an international one.

LOCATING EDUCATION-RELATED RESOURCES IN SPECIAL VIRTUAL LIBRARIES

Special collections are set-up and maintained with a particular group of users in mind. Special libraries create or adopt specialized classification schemes which provide a structure and a terminology owing at least as much to scientific as to literary warrant. Specialized classification schemes reflect more accurately the internal organization of the discipline, and keep up to date more easily than do universal structures. Domain specialists, already familiar with physical collections entirely devoted to their field of practice, will expect special virtual libraries to provide them with the same level of service and the same quality and relevance of resources. And so will educators and education specialists when they explore virtual collections in education.

Virtual libraries in education are set-up and maintained by governments, universities, and official agencies sharing an interest and/or responsibilities for education and training, as well as by professional associations of educators and education specialists. There are dozens of such libraries or portals on the Web, which exhibit much duplication in collection contents. As is often the case with physical collections, virtual special collections are not necessarily easy to find; indeed, special virtual libraries and information gateways are "very poor at self-promotion."[10]

Resources found in virtual libraries in education may have been selected and organized for the benefit of educators only, for an audience of parents and other taxpayers, for actual and potential students, for mixed audiences of specialists and non specialists. Consequently, conceptual structures and terminology will have to be as accessible as those that are used in general directories.

Five of the best known virtual libraries of education-related resources have been used in our sample. We have considered only those libraries that include a clearly marked reference section containing sources and documents, excluding commercial portals such as *Education World* (http://www.education-world.com) because they put more emphasis on news, products, chat lines, etc. Of those five libraries, three are maintained in the United States, one in Australia, and one in the United Kingdom; only one, *Education Index*,[9] presents itself as a commercial venture. Collections are generally small: *AskEric*[10] and *Education Index* both supply approximately 3,000 catalogued resources. Table 3 lists first-level categories in all five structures.

On the whole and as expected, organizational schemes in special virtual libraries are more homogeneous, more focused, and in the top levels of the hierarchies, contain only education specific categories corresponding to true topics rather than to types of resources. But our sample shows that there is quite a lot of room for variations, even at the macrostructure level.

Our first library, the *Education Virtual Library*,[11] the easiest to find since it forms part of the W3 virtual library (http://vlib.org) is maintained in Australia. Its editors have chosen to partition their collection using four facets only: education level, type of resource, type of sites, country (geographical location). A single layer of further subdivision is available. *Education Index* offers the possibility of searching under one of 55 subjects (Agriculture, Arts, and surprisingly Education, etc.) or, in its interesting Lifestage section, under one of 11 categories corresponding for the most part to educational levels. *AskEric*, and *SOSIG*[12] offer lists of categories that represent most explicitly major themes and areas of research in education. *GEM*,[13] the popular *Gateway to Educational Materials* has a structure that emphasizes curriculum subjects, with only Educational technology and Vocational education disrupting the apparent logic of this arrangement.

As was the case in general directories, educational levels are used at or near the top of hierarchies in all but one classificatory structure. This type of organization uses as partitioning criterion a characteristic that will be universally recognized and it is efficient. However, the benefit of this option are greatly reduced if the main or sub-categories become too specific. Middle or College education, for example, correspond to different realities within various education systems, and may not exist at all in some places. The *Education Virtual Library* keeps it simple and more accessible, presenting only four educational,

TABLE 3. First Level of Subdivision in Virtual Libraries in Education

Education Virtual Library	*Education Index*	*AskEric*	*SOSIG Education*	*GEM*
Education (General) By education level Primary (K1-6) Secondary (K7-12) Tertiary Postgraduate By resources provided Bibliography Books Course details Databases Funding Lectures and tutorials Teaching Methodologies Software Educational Technology By type of site By country	Prenatal and infant Preschool Primary education Middle education Secondary education College education Distance learning Graduate education Continuing education Parenting + 55 subject categories such as Agriculture, Arts, Education, etc.	Counseling Educ. levels Educ. management Educ. technology ERIC Evaluation Family life General education Librarianship Specific populations Subjects Teaching	Adult education Educ. policy Educ. theory Elementary educ. Further educ. Higher educ. Primary educ. Secondary educ. Special educ. Teaching methods	Arts Educational technology Foreign languages Health Language arts Mathematics Philosophy Physical education Religion Science Social studies Vocational education

and universal, levels: the primary (K1-6), the secondary (K7-12), the tertiary, and the postgraduate.

Hierarchies are shallow, even more so than in most general directories. Even *AskEric*, which is maintained by an organization with a long history of information management in the field of education, does not offer more than three levels of subdivision (e.g., General education > Learning theories > Experiential learning). At all hierarchical levels, this leads to long lists of resources, presented in alphabetical order of name/title; this is certainly appropriate for browsing and discovery, but not very useful for identification of resources on specific topics. One could venture that *Open directory/Google* probably offers a better service at this level. It is interesting to note that although regional or national directories could prioritize subordinates and display them in more significant places, the process has not been abused; most structures are truly conventional and potentially accessible to a wide audience.

Variations in terminology exist, but they rarely reflect variations in concepts. In fact, such variations as Special education/Specific populations, Educational administration/Educational management, or Teaching/Teaching methods/Teaching methodologies are most unfortunate. They do nothing to add to the clarity of the structure, and they complicate needlessly the task of the searcher who must apply his own vocabulary control methods when browsing several collections.

As was the case in general Web directories, it is not easy to isolate resources on education from instructional resources. Since it puts such emphasis on subjects, *GEM* of course makes it quite clear that it provides mainly instructional materials. On the other hand, *AskEric*'s main categories suggest that it offers lots of resources that most certainly are not for direct use in the classroom. It is not entirely clear what is included in the other collections, but it is likely that resources classified under a specific educational level will be of more interest to practitioners than to researchers.

To establish a parallel between new organizational structures and traditional ones, we chose the organizing scheme provided in the *Encyclopedia of Educational Research*,[14] a reference source widely used around the world. The *Encyclopedia* assigns articles to one of the 16 broad categories listed in Table 4. The *Encyclopedia* offers a three-level deep hierarchical structure which could actually suit quite well virtual libraries in education (e.g., Agencies and Institutions > Private companies in education > Textbook publishing companies; Organizational structure and governance > Educational administration > Financing schools).

All facets of education, with the exception of geographical location, are put to good use in this environment which takes away the emphasis on educational levels characteristic of most other organizing schemes in the field. Main categories are more precisely delimited and will make it easier for the researcher to identify

TABLE 4. Main Categories in the *Encyclopedia of Educational Research*

Agencies and institutions related to education
Context of education
Counselling, medical, and psychological services
Curriculum, elementary and secondary
Education of exceptional persons
Education related to identifiable groups
Educational measurement and assessment
Internal operational policies and practices
International differences in education
Levels of education
Methods of inquiry
Occupationally oriented education
Organizational structure and governance
Policymaking arenas
Teachers
Teaching, Instructional systems and strategies

the best pathway to the lower levels of the hierarchy, where relevant resources may be found. Also of interest in this structure is the use of categories such as Agencies related to education, Context of education, and International differences in education which are nowhere to be found in the virtual libraries making up our sample. Furthermore, with the exception of *AskEric*, none of the virtual collections offers the one or more categories needed to include resources covering peripheral but important areas of education, such as counseling and psychological services. Virtual libraries in education appear to be taking a more restrictive view of what is an education-related resource than does the *Encyclopedia*; here again, general directories may be more efficient and useful as they will at least lead users to relevant resources classified in sociology, psychology, linguistics, etc., through their rudimentary cross-referencing system.

This leads us to suggest that organizing structures used in virtual libraries in education are more difficult to use and possibly less efficient than subject trees developed for general directories, and even where subject specialists are concerned. Some special virtual libraries do not even provide keyword access to the classificatory structure, as most general directories do. And when a keyword search feature is available, there are no explanations as to what exactly is being searched, how it is being searched, and whether any form of controlled vocabulary is available in the background.

LOCATING RESOURCES ON THE PROBLEM-BASED APPROACH TO LEARNING, TEACHING AND TRAINING

Educators and education specialists use virtual libraries to browse collections of resources in an area of interest, to keep on top of what is happening in their specialty, and to find clusters of related resources. It remains difficult for them to locate specific subjects in the various home-grown classificatory structures available. As a rule, it seems easier to uncover instructional materials and to establish further distinctions using educational levels or curriculum subjects as specifying criteria than it is to find information about instructional theories and methods.

A searcher looking for Web resources on problem-based learning (PBL), for example, is most likely to first input keywords into a search box to see what is available. Doing this in *Google*, without any search limitations, will bring back approximately 124,000 references, but the same search in *Yahoo!* fetches only two; neither result is satisfactory, and a search through subject trees may be worth a try.

Virtual libraries in education have little to offer to the individual looking for resources on a specific topic. *AskEric* provides an alphabetical list of topics that covers only the headings appearing in the subject tree. If any information on PBL is available, it is likely to be found under General Education > Learning theories. The next hierarchical level, however, offers a restricted choice of two headings: Experiential learning and Multiple intelligences.

GEM offers multiple access points to its catalog of resources. A keyword search, without limitations, retrieves a dozen descriptive records in which the phrase "problem-based learning" can be found. All but the first one of these references are about teaching a subject using the approach, not about the approach itself. *GEM* also offers the possibility of browsing an index of assigned descriptors. In the index, our searcher will find both problem-based learning and problem based learning, each term leading to different sets of resources. Out of the 10 resources thus retrieved, two turn out to be on PBL. The resources would have been next to impossible to find through a simple process of navigating the structure; they appear in different sub-categories in the Educational technology category.

We have seen that the *Education Virtual Library* has the simplest approach to classification. Any resource on PBL should logically be found in the sub-category Teaching methodologies, within the "By resources provided" section. Since the structure is not developed any further, however, one has to go over a long list of records for potential access to one or two resources on the subject of interest. A direct keyword search on problem-based learning brings back nothing, but this says very little as to what is actually available in the database; the user does not know what is being searched and how it is being searched: finding nothing through a keyword search does not mean there are no resources on the topic in the library.

Of all the virtual libraries in our sample, it is *Google*, a general directory, that provides the best service when one uses the hierarchical structure to reach a specific topic. *Google*'s path to problem-based learning is logical: Home > Reference > Education > Methods and theories > Learning theories > Problem-based learning. At the lowest level of the hierarchy, 23 resources are described, all of which are relevant. One should note that the same search in the *Open Directory* will retrieve 22 relevant resources, but since these resources are arranged alphabetically rather than in relevance order, the *Google* search is ultimately more efficient. The fact that *Google* is a general directory is particularly interesting; in traditional libraries, universal classification schemes are rarely considered appropriate for use with specialized collections in a single domain of knowledge.

Indeed, traditional bibliographic classification schemes do not fare much better when it comes to locating information on a specific topic in the field of education. In DDC, PBL does not appear in the index and not even in notes. Resources on PBL are classified under 371.39, Education > Schools and their activities > Methods of instruction and study > Other methods of instruction. It is only through subject headings that have been editorially linked to the classification scheme that the user will get access to this class number and will be able to locate resources of interest. In LCC, resources on PBL are found at LB1027.42, Education > Theory and practice of education > Teaching (Principles and practice) > Problem-based learning. There, it is squeezed between Lesson planning (LB 1027.4) and Project method (LB 1027.43), and appears as a coordinate of Religious aspects, Active learning, Classroom observation.

CONCLUSION

We began this paper by stating two questions relating to the accessibility of education-related resources on the Web in a context of global exchanges: (1) Are education-related resources available on the Web organized in such a way as to maximize efficiency of identification and retrieval? (2) In virtual libraries with specialized collections on education, do categorization schemes and terminology reflect anything else than local perspectives and systems? Our observations allow us to offer provisional answers, which could in turn be used as starting assumptions in a more complete investigation of the subject.

On a structural level, all subject trees that were examined compare favorably to one another in terms of general accessibility, internal logic, and ease of navigation. Most structures are indeed pretty conventional and not entirely different from those that are found in DDC, UDC, LCC or in major reference works in the field. It is interesting to note that the subject trees proposed by general directories are at least as logical, and often more developed, than the ones that are used to organize special virtual collections. Several facets used to partition sets of resources, educational levels, type of education, and target audience, to give a few examples, are universal in nature (though of course specific values may not be).

Hierarchical structures are generally shallow, making it rather difficult to discover resources on a specific topic; in our sample, a few general directories actually provide higher levels of specificity than do virtual libraries in education. By nature, and because they are supposed to be eminently flexible, home-grown organization schemes have a high potential for exhaustivity. But because their expansion remains conditional to that of actual collections of resources, all of them are currently weakened by significant gaps in their hierarchical structures as well as within the inventories of coordinate classes at every level. The lack of cross-references and of scope notes is also likely to reduce their effectiveness.

Categories and terminology, in most structures, do not reflect strictly local perspectives. Where values given to such variables as educational level are not too specific (dividing K-12 into primary, middle and secondary education, rather than just primary and secondary education, for example), the potential for global exchange of information and resources is considerable among education specialists who work in, or can at least understand, the English language. Slight variations in terminology may unfortunately make it harder to find pertinent resources through manual browsing or through an automated or semi-automated meta-search.

Education-related resources on the Web appear to be equally accessible (or unaccessible) to international as to local audiences. The organization of Web-based resources in education is obviously no easy task. The difficulties of combining the various facets of the field into a logical, flexible, and intuitive classificatory structures have transferred themselves from the traditional library environment to the virtual one. Older systems and home-grown structures exhibit similar strengths and weaknesses. It is likely equally difficult, but far from impossible, for educators and education specialists alike to locate the most pertinent resources in the virtual library than it was, and still is, in the traditional one.

REFERENCES

1. LaVelle, Linda, and Jon Nichol. Editorial: Intelligent information and communications technology for education and training in the 21st century. *British Journal of Educational Technology* 31(2):99-107 (2000).

2. Auricombe, Stéphanie. Recherche et usage de l'information documentaire: Analyse des pratiques des chercheurs et enseignants-chercheurs sur la formation du CNAM. *Perspectives documentaires en éducation* 52:61-69 (2001).

3. Chan, Lois Mai, Xia Lin, and Marcia Lei Zeng. Structural and multilingual approaches to subject access on the Web. *IFLA Journal* 26(3):187-197 (2000).

4. Ellis, David, and Ana Vasconcelos. The relevance of facet analysis for World Wide Web subject organization and searching. *Journal of Internet Cataloging* 2(3/4):97-113 (2000).

5. Weinberg, Bella Hass. Complexity in indexing systems abandonment and failure: Implications for organizing the internet. In *Proceedings of the 59th Annual*

Meeting of the American Society for Information Science, Baltimore, Maryland, 21-24 Oct. 1996, 84-90. Medford, NJ: Information Today, 1996.

6. Koch, Traugott et al. 1997. The role of classification schemes in Internet resources description and discovery. Available at http://www.ukoln.ac.uk/metadata/DESIRE/classification/ [accessed 26 July 2002].

7. Wheatley, Allan. Subject trees on the Internet: A new role for bibliographic classification? *Journal of Internet Cataloging* 2(3/4):115-141 (2000).

8. Chan, Lois Mai, Xia Lin, and Marcia Lei Zeng. Structural and multilingual approaches to subject access on the Web. *IFLA Journal* 26(3):187-197, p. 189 (2000). Broughton, Vanda, and Heather Lane. Classification schemes revisited: Applications to Web indexing and searching. *Journal of Internet Cataloging* 2(3/4):143-155 (2000).

9. http://www.educationindex.com [accessed 26 July 2002].

10. http://www.askeric.org [accessed 26 July 2002].

11. http://www.csu.edu.au/education/library.html [accessed 26 July 2002].

12. http://www.sosig.ac.uk/education/ [accessed 26 July 2002].

13. http://www.thegateway.org [accessed 26 July 2002].

14. *Encyclopedia of Educational Research.* Sponsored by the American Educational Research Association. 6th ed. New York: MacMillan, 1992.

Text Mining and Data Mining in Knowledge Organization and Discovery: The Making of Knowledge-Based Products

L. J. Haravu
A. Neelameghan

SUMMARY. Discusses the importance of knowledge organization in the context of the information overload caused by the vast quantities of data and information accessible on internal and external networks of an organization. Defines the characteristics of a knowledge-based product. Elaborates on the techniques and applications of text mining in developing knowledge products. Presents two approaches, as case studies, to the making of knowledge products: (1) steps and processes in the planning, designing and development of a composite multilingual multimedia CD product, with the potential international, inter-cultural end users in view, and (2) application of natural language processing software in text mining. Using a text mining software, it is possible to link concept terms from a processed text to a related thesaurus, glossary, schedules of a classification scheme, and facet structured subject representations. Concludes that the products of

---

L. J. Haravu is Information Consultant, 69 Krishnapuri Colony, Secunderabad 500026, India (E-mail: jharavu@hd2.vsnl.net.in). A. Neelameghan is Honorary Visiting Professor, Documentation Research and Training Centre, Indian Statistical Institute, Bangalore, India.

Address correspondence to: A. Neelameghan, 216, 4th Main Road, 16th Cross Road, Malleswaram West, Bangalore 560055, India (E-mail: anm2002@vsnl.net and srels@vsnl.com).

[Haworth co-indexing entry note]: "Text Mining and Data Mining in Knowledge Organization and Discovery: The Making of Knowledge-Based Products." Haravu, L. J., and A. Neelameghan. Co-published simultaneously in *Cataloging & Classification Quarterly* (The Haworth Information Press, an imprint of The Haworth Press, Inc.) Vol. 37, No. 1/2, 2003, pp. 97-113; and: *Knowledge Organization and Classification in International Information Retrieval* (ed: Nancy J. Williamson, and Clare Beghtol) The Haworth Information Press, an imprint of The Haworth Press, Inc., 2003, pp. 97-113. Single or multiple copies of this article are available for a fee from The Haworth Document Delivery Service [1-800-HAWORTH, 9:00 a.m. - 5:00 p.m. (EST). E-mail address: docdelivery@haworthpress.com].

http://www.haworthpress.com/store/product.asp?sku=J104

Digital Object Identifier: 10.1300/J104v37n01_08

text mining and data mining could be made more useful if the features of a faceted scheme for subject classification are incorporated into text mining techniques and products.

KEYWORDS. Text mining, data mining, knowledge discovery, natural language processing software, multilingual, multimedia

INTRODUCTION

The Internet, intranets, e-mail and groupware make more data than ever before available to the knowledge worker. Customer/user comments, communications between staff members of an organization and peers in a professional group, internal research reports, trade and technical publications, and competitor and other web sites are just a few examples of available heterogeneous electronic data. It is, therefore, no surprise that the literature of knowledge management (KM), information retrieval, corporate portals, digital libraries and web-based information and document management technologies is replete with concerns about our information overloaded, web-centered, digital world, and the need for better methods of knowledge organization.

Information managers try to lower the cost of tasks that require discourse/document analysis, if possible by using automated methods, to provide better service to clients and improve the quality of information provided. Information users need to have direct access to relevant information, for rapid awareness of content, and the discovery of new ideas and relationships. For meeting these needs a rapidly growing class of software products called enterprise KM products has come up, e.g., the Semio Corporation.[1] Numerous vendors have entered the KM market with a wide variety of products purported to manage and control the great quantities of textual and other information that drive organizations of all kinds. The tools and products in the KM market include, among many others, search engines, natural language processing software, document management systems, and groupware products.

Many of the methods for knowledge organization in the web environment are based on principles that librarians have long discovered, understood and used. For instance, classification schemes, subject headings, authority files and thesauri. In addition, library and information professionals have made significant contributions to the theories that underlie classification schemes and thesaurus development long before the arrival of the web era. It would be useful to see if some of these theoretical insights can indeed be applied in the context of new methods now being developed to manage the great quantities of textual and other information that drive the Web.

In this paper we present two approaches to the creation of knowledge products. First, the possibility of building knowledge products in a narrow domain somewhat like the expert systems that were being built earlier, but with some important differences. There are already several domain-specific knowledge-based products on the scene, e.g., FAQ databases, and customer support call center logs. Second, there is the possibility of using knowledge discovery methods, such as text mining. We believe that there is need for both approaches in knowledge organization and in providing access to knowledge sources. However, there is also need to clearly state what a knowledge product is or should be, and we present some thoughts on this. Some suggestions for the possible application of classification theory in text mining efforts are also offered.

KNOWLEDGE-BASED PRODUCTS

Five hundred years after Gutenberg's printing press sparked the mass media revolution, the printed document or an electronic version of it still largely governs the way people perceive information. But now we are also witnessing a convergence of media technologies that make representation, storage and distribution, not only of text but also of audio and video, as easy as that of text. This has enabled advancement beyond the 'document-oriented' paradigm. It is now possible to develop products that are truly knowledge-based.

We define a knowledge-based product as follows. It should:

- have captured the tacit knowledge of one or more experts in a domain of study or practice;
- be the result of collaboration between domain specialists and information specialists;
- promote collaboration between and among users of the products and domain specialists;
- be rich in content and if possible have a wide reach within the potential user community;
- enable quick and easy access to information about the domain;
- be possible for users of the product to learn new skills, gain insights (or improve skills) in the domain targeted by the product;
- promote cross-cultural information access, understanding and communication, where necessary; and
- continuously evolve with new inputs from interactions that take place in using it.

The idea of knowledge-based products arose out of concerns, primarily in the corporate world but also in other spheres (e.g., government), of the information overload phenomenon to which information seekers are subjected. The ongoing need to manage knowledge and discover the nuggets of knowledge in a sea of information has led to the search for better methods of organizing information for knowledge discovery (KD). The term *knowledge organization system* encompasses all types of schemes for organizing information and for promoting knowledge management. These include taxonomies, classification, clustering and categorization schemes that organize materials at a general level, subject headings that provide more specific access, authority files that control variant forms of key information, such as geographic names, highly structured vocabularies, including thesauri, ontologies, and coding schemes, and less traditional tools, such as semantic networks and word nets. One kind of knowledge product that had many devotees during the 1970s and 1980s, namely Expert Systems using artificial intelligence (AI) principles, did not make a significant dent primarily because of the difficulties and the cost of capturing domain knowledge in an ongoing manner.

The fact that more than 80 percent of the content on the Web is text has given rise to automated text mining solutions. As described by Chen,[2] the Gartner Group, a consulting firm in KM, proposes a multi-tier KM architecture. At the lowest level, an intranet and an extranet with platform servers, network services, and distributed object models are used as the foundation for KM applications. Databases and workgroup applications constitute the next level. Above this layer are the text and database drivers to handle various corporate data and information assets, Knowledge Retrieval (KR) functions and concept and physical knowledge maps. Above this is a web user interface.

Notable about this architecture is that it consists of applications and services that are layered and have complementary roles. No single infrastructure or system is capable of serving an organization's complete KM needs. Second, KR is considered as the newest addition to the existing IT architecture and is its core.

The Gartner group presents the KR function along two dimensions: a semantic and a collaboration dimension. In the former, linguistic analysis, thesauri, dictionaries, semantic networks and clustering (categorization/table of contents) are used to create an organization's Concept Yellow Pages. These are used as organizational knowledge maps (conceptual and physical). The techniques proposed consist of both algorithmic and ontologic generation and usage. The collaboration dimension's goal is to achieve "value recommendations" identified by experts and trust advisers, community building activities, and collaborative filters. Domain experts who hold valuable tacit knowledge can be explicitly identified and consulted for critical decisions (Figure 1).

FIGURE 1. Semantic and Collaboration Dimensions

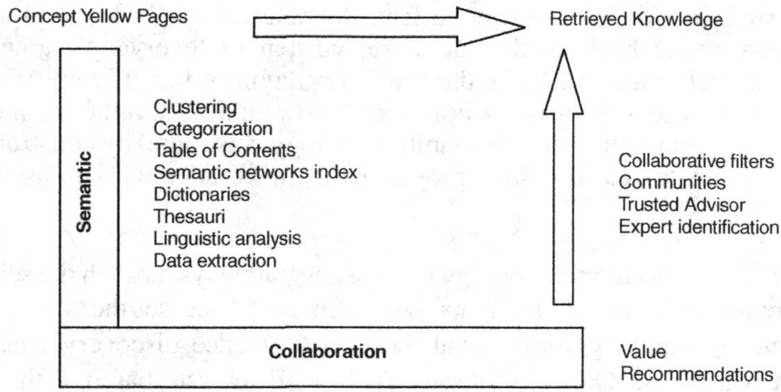

TEXT MINING

Knowledge Discovery in Databases

During the past couple of decades many papers have been devoted to Knowledge Discovery (KD). Various software packages for data and text mining and related processes are available as aids to KD. Roy Davies[3] has reviewed the literature on the relation between information retrieval and classification and KD. Don Swanson in a series of papers [4,5,6,7,8,9] has argued "that some knowledge which has never been stated explicitly or even implicitly (though it may be implicit in the literature as a whole) may be readily inferred from what has already been published." Other authors, too, have discussed similar ideas. They have used source linking, citation indexes and related tools and methods in their studies. Application of statistical techniques, especially in citation studies, bibliometric coupling, correlation, pattern recognition and other areas of informetrics and scientometrics, help in KD.

"Knowledge discovery in databases (KDD) revolves around the investigation and creation of knowledge, processes, algorithms, and the mechanisms for retrieving potential knowledge from data collections."[10] "Classification schemes have properties that enable the representation of entities and relationships in structures that reflect knowledge of the domain being classified."[11] In this context, hierarchies, trees, paradigms, and faceted classification can reflect structures, discover, and create new knowledge. How to find interesting previously unknown implicit information in scientific literature is examined in the paper

"Implicit text linkages between Medline records: using Arrowsmith as an aid to scientific discovery" by Swanson and Smallheiser.[12] As stated by Cory:

> Extracting hidden knowledge from humanities databases is especially problematic because the literature, written in 'everyday' rather than technical language, lacks the precision required for efficient retrieval, and because humanities scholars seek new analogies rather than causes . . . an illuminating new humanities analogy was found by constructing a search statement in which proper names were coupled with associated concepts.[13]

Small[14] presents a "methodology for creating pathways through the scientific literature following co-citation links." Also, Small[15] discusses the "implications of information pathways for retrieval, the unity of science, discovery, epistemology and evaluation." Quin He[16] discusses co-word analysis, based on the co-occurrence frequency of pairs of words or phrases, for discovering links among subjects. Such studies can also help in tracing the development of science. Ahonen[17] discusses "a method of extracting *maximal frequent sequences* [MFS] in a set of documents. An MFS is a

> sequence of words that is frequent in the document collection . . . that is not contained in any other longer frequent sequence. A sequence is considered to be frequent if it appears in at least *n* documents where *n* is the frequency threshold given.[18]

The technique is used to discover other regularities and similarity mapping in document collections. This could assist information retrieval, hypertext linking, clustering, and discovery of frequent co-occurrences. Pinto and Lancaster[19] conclude: "the wide availability of complete text in electronic form does not reduce the value of abstracts for information retrieval activities even in such more sophisticated applications as knowledge discovery." In "Template Mining for Information Extraction from Digital Documents,"[20] Chowdhury points out that with the rapid growth of digital information resources, a number of information extraction (IE) systems from natural language text, particularly in the areas of news/fact retrieval and in domain-specific areas such as in chemical and patent information retrieval, have been developed. A template mining approach involving a natural language processing (NLP) technique is used to extract data directly from text if either the data and/or text surrounding the data form recognizable patterns. When text matches a template, the system extracts data according to instructions associated with that template. Chowdhury[21] reviews template mining research, which also shows how templates are used in Web search engines–such as Alta Vista–and in meta-search engines–such as Ask Jeeves–for helping end-users generate natural language search expressions. Some potential areas of application of template mining for extraction of different kinds of information from digital documents are highlighted, and how such applications are used are indicated. It is suggested that, in order to facilitate template mining, standardization in the presentation and layout of information within digital documents has to be ensured, and this can be done by generating various templates that authors can easily download and use while preparing digital documents.

Text mining is receiving considerable research and development attention. Content searching using a search engine based on a search term–keyword or string–does not address the information overload problem adequately enough even with methods that list the retrievals according to one or more other ranking methods. This has led to the need to differentiate between search and discovery. A search engine's main function is to locate documents based on the user's keywords. A discovery engine on the other hand attempts to extract relevant textual data from a corpus of text and then provides a graphical, dynamic and navigable index. (See also "Application of Text Analysis Software" under the section on "Case Studies.") The visual presentation of concepts is aimed at promoting a better understanding of the underlying content and structure of the textual data, leading hopefully to improved retrieval, and hence, productivity of the knowledge worker.

Figure 2 shows the difference between a search engine and a discovery engine as depicted by the Semio Corporation.[22]

Text mining is best suited for "discovery" purposes, i.e., learning and discovering information hidden in the documents of an organization's unstructured repositories. Reasons for using text mining include:

- Uncovering a "narrative" in an unstructured mass of text
- Learning about a topic
- Exploring how an environment, e.g., market, is evolving
- Looking for new ideas or relations in topics.

Text mining is useful because of the enormous amount of knowledge, either within an organization or outside of it, that resides in text documents. Since most organizations rely on textual information, both from outside and inside the organization, working with this sea of text can become extremely difficult. The whole collection of text is simply too large to read and analyze easily. Furthermore, it changes constantly and requires ongoing review and analysis if one is to stay current. Text mining addresses these problems, providing tools to analyze and learn from this kind of dynamic information.

However, text mining is not an end in itself; it is a support tool and complements search engines. A text mining product supports and enhances the knowl-

FIGURE 2. Difference Between Search Engine and Discovery Engine

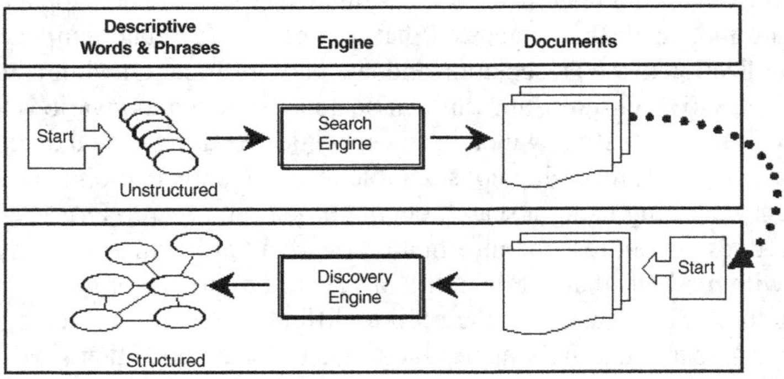

edge worker's creativity and innovation with *open-ended* exploration and discovery. The individual applies intelligence and creativity to endow *meaning* and *relevance* to information, turning information into knowledge. Text mining advances this process, empowering the knowledge worker to explore and gain knowledge from a knowledge base.

There are several types of industry players in text mining: IR vendors such as Verity, Excalibur, and Dataware are refining their product functionalities from text retrieval to text mining. There are also niche document management players such as PCDOC and Documentum who have developed successful products for managing document content and workflows. Large IT platform companies such as Oracle, Lotus, and Microsoft are aiming to improve the KR functionalities of their database or workgroup products. These companies may lack in significant linguistic and analytical abilities. The last type of vendor consists of small, new companies such as Autonomy, Perspecta, InXight, Semio and KCC. These have new analytical and linguistic technologies but may lack in execution experience and integration ability.

According to Chen,[23] the approaches of consultants and refinements being sought by IT vendors, described briefly above, are evidence of the trend away from the use of simple and basic search and retrieval techniques to KR using text mining technologies.

Text processing and analysis is significantly more difficult than processing and analysis of structured data as in DBMS systems. The status of text mining today is much like that of DBMS twenty years ago. The real challenges and the potential payoffs for an effective universal text solution are equally appealing. It is inevitable that whoever dominates this space will become the next Oracle (in text). The above formulation is obviously targeted to text-oriented sources of knowledge. When it comes to multimedia products, which are likely to be predominant in the future, text mining alone will not be adequate.

Knowledge products, as defined earlier, are products that utilize both the semantic and collaborative dimensions for their development, albeit in a limited and specific domain. In this sense, such knowledge products could well become an ongoing and integral part of an organization's knowledge resources. We believe that such knowledge products operate also along three other dimensions, namely, information access, communication and collaboration as shown in Figure 3. These are meant to provide access to information, enable learning and collaboration and communication between people with common interests, and the sharing of knowledge in a specific domain, ideally in an ongoing manner and evolving with time.

Text Analysis and Mining Techniques

First, text mining requires natural language processing abilities. Second, while data mining (see also the section on Data Mining which follows) attempts to identify causal relationships through classification or supervised learning techniques, text mining aims to create organizational knowledge maps or concept yellow pages. Third, text mining deals more with diverse and eclectic collections of systems and formats (e-mail, web pages, Notes databases, newsgroups, etc.). Both data mining and text mining adopt significant analytical methods and their results and are often highly visual and graphical. Data visualization and information visualization techniques attempt to create an interface that is well suited for human decision-making.

At the heart, text mining is a cross between IR and AI. IR has gone through several generations of development. In the 1970s, computational techniques based on inverted indexes and vector spaces were developed and tested on computer systems. Also, probabilistic retrieval methods based on Bayesian statistics were developed. Although more than 30 years old, this still forms the basis of modern IR systems. In the 1980s, coinciding with the developments of new AI techniques, knowledge-based and expert systems that aim to emulate domain specialists were developed. User modeling and natural language pro-

FIGURE 3. Information Product, Information Access, Communication, and Collaboration

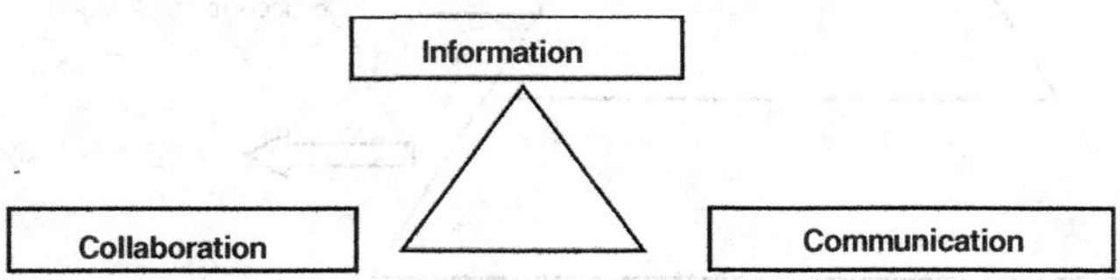

cessing (NLP) techniques were developed to assist in representing users and documents. These were applied to improve online searching.

Realizing the difficulties of creating domain-specific knowledge bases and heuristics, researchers in the 1990s adopted new machine-learning techniques for information analysis. AI techniques such as neural networks, genetic algorithms, and symbolic learning were tested in IR as described by Chen.[24] Text analysis includes such features as natural or statistical language processing, indexer or phrase creator, entity extraction, conceptual associations (automatic thesauri), domain-specific knowledge filter (using vocabularies or ontologies), automatic taxonomy creation (clustering), multi-document and multi-language support. Core text mining analysis can be classified into four main layers: linguistic analysis and NLP, statistical or co-occurrence analysis, statistical and neural networks clustering/categorization, and visualization (Figure 4).

At the lowest level, linguistic analysis and NLP techniques aim to identify key concept descriptors (who/what/where/when) embedded in textual documents. Different types of linguistic analysis techniques have been developed. Word and inverted indexing can be combined with stemming, morphological analysis, Boolean, proximity, range and fuzzy search. The unit of analysis is 'word.' Phrasal analysis, on the other hand, aims to extract meaningful noun phrase units or entities (e.g., people names, organization names, location names). Both linguistic and statistical analysis techniques are plausible. In addition, semantic analysis based on techniques, such as semantic grammar and case grammar, can be used to represent semantics (meaning) in sentences. Semantic analysis is domain specific and lacks scalability. This often requires a significant knowledge base or a domain lexicon creation ef-

FIGURE 4. Layers of Core Text Mining

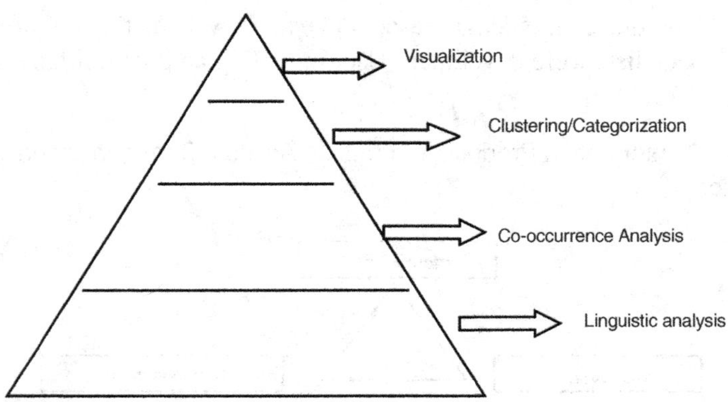

fort and hence it may not be suitable for general-purpose text mining across a wide spectrum of domains.

Based on significant research in the IR and the computational linguistics communities, it is generally agreed that phrasal-level analysis is more suited for coarse but scalable text mining applications. Word-level analysis is noisy and lacks precision. Sentence level is too structured and lacks practical applications. It is not coincidental that most of the subject headings and concept descriptors adopted by library classification schemes are noun phrases. Based on statistical and co-occurrence techniques, link analysis is performed to create automatic thesauri or conceptual associations of extracted concepts. Existing human-created thesauri can also be integrated with system-generated thesauri.

Statistical and neural network-based clustering and categorization techniques are often used to group similar documents, queries or communities in subject hierarchies, which could then serve as corporate knowledge maps. Hierarchical clustering (single link or multi link) and statistical clustering (multi-dimensional scaling, factor analysis) techniques are precise but often computationally expensive. Neural network clustering by Self-organizing Map (SOM) technique, as described by Kohonen,[25] performs well, is fast and is most suited for large scale text mining tasks. In addition, SOM lends itself to intuitive graphical visualization based on such visual parameters as size (a large region represents a more important topic) and proximity (related topics are grouped in adjacent regions).

McCormack,[26] an anthropologist, attempted to discover the emotional attitudes, outlooks and cultural patterns of certain 'saints' of South India, by analyzing the content of their writings, and then "making a frequency count of selected categories of metaphors in *vacanas* (religious literature, wisdom literature) . . . The categories chosen were metaphors about animals, persons, natural objects (including plants), and subjects of cultural interest." The method was adapted to computer technology by Colby.[27]

Visualization and human-computer interaction (HCI) help to reveal concept associations and visualize knowledge maps. Different representation structures (tree, network) and interaction techniques (e.g., zooming, spotlight) can be adopted to reveal knowledge more completely.

Richness versus Reach

Another perspective that accelerated the enthusiasm for KM and the development of knowledge products is the 'richness versus reach' thesis of Evans and Wurster.[28] They pointed out that the nature of communication has drastically changed. Until now, one had a choice of richness or reach, but one could not achieve both simultaneously. A face-to-face conversation, for instance, is rich in content, nuance and interactivity but poor in reach. A radio or TV broadcast has great reach but is poor in interactivity and nuance. Communication strategies were always an either/or choice. With the Internet, it is argued that we can craft systems that provide both richness and reach. This has necessitated a rethink on how information and knowledge are shared within organizations, an important concern of businesses wishing to harness knowledge. Knowledge products targeted to specific domains, together with the use of the Web as the delivery medium, we believe can provide the richness and reach sought for in organizations.

DATA MINING

Data mining is a step within the knowledge discovery in the databases (KDD) process through which an organization's data assets are processed and analyzed to gain insights to assist in decision-making. KDD originates with data held in the organization's data management systems or data warehouses. The steps to knowledge discovery include data selection, processing, transformation, data mining, interpretation and evaluation leading to discovery of new intelligence or knowledge. In an institution, the internal data assets and those obtained from external sources and warehoused are processed and analyzed in depth to gain insights on the research object, event or situation.

Data mining techniques used have to be specific to the domain and also depend on the area of application. Important requirements are that the data collected should be relevant and of a high-quality. (See also the section on Text Mining earlier.) Some analytical techniques used in data mining include statistical methods, such as regression analysis, discrimination analysis, factor analysis, principal component analysis, word usage and co-occurrence analysis, and time-series, as well as mathematical modeling. In-depth classification and related indexes are also helpful in data mining.

CASE STUDIES

As indicated earlier, two case studies are presented: (1) the development of a multimedia multilingual CD product, and (2) application of text analysis software.

Multimedia CD

Saint Tyagaraja–A Multimedia Presentation is a multimedia knowledge product on the life and selected works of one of the greatest composers of classical Carnatic music (South Indian music of the 18th century in India, namely, Tyagaraja). A paradigm pioneer in the field of Carnatic music, his contributions–compositions, art models and other innovations–continue to influence present day composers, and the theory and practice of Carnatic music even 150 years after his death.

The product (Saint Tyagaraja)[29] was the collaborative effort between two musicians/musicologists and an information professional. It took over three years for the product to be completed and launched in the market. The planning of the content, access to the content and the learning elements built into the product resulted from interactions, not only between the three developers, but also from several practising musicians, Tyagaraja specialists, linguists, music lovers, teachers and students of music. Interactions were usually conducted on a one-on-one basis, but on occasion, there were also interactions with a group of potential users. Importantly, the method used to elicit opinion was that ideas and knowledge for the product were based on product demonstration (in the state of development at the time of the interaction) to an individual or a group. Valuable suggestions for the navigation, content, and emphasis, apart from insights that we had not included in the product were received via these interactions. This has enabled the capture of tacit knowledge of many specialists and potential users into the product.

The product has other characteristics of what we define to be a knowledge product. These are discussed:

- The CD has information on 108 kritis (devotional songs) representing different themes, ragas (melodic matrices or patterns), talas (rhythm or beats) and art models used by Tyagaraja. Each kriti record has elaborate summaries and notes for the kriti. An important value-added component in the product is the insightful special commentaries for each of the kritis. The special commentaries provide valuable insights into the subtleties (e.g., of the raga), nuances, scriptural background, emotions and feelings that are behind the composition; and the place and time in a concert that the kriti is best sung. This again is an example of the capture of the tacit knowledge of experts and its presentation to users. Importantly, the product allows users not only to view the special commentaries but also listen to it. This option, we believe, enables a better understanding and appreciation of the kriti because of the tonal inflections and emphasis that is available and possible in the spoken word as compared to the written word. The special commentaries (written and spoken) contribute to the richness of the content in the product.
- Another important feature in the product is the presentation of the lyrical content of each of the kritis. The contextual meaning of each Telugu word or phrase used in a kriti is explained in English. The user can view the meanings while he listens to the music. This, we believe, adds to the user's musical experience and his understanding of the kriti and its musical rendition. This feature again adds to the richness of the content in the product and enables the listener to learn from experienced singers of the kritis.
- The product also attempts to foster understanding and appreciation of the kritis across linguistic and cultural borders within India and internation-

ally. It does this by allowing the listener to view the text of the kritis while listening to the music in any of 3 Indian language scripts (Telugu, Tamil, and Devanagari). Western audiences can see the text of the kritis in the Roman script. The product allows listeners simultaneously to listen to the music, see the meanings of lyrical content words/phrases and the text of the kritis in a chosen language. This kind of integrated access is only possible in multimedia products. Another noteworthy feature that promotes learning is the possibility for users to listen to illustrative renderings of selected phrases (in kritis) that are commonly mispronounced by singers who do not know Telugu.
- The product allows the user to navigate the kriti database either in browse mode or by searching by raga, tala, theme, keyword, lyrical content word, etc. The application also provides for an advanced search where the user can combine terms from different fields. It is also possible for users to do free-text searching in the summary or special commentary fields.

In its present form, the product is a standalone one for use on PCs. This does limit its reach. Making available the content on the Internet would obviously widen its accessibility and reach to interested audiences globally. More importantly, it would be possible to expand the collaboration and communication dimensions of the product and enable the product to evolve with new input.

Application of Text Analysis Software

A text with color diagrams and dealing with concepts in Cosmic Creation in Jewish, Buddhist and Hindu religions downloaded from the Internet, was subjected to an analysis by the text mining software TextAnalyst 2.0 (trial version) of Megaputer Intelligence Inc. by Ananyan and Kharlamov.[30] This software takes text files as input and produces a semantic network of important concepts in the text, hyperlinked to the sentence(s) in the original text file. It uses weighting algorithms to identify terms and term relationships. It also produces a summary, essentially sentences extracted on the basis of weights that the software assigns to terms mined in the text. The result of the mining can be exported as html files or as a comma separated file (for use with MS-Excel). The length of the summary can be controlled. Queries in natural language and structured queries are accepted. The keywords and texts are hypertext linked facilitating navigation. The software can work on texts in languages other than English provided the strings or terms not to be indexed are identified and listed by Megaputer Intelligence, Inc.[31] We also applied TextAnalyst to internal documents. The outputs–summary was acceptable to end-users and authors, and the hypertext linking from the index terms to the text and vice versa, the hierarchical tree structures, etc.–were useful in preparing knowledge organization products such as a thesaurus.[32]

CONCLUDING REMARKS

Classification theorists, notably S. R. Ranganathan,[33] have always maintained that the universe of knowledge is a dynamic continuum. It is ever growing; new branches may stem from any of its infinity of points at any time; they are unknowable at present. They cannot be anticipated; their filiation can be determined only after they appear. This view is similar to that of modern day thinkers in KM (e.g., Allee[34]) who view knowledge as a complex self-organizing system, that is, one that is far more organic than mechanical. In this view, knowledge evolves as our purposes change in creative response to our environment. It reconfigures and expands as we exercise our will and intent (e.g., through deliberate research and development) to influence and shape that environment in various ways. Because text mining does not assume or use, *a priori*, any scheme or taxonomy, that is, the discovery engine examines the corpus each time a query is made, it is potentially capable of discovering new relationships and network nodes that hitherto were not known. In this sense, text mining recognizes the dynamic nature of knowledge evolution and growth, and therefore also the need for a dynamic means for discovering knowledge in a large text mining solution to be guided by the set of fundamental categories. Can the linking between text mining and categorization based on a set of fundamental categories be automated? Satyapal and Satyapal,[35] in their work of semi-automatic synthesis of Colon Class number, have automated the process of identifying and assigning the terms resulting from the analysis of the subject(s) of a document, to the appropriate Fundamental Categories (P,M,E,S,T plus Speciators) of Ranganathan's General Theory of Knowledge Classification.

One of the disadvantages of text mining solutions is that the resulting indexes (or semantic network, or cluster) do not always present a hierarchical view of mined text. Such a view is useful to a user so that he can quickly narrow or broaden his search. If a text mining solution can use a taxonomy (manually or automatically generated), it may be possible for the results to be shown in an explicit hierarchical structure. The work of Neelameghan[36] to hyperlink terms from a subject analysis (document or query) to corresponding sections of a scheme for classification or thesaurus, and Gaikaiwari's[37] work should be of interest. Using software, such as TextAnalyst, it is possible to link concept terms from a processed text to a related thesaurus, glossary, schedules of a classification scheme, and facet structured subject representations.

Most text mining solutions in the final analysis attempt to map the multidimensional knowledge into a two-dimensional structure, i.e., pre-coordinated strings of linked text that are recognized by the text mining software. Can these solutions use principles of facet sequence already developed in classification theory by Ranganathan and others? If this is possible, then the output of text mining software would be more consistent and meaningful (because they will be governed by a set of syntactical rules and not merely by the presence or absence of words or phrases in a body of text) and not dependent only on the automated statistical and/or linguistic analysis methods that such solutions use.

REFERENCES

1. Semio Corporation. 2002. Text mining and the knowledge management space. (Web document: http://www.dmreview.com/master.cfm?NavId=6180&WhitepaperID=80).

2. Chen, Hsinchun. 2001. *Knowledge management systems: a text mining perspective*. Tucson, Arizona: Knowledge Computing Corporation.

3. Davies, Roy. 1989. The creation of new knowledge by information retrieval and classification. *Journal of Documentation*, 45 (4): 273-301.

4. Swanson, D.R. 1986a. Fish oil, Raynaud's syndrome and undiscovered public knowledge. *Perspectives in Biology and Medicine*, 30 (1); 1986; 7-18.

5. ___. 1986b. Undiscovered public knowledge. *Library Quarterly*, 56 (2): 103-118.

6. ___. 1987. Two medical literatures that are logically but not bibliographically connected. *Journal of the American Society for Information Science*, 38 (4): 228-233.

7. ___. 1988a. Historical note: information retrieval and the future of an illusion. *Journal of the American Society for Information Science*, 39 (2): 92-98.

8. ___. 1988b. Migraine and magnetism: eleven neglected connections. *Perspectives in Biology and Medicine*, 31 (4): 526-557.

9. ___. 1989. Online search for logically-related noninteractive medical literatures: a systematic trial-and-error strategy. *Journal of the American Society for Information Science*, 40 (5): 1989; 356-358.

10. Norton, M. Jay. 1999. Knowledge discovery in databases, *Library Trends*, 48 (1): 9.

11. Kwaśnik, Barbara H. 1999. Role of classification in knowledge representation and discovery. *Library Trends*, 48 (1): 22.

12. Swanson D. R. and Smallheiser, Neil R. 1999. Implicit text linkages between Medline records: using Arrowsmith as an aid to scientific discovery. *Library Trends*, 48 (1): 49-59.

13. Cory, Kenneth A. 1999. Discovering hidden analogies in an online humanities database. *Library Trends*, 48 (1): 60.

14. Small, Henry. 1999. A passage through science: crossing disciplinary boundaries. *Library Trends*, 48 (1): 72.

15. Ibid.

16. Quin He. 1999. Knowledge discovery through co-word analysis. *Library Trends*, 48 (1): 131-159.

17. Ahonen, Helena. 1999. Knowledge discovery in documents by extracting frequent word sequences. *Library Trends*, 48 (1): 160.

18. Ibid.

19. Pinto, Maria and Lancaster, F.W. 1999. Abstracts and abstracting in knowledge discovery. *Library Trends*, 48 (1): 234-248.

20. Chowdhury, Govinda G. 1999. Template mining for information extraction from digital documents. *Library Trends*, 48 (1): 182.

21. Ibid.
22. As in 1.
23. As in 2.
24. Ibid.
25. Kohonen, Teuvo. http//www.informatik.uni-trier.de/~ley/db/indices/a-tree/k/KohonenTeuvo/html.
26. McCormack, William. 1969. On Lingayath culture. In *Speaking of Siva*. Translated with an introduction by A.K. Ramanujam. London: Penguin Books; 1973, Appendix II, p. 175-187.
27. Colby, B.N. 1969. Cultural patterns in narrative. *Science*, 151, 9166, Feb. 18; p. 793-798.
28. Evans, P.B and Wurster, T.S. 1997. Strategy and the new economics of information. *Harvard Business Review*, 75 (15): p. 70-82.
29. *Saint Tyagaraja, a multimedia presentation; a unique portrayal of 108 krithis of Tyagaraja*. 2001. Electronic resource/Developed by B.R.C. Iyengar; T.N. Rajan; L.J. Haravu. Electronic optical disc, Electronic text data, Electronic image data, Electronic sound, Electronic numeric data. Secunderabad, India, L.J.Haravu, cop.2001.1, Electronic optical disc (CD-ROM): sd., col.: 12 cm., 1.User manual.
30. Ananyan, Sergei and Kharlamov, Alexander. 2002. Automated analysis of natural language texts. (Web document: http://www.megaputer.com/tech/wp/tm.php3).
31. Megaputer Intelligence, Inc. 2002. *TextAnalyst 2: user manual*.
32. Haravu, L.J. and Neelameghan, A. 2002. Content summarization and indexing of internal document using a text mining software. *National Seminar on Cataloguing of Digital Resources, Bangalore, 9-11 August 2002. [Papers]. Bangalore, India*: Sarada Ranganathan Endowment for Library Science; Paper F.
33. Ranganathan, S.R. 1967. Prolegomena to library classification, ed. 3, assisted by M.A. Gopinath. Bangalore, IN: Sarada Ranganathan Endowment for Library Science. V1, chapter PM, sec. 7.
34. Allee, Verna. 1997. *The knowledge evolution: expanding organizational intelligence*. Boston, MA: Butterworth-Heinemann.
35. Satyapal, B.G., and Satyapal, Sanjivini. 2002. Postulational approach to classifying documents: use of SATSAN AUTO-MATRIX version 1–program for synthesis of colon class number. *Information Studies*, 8 (2): 92-113.
36. Neelameghan, A. 2002. Digitized schemes for subject classification and thesauri: complementary roles. *Information Studies*, 8(1); 25-42.
37. Gaikaiwari, Madhusudan. 2002. An interactive application for faceted classification systems. *Information Studies*, 8(1); 43-56.

Information Organization to Assist Knowledge Discovery: Case Studies with Non-Bibliographic Databases

A. Neelameghan
Hemalata Iyer

SUMMARY. Enumerates various paths that may lead to knowledge discovery (KD). Most of these paths begin from knowing what exists. To know what exists about an entity requires comprehensively assembling relevant data and information, in-depth analysis of the information, and identifying relations among the concepts in the related and even apparently unrelated subjects. Provision has to be made to reorganize and synthesize the information retrieved and/or that obtained through observation, experiment, survey, etc. Information and communication technologies (ICT) have considerably augmented the capabilities of information systems. Such ICT applications may range from the simple to sophisticated computerized systems, with data

---

A. Neelameghan is Honorary Visiting Professor, Documentation Research and Training Centre, Indian Statistical Institute, Bangalore, India. Hemalata Iyer, PhD, is Associate Professor, School of Information Science and Policy, University at Albany, SUNY, Albany, NY 12222 USA (E-mail: hi651@csc.albany.edu).

Address correspondence to: A. Neelameghan, 216, 4th Main Road, 16th Cross Road, Malleswaram West, Bangalore 560055, India (E-mail: anm2002@vsnl.net and srels@vsnl.com).

[Haworth co-indexing entry note]: "Information Organization to Assist Knowledge Discovery: Case Studies with Non-Bibliographic Databases." Neelameghan, A., and Hemalata Iyer. Co-published simultaneously in *Cataloging & Classification Quarterly* (The Haworth Information Press, an imprint of The Haworth Press, Inc.) Vol. 37, No. 1/2, 2003, pp. 115-130; and: *Knowledge Organization and Classification in International Information Retrieval* (ed: Nancy J. Williamson, and Clare Beghtol) The Haworth Information Press, an imprint of The Haworth Press, Inc., 2003, pp. 115-130. Single or multiple copies of this article are available for a fee from The Haworth Document Delivery Service [1-800-HAWORTH, 9:00 a.m. - 5:00 p.m. (EST). E-mail address: docdelivery@haworthpress.com].

http://www.haworthpress.com/store/product.asp?sku=J104

Digital Object Identifier: 10.1300/J104v37n01_09

gathered using aerial photography, remote sensing, satellite imagery, large radar and planetary telescopes and many other instrument records of phenomena, as well as downloading via the Internet. While classification helps in data prospecting and data mining, for it to assist the KD process effectively it has to be supplemented with good indexes, hypertext links, access to statistical and modeling techniques, etc. Computer software assists text analysis, complex data manipulation, computation, statistical analysis, concept mapping, etc. But manual information systems can also assist KD. Enumerates several prerequisites to KD and relevant tools and techniques to be incorporated into information support systems. Presents case studies of information systems and services that assisted KD.

KEYWORDS. Knowledge discovery, non-bibliographic databases, information technology, communication technology, knowledge organization tools

KNOWLEDGE DISCOVERY AND KNOWLEDGE GENERATION

Knowledge discovery (KD) has occurred and continues to occur in different cultural, economic and technological environments. Before discussing how information organization can assist KD, it will be helpful to overview the KD process, the context and environments in which discovery and new knowledge generation take place, and the types of, and paths to, KD.

Knowledge discovery, knowledge acquisition, creation of new knowledge and its communication, are essentially human characteristics. These are the means of human survival and progress. Findings from archaeological and palaeontological studies, and of relics and remnants of ancient records, attest to the achievements in the sciences, engineering, technology, and the arts of early civilizations across the globe. Parts of the valuable knowledge transmitted orally from generation to generation are being rediscovered today.

Knowledge is embodied in nature, human intellect and skills, and in artifacts, cultural practices, traditions, conventions (tacit knowledge) and the arts of a community, as well as in records of information. Knowledge is the most valuable asset of a society. Hence, the attempts to patent natural and man-made entities and to copyright records. Archaeological, palaeontological, historical and archival studies attempt to piece together our knowledge about the *past*. We collect information about the *present*–what is happening now–through observation, survey, experimentation, exchange of ideas among people, through media and by examining information sources. By using forecasting techniques and futuristic studies we try to obtain information about likely trends and state-of-the art in a field during a period and/or in a particular country, in the *future*. In all of these, one needs to have information about what exists or existed for comparison, to find out what is new and also to build upon, rather than to duplicate, what is already known. Thus, the present has roots in or links to the past, and the future links to the present.

An inquiry and the associated search for information is an attempt to discover knowledge that may fill in a gap in the seeker's knowledge base or even a gap in the subject field as a whole. But every search for information need not necessarily lead to KD. The discovery may arise from a directed search or it may be a serendipitous, that is a chance, discovery. Even in the latter case, as Louis Pasteur had said, "Chance only favors the prepared mind." The search/research may begin with a conjecture, an assumption, or an existing theory, to be confirmed, rejected, or modified by collecting relevant data/evidence (from experiments, surveys, and source records). The data is processed and organized to draw inferences, identify patterns of relationships among concepts, or formulate empirical principles (statistical and operations research methods can assist in these tasks). Earlier conjectures, and theories may be refuted, or confirmed, or their limitations exposed. If an earlier theory/conjecture is confirmed or its limitations found, there may be further movement along the spiral toward greater generalization, wider application and identification of limitations, and so on (cf. geocentric theory refuted and replaced by Galileo's heliocentric theory; and progress from Copernicus's collection of data to Kepler's laws of planetary motion to Newton's generalized laws to Einstein's more comprehensive relativity theories). In more recent times the conjectures about the moon's surface had to be changed in the light of the data/evidence obtained through some of the Apollo missions as indicated in Ian Mitroff's, "The moon scientists," cited by Neelameghan[1] in 1979.

KNOWLEDGE DISCOVERY ENVIRONMENT

Knowledge discovery and the generation of new ideas can be aided by information support systems and services. But they may also require or be helped by, several other environmental factors.

Inter-Disciplinary Interactions and KD

Prior to the 19th century, a scholar in a subject, a scientist for instance, might have been knowledgeable about most of what was then worth knowing in the subject. As the amount of knowledge in a subject was then relatively small, the scholar had a pretty good map of the subject and knew the holes and gaps therein. By the early 20th century not only some of the knowledge gaps got filled in, but also the amount of knowledge in a subject and its components increased substantially and at an accelerated pace. The boundaries of subjects were extended and interdisciplinary interactions arose. It became more and more difficult for any one scholar to be knowledgeable about even a small part of a subject and also to keep abreast of the new developments, especially in the frontier areas that attracted an increasing number of research studies. More than ever before, teachers, students, scholars, and practitioners came to depend on information support services to keep themselves updated about developments in the subjects of their respective interests, to fill in gaps in their knowledge base and to discover new knowledge.

Interdisciplinary interactions and connections arise in a number of ways. For example, researchers in a subject:

- using the principles and theories of a 'parent' or of another subject; e.g., principles of genetics provide a basis in medical studies;
- applying methodologies, tools and techniques developed in or for another subject; e.g., systems analysis applications in library studies; mathematical modeling in aerodynamic studies;
- using data collected in another field or for another purpose: e.g., population data used in education planning, and in housing planning.

Other types of inter-disciplinary links include:

- comparative studies between two or more subject areas; e.g., comparison of certain principles of physics and those of Vedanta;
- differentiation studies between two or more subject areas; e.g., study of differences between the African elephant and Indian elephant;
- studies on the impact of one subject field on another; e.g., contribution of information technology to national economic development;
- evaluation of a discourse from the point of view of another field; e.g., Sufism from a Christian religious perspective.

In studies of the above nature, the potential for discovering or generating new ideas is high. On a personal note: In February 2002, in an e-mail (to Neelameghan), Dr. Michael Medland wrote:

> I have read your paper on dynamism and stability in knowledge organization: S. R. Ranganathan's contributions. I found it enlightening and in-

> teresting. My own work deals with developing KOTs (knowledge organization tools) and teaching them to young children. I am trying to integrate the kinds of things you are saying . . . with some of my own. I believe that the integration would be helpful to both library science and education psychology, especially, with the explosion of information that is taking place . . . I am from education psychology and only discovered the most interesting ISKO text I mentioned previously in the book give-away bin at the university I taught last year . . . [2]

In a later communication he reported success:

> I have already tried my analysis on English-speaking four-year-olds. Most four-year-olds have the knowledge categories already. I want to try and teach them to talk about the categories (the knowledge ontology) and use them to analyze and synthesize knowledge, to accelerate their learning about and acting on the world, individually or in groups (a value statement).[3]

This cross fertilization of ideas was certainly KD for the author and to Medland as well.

Such relations between subjects, which S. R. Ranganathan called Phase Relations (differentiated from Facet Relations), may eventually give rise to new interdisciplinary subjects. Several modes of formation of such subjects have been identified: Fission, Fusion, Lamination, Agglomeration, Distillation, etc. The recognition of the modes of formation facilitates knowing the roots, the connections and relations among the new subject(s) and the inter-linked subjects on the one hand, and for the arrangement of new subjects in a helpful sequence in knowledge organization tools such as classification schemes, thesauri, concepts maps, etc.[4]

New Knowledge in One Context but Known Knowledge in Another

Some South Pacific Islanders recognize only three primary colors (as opposed to the conventional five elsewhere); but the same group recognized, differentiated, and named some thirty-five varieties of one species of fish necessary for their survival and living in the island environment (even though they were not found in scientific writings on the species).[5] The discovery of the detailed differentiation and classification of a particular fish species could be KD to the scientist specializing in the subjectthough already known to the Islanders.

Enrico Fermi split the atom and observed the chain reaction, but he did not have a name for the phenomenon. He mentioned what he had found to his ten-year-old daughter who was reported to have said that the kind of division was known in her biology lessons as *fission*! In this case, Fermi had an additional KD–a phenomenon in cell biology similar to what he had observed in splitting atoms.

A reputed researcher and his colleague noted the occurrence of ribose (a carbohydrate) in free form, in the filaments of a particular fungus, an apparently unknown phenomenon (c.1960). They prepared a paper for the journal *Nature,* claiming first report on such occurrence of ribose. Before mailing the paper, the researchers, as usual, asked the library to check whether any similar observation had been reported earlier. Several hours of checking abstracting journals led to an abstract of a paper published in a relatively unknown serial several years earlier on the occurrence of ribose in free form in the ribs of wings of crows! The abstract was sent to the senior researcher. After a couple of days when he happened to visit the library he was asked about his paper. He thanked the library for 'saving his reputation.' What about the paper? It goes through except that the claim was now restricted to *first report of free ribose in the filaments of a particular species of fungus* [personal experience].

Is Discovery of Duplication of Research a KD?

In the late 1950s, from the bibliographical records that were prepared in the technical information centre of an antibiotics research center, it was noted that almost identical antibiotic substances were being reported from different laboratories around the world. About two decades later, Neelameghan et al.[6] applied statistical methods to study the relation between the total number of antibiotics reported during a year and the number found to be duplicate, triplicate, etc., of already reported ones. The pattern of distribution of duplicate discoveries over a period of about sixty years conformed to a modified Poisson Distribution, and to the Square-Cube law. The late Derek De Solla Price, when contacted, said that the finding was the first practical confirmation of his conjecture and suggested that the work be published in 1970 in *Nature.*[7]

This knowledge was useful in forecasting the chances of a reportedly 'new' antibiotic being a duplicate discovery. It also led to examining the reasons for the duplication: R&D for isolating new and useful antibiotics is mostly directed research; groups in research laboratories across the world went through similar paths and used similar procedures. The research may not be communicated immediately but only after examining patenting possibilities, etc. In some cases the reports are not in English–Japanese, Polish, etc. These factors increased the chances of duplication of 'antibiotics discovery.'

Duplication could also arise because one and the same antibiotic may be produced by different organisms and different antibiotics by one and the same organism in different culture substrates. This has to do with the genetic characteristics and the products of the biochemical cycle of the micro-organisms.

Discovery of Non-Existence of an Entity Is KD

In the early part of the last century, a mission was organized to study the snakes in Iceland, there having been no prior reports on this subject. The team did a thorough search and research on the island and after two years of effort submitted a one line report: "There are no snakes in Iceland." Besides this discovery, a positive aspect of the report was, perhaps, that it would prevent duplication of any similar studies being undertaken on the island.

Knowing About Earlier Failures–Impediment to Innovation, Creative Work?

Nobel Laureate E. O. Lawrence was asked whether he had looked into reports of past work before he came up with the concept of the cyclotron. He is reported to have said that if he had done that he might not have conceived of the new machine because of the several failed attempts reported earlier!

During his tenure as Director of the Cavendish Laboratory (CL), Lord Rutherford attracted young bright researchers in diverse disciplines to work in the laboratory. The young researchers, from time to time, would propose ideas to work upon. Although Lord Rutherford had experimented with quite a few of those ideas but without any new discoveries, he encouraged the researchers to go ahead. He thought he might not have explored all possibilities and there might be new developments which the young researchers could work upon. During the period of his stewardship, the CL produced several Nobel Prize winners.

PATHS TO KNOWLEDGE DISCOVERY

The quintessence of reference work and service, as conceived by S. R. Ranganathan, anchored and guided by his Five Laws of Library Science, is to assist KD. There are different paths to KD. New ideas may emerge, for instance, from:

- Observing the unusual in the usual or non-conformity to the expected. For example, Alexander Fleming's observation of inhibition of bacteria by fungal toxin; and C. V. Raman's noting of a kink in the spectral curve and the eventual formulation of the Raman Effect (cf. also medical diagnostic work-study of records of symptoms, and instrument records of patients).

- Organizing or reorganizing a mass of data to identify patterns of relations among them or correlating sets of known data and formulating generic principles for the observed relation, pattern, regularity, etc., or drawing inferences thereof. For example, the formulation of the principles of planetary motion by Johannes Kepler by reorganizing the vast amount of data on the position of planets collected and recorded by Nicolaus Copernicus earlier. Further generalization is exemplified in the theory of universal gravitation by Isaac Newton; Charles Darwin's postulation of the Survival of the Fittest theory; and Carl Linnaeus' taxonomy of plants/organisms to disclose relations among family, genus, and species.
- Observing an entity from a new or a different angle (cf. De Bono's *Lateral thinking*).[8]
- Finding a pattern common to, or relations among, events or entities in diverse fields; for example, the cyclic movement in geology, climate/weather, in biological organisms, business, etc. Such findings may arise by application of statistical and operations research techniques to a mass of data in diverse fields; e.g., Zipf, Bradford, Lotka and Pareto distributions[9] (cf. also study of *modus operandi* and other pattern analysis of records of crimes).
- Formulating a principle or theory that explains phenomena observed in different fields or contexts; e.g., Newton's Law of Gravity.
- Relating or applying an observation in one situation to a different event(s) or situation(s). One may be obsessed with the need to find a solution to a problem, or the problem may be lying at the subconscious level, and the solution may be found from an observation in quite a different situation; e.g., the Greek mathematician Archimedes relating his observation of the rise of water in the bath tub when he entered it and the level receding when he got out of it to a method of determining whether the king's crown was of pure gold or alloyed with silver, etc. Other examples include: August Kekule relating the appearance in his dream of a snake trying to catch its own tail to the Benzene ring structure; and. S. R. Ranganathan applying his observation, in a London store, to the assembling of unit metal pieces in different ways to produce different mechanical toys to connecting different concepts–facets and isolates–to create subject structure representations.
- Refutation of, or discovering faults and limitations in, an existing theory, assumption, or finding. This attests to the value of careful evaluation and constructive criticism of a proposition, theory, or experimental work.
- When a new concept is added to an existing corpus of knowledge, only a few of its relations to other concepts within the field may be realized, much less so with concepts in other fields. Thus, when these latent relations are recognized chances for KD arise.

- Trans-sensory and trans-intellectual knowledge (intuitive and revealed knowledge).
- Serendipity.

The knowledge or insight gained *via* any of the paths may trigger new lines of search and research; show the limitations of existing knowledge; disclose discrepancies in data obtained by different methods, duplication of findings; and help in problem solving, decision making, taking alternative course of action, and so on.

Each of these paths involves, almost invariably, knowing what exists and the lacunae thereof. To know what exists in a specific area of study implies not only assembling relevant comprehensive data and information, but also their in-depth analysis and identification of relations among ideas in an area to those in its sub-areas, as well as in the related and even apparently unrelated areas. It should also be possible to reorganize and synthesize the data retrieved and/or that obtained through observation, experiment, and survey. The capabilities of information support systems for KD have been considerably augmented by the application of information and communication technologies (ICTs). This may range from the simple to the sophisticated computerized systems, with data gathered using aerial photography, remote sensing, satellite imagery, large radar and planetary telescopes and other instrument records of phenomena (e.g., electron microscope, X-ray photography, endoscope, oscilloscope, etc.). And there are programs and softwares for complex data manipulation, computation, statistical analysis, and mapping. But *KD can also be well supported by manual systems prepared and used by information professionals* (see also case studies which follow).

KNOWLEDGE DISCOVERY WITH BIBLIOGRAPHIC DATABASES

During the past couple of decades several papers have been devoted to KD. Software for data mining and related processes is available as aids to KD. Roy Davies[10] has extensively reviewed the literature on the relation between information retrieval and classification and KD. Application of statistical techniques especially in citation studies, bibliometric coupling, correlation, pattern recognition and other areas of informetrics and scientometrics helps in KD. Brief notes on the papers in the special issue of *Library Trends*, 1999[11] on data mining, data discovery, and the related techniques are given in the paper by Haravu and Neelameghan in this volume.

Knowledge discovery requires providing for data prospecting or exploration. Generally, in an information system the search and discovery process, to be economical with a reasonable chance of being productive, has to provide for data prospecting (data exploration) in order to identify and mark the boundaries of the search area(s) likely to yield acceptable results. Classification and clustering techniques are tools useful for marking out such areas for search. The contents of the sources may be classified and pre-organized, and to help the user to select one or more search areas, subject indexes are provided. Content organization (or reorganization) may also be done in presenting the retrieved information. Alternatively or in addition, the user may be provided (online and/or manual) a map of the subject divisions (with its own index), using, for example, a scheme for subject classification, knowledge/subject maps, and thesauri (conventional, faceted, classaurus, etc.). Depending upon the field of search and user's requirement, provision of access to other facilities, such as an online dictionary or glossary, would also help, as well as the restructuring and organization of the data (pre- and/or post-retrieval).

KNOWLEDGE ORGANIZATION TOOLS AND METHODS TO AID KD

Methods and tools of information organization and presentation, to assist in the retrieval process and in KD, include the following:

- Linking sources of data/information (e.g., cross referencing and hypertext links). Inter-linking of concepts (hyper links) or items of information within and across databases, which, incidentally, overcomes certain limitations of a preclassified arrangement of records
- Citation links, URLs, e-mail and other contact addresses (experts, corporate bodies)
- Linking of concepts and knowledge mapping[12]
- Knowledge/subject maps; scientographs[13,14]
- Thesauri (conventional-, faceted-, root-, classaurus) and hyper linking between thesauri, classification schemes, etc. Neelameghan and Prasad[15] have shown how in a user interface: (1) a thesaurus for a very specific subject 'Energy flow in an eco-system' can be linked (hypertext link) to a thesaurus for a more general subject (biosciences); (2) a term in the index to a classification scheme may be hyperlinked to a corresponding terms in a thesaurus; (3) relations in a concepts map can be shown in the related thesaurus
- In-depth analysis, restructuring and indexing (see case studies). The indexes may be a conventional alphabetical index, or POPSI, PRECIS, KWAC, KWIC. In these alphabetical concordance type indexes, the occurrence (juxtaposition) of a concept in a different contextual environment of concepts can be helpful in triggering new ideas

- Use of analytico-synthetic methodology and principles of classification (see case studies)
- User interfaces and search engines for concurrent multiple access to one or more databases of different types
- Tools to help users to understand the specialized vocabulary (especially in multilingual multicultural databases and user groups) (see case studies)
- Facilities for using different media and different types of presentations, including mapping of the data/information (text, table, formula, graphics, image, and sound)
- Geographical information systems (GIS) (see case studies)
- Data mining and text mining and facilities to store the processed data for future use (data warehousing) (see also paper by Haravu and Neelameghan in this volume)
- Word use analysis to discover linguistic/cultural behavior of authors (see paper by Haravu and Neelameghan in this volume)
- Informetric, scientometric and operations research tools for further processing of the retrieved data; for comparison, correlation, pattern recognition, modeling and simulation[16,17]
- Artificial intelligence applications (see also paper by Haravu and Neelameghan in this volume)
- Mind mapping–a visual thinking technique described by Buzan and Buzan.[18] Mind maps are used to organize individual or collective thought and represent it visually. A mind map consists of a central word or concept, around which 5 to 10 main ideas that relate to that word are drawn up. Each of those 'child' words in turn attract 5 to 10 main ideas that relate to each of them. In this way an exponential number of related ideas can quickly be produced with little mental effort.

CASE STUDIES

The case histories presented here are from our personal experience describing specialized information support systems for assisting researchers and scholars and how they were used in knowledge discovery.[19]

Case 1

Case 1 illustrates the usefulness of inter-linking within and across databases, multiple database search facilities, alternative search routes, and the use of an online glossary in relation to multilingual, multicultural databases.

The information support system is a multi-media information system containing about 18,000 extracts and associated databases of life sketches, plus pictures, and bibliography of source documents to support spiritual studies (accessible on the Internet, but the case study relates to the PC version).[20] An online thesaurus and glossary of specialized terms from Sanskrit, Pali, Arabic, etc. (in English transliteration) are provided. The databases are hyperlinked as are records within a database.[21]

An example of a *user's query* was for information on the concept of 'Enlightenment in Zen Buddhism.' One of two approaches to formulating a search expression might be adopted: (1) to look up the term 'Buddhism' or 'Zen Buddhism' in the related online thesaurus. Under 'Zen Buddhism,' 'Enlightenment,' 'Satori' and other RT terms are given. Either or both of these terms may be used as search term; and (2) to use the Boolean search expression 'Buddhism and Zen and Enlightenment.' The user adopted the latter approach.

Retrieval/Hits found were as follows: Buddhism (983 extracts), Zen (107), Enlightenment (139); combination of concepts: resulted in 4 extracts. One of the retrieved records dealt specifically with 'Satori,' a term for enlightenment in Zen. Further search with 'Satori,' retrieved 9 extracts. One of the texts displayed, discusses Satori in relation to 'Prajna,' a Sanskrit term. The user was interested but needed a definition of 'Prajna.' The online glossary of terms was called up using a linking program. The cursor was moved on the term 'Prajna' in the extract, and selecting it retrieved the relevant record from the GLOSS database and displayed it in a window. The user, interested to know more about 'Prajna,' selected the term and all extracts dealing with 'Prajna' were retrieved. In this way the user interface permits movement from one record to another dealing with the same concept or related concepts from any of the records retrieved from the same or other databases in the system, and permits the user to learn and discover relations between 'satori' and other concepts in Hinduism, Christianity, etc., even if the thesaurus does not show such links or relations. The knowledge proved helpful in the comparative studies in which the user was engaged.

Case 2

Case 2 relates to an information support system for researchers in antibiotic substances. At the time the work was started (1960), some 2000 antibiotic substances (produced by micro-organisms) had been reported in literature, although fewer than ten of them were being used extensively for therapeutic purposes and produced on a commercial scale. A bibliography on cards of about 14,000 references had been compiled with weekly updates from the *Current Awareness List* (weekly), and *Patents Abstracts* (fortnightly). As desired by the researchers, the antibiotics record forms, one for each antibiotic, were classified and organized into four main classes according to the type of source micro-organism, and serially numbered with gaps for insertion: (1) Bacteria, 1 to 199; (2) Actinomycetes, 200 to 999; (3) Fungi, 1000 to 1499; and (4) Lichen, 1500 to 1599. Almost all of the attributes were treated as potential access points. Indexes to source micro-organism, physical and chemical properties (solubility in water, alcohol, etc.), special tabulated chart of UV spectrum peaks, infrared data, optical rotation, molecular structure and components, which can serve as indexes to these attributes data, were prepared. The printed indexes were to be compact, easy to use and made available to users for personal use, if desired. In the chart for UV maxima (λMax) (Figure 1), each box represents one wavelength on the horizontal row in units (0 to 9) and the numbers 210, 220, 230, etc., in the first vertical column denote the beginning of the range. Serial numbers of the data sheets (which are unique ID numbers for the antibiotics) are posted in the appropriate boxes such that the ID numbers of antibiotics having the same UV maxima fall in the same square. Thus, for a substance isolated in the laboratory which shows a UV maxima of 236 and 276, it is quickly seen that an antibiotic already exists with those UV maxima. Similar charts for melting point, molecular formulae, etc., were prepared.

These charts enabled quick comparison of attributes of a substance on hand (from laboratory work) with those already known. Search and comparison by a combination of three or four attributes (source organism, UV spectrum, melting point, optical rotation, solubility) of the substance on hand may point to 3 or 4 known antibiotics (out of some 2,000) or none at all. In the latter case the possibility of discovery of a new antibiotic, or a new source for a known antibiotic or other differences in attributes arise. Original papers are then studied to arrive at decisions about the new findings. The system enabled us to find duplicate discoveries of antibiotics, some more than once. In a 10 in × 10 in. chart with 1 in. × 1 in. each box size, about 15,000 items could be conveniently posted.

FIGURE 1. Ultraviolet Absorption Maxima Index (Incomplete)

λMax	0	1	2	3	4	5	6	7	8	9
210	31 41	166 207 208 253	29	7				7 129	70 214	
220	121	26			53	12 69	69 129			70
230	9 77 121 165	165	88 89 111		51 165	52 78	39 53 88 111	41 70	161 215	158 161

Case 3

Case 3 is an example of the application of a depth classification scheme for classifying and organizing micro-documents. A large number of schemes for classification, especially relating to specific Commodity Production Engineering, were designed and developed according to Ranganathan's[22,23] Generalized Facet model. The schemes were used for the analytical presentation of product data and to create structured abstracts of micro-documents. The example given here is in the field Automobile Production Engineering. The number of attributes to characterize an automobile was about 230. A database was created based on this analysis. Every term (excluding apparatus words) in the structured abstract was indexed so that the system could respond to such search queries as: Which automobile uses a Synchromesh Transmission Gear Box? What are the uses of Borg and Beck Transmission Clutch with Diaphragm Disc Engagement? With hypertext linking (see Case 4) between records within a database and those in two or more databases, the approach was particularly useful in the analysis of patents information, comparative study of automobile products, discovery of market for, or applications of, particular devices, etc.

Case 4

Case 4 illustrates the use of geographical information system (GIS) in checking reported data with GIS pictures, discovering discrepancies and drawing inferences for further action. GIS is a useful tool to present, in an integrated way, text, tabulated data, graphics, and pictures. A large amount of information can be visualized in a small space, for example, the cropping pattern of a region consisting of over 700 villages. A data table will run to several pages and it will be difficult to get a synthetic or comparative picture of the pattern or situation from it. A cartographic picture or thematic map can provide an organized visual translation of the pattern, from the lightly shadowed to the darkly shadowed area, of irrigated areas during rainfall season of a particular period. Visual perception rules being innate to human beings, they are universal and can be used in communicating even with non-literate people and with people whose native language may not be the same as that of the communicator. It is relatively easier to compare maps and draw inferences using maps of particular theme. A loose-leaf atlas of the maps can be prepared. Those of interest for a particular purpose can be retrieved, classified, organized and presented in interesting ways, for example, by superimposition of maps. Such flexibility is difficult to achieve with conventional printed maps and textual information systems. GIS also permits examining changes in the features of the object when one or more relevant parameters are changed.

In summary, some of the special advantages of GIS in this context are:

- Large amounts of information can be visualized in a small space
- Focusing attention on particular features of the mapped area
- Drawing attention to unreliable data
- Easier identification of areas with development potential or that require special attention
- Identification of under-utilization of development resources
- Superimposition of development indicators
- Identification of gaps
- Representation of qualitative information
- Locating areas of high production
- Regional comparisons.

GIS applications with examples are discussed by Neelameghan[24] in another paper in 1996.

CONCLUDING REMARKS

There are several paths to knowledge discovery (KD). Appropriate information support systems can assist the processes of KD. In the different case studies presented above, different types of information support services are briefly described. The usefulness of an innovative but manual system is discussed; the use of knowledge organization tools are presented in other case studies. The importance of discourse analysis (using analytico-synthetic methodology, and text mining software) is emphasized. A knowledge of the subject fields is necessary in interacting with and understanding end-users' information needs, in developing the systems and user interfaces, and in designing the knowledge organization tools.

REFERENCES

1. Neelameghan, A. 1979. "Expressions of time in information science and their implications." In: *Time and the sciences*, edited by Frank Greenaway (At the cross roads of cultures). Paris: Unesco, p. 103-118.

2. Medland, Michael. 2002. Department of Foundations, Research and Reading, East Carolina University, Greenville, NC 27858 USA. [*Personal communication*]. E-mail: mb_medland@hotmail.com.

3. Ibid.

4. Neelameghan, A. 1992. "Ranganathan's generalized model of subject structure and modes of formation of subjects. In: *Cognitive paradigms in knowledge organization: Second International ISKO Conference, Madras, 26-28 August 1992*, edited by A. Neelameghan and others. Bangalore, India: SRELS, p. 269-285.

5. Farb, Peter. 1974. *Word play: what happens when people talk.* New York: Alfred A. Knopf.

6. Neelameghan A., Buche, V.V. and Gupta, B.S.S. 1970. "Distribution pattern of the duplication of discoveries." *Nature* 227: 1060.

7. Ibid.

8. De Bono, Edward. *Lateral thinking: a textbook of creativity.* London: Ward, Lock & Co.

9. Ravichandra Rao, I.K. 2000. *Quantitative techniques for content analysis. Content organization in the new millennium. Seminar on Content Organization in the New Millennium, Bangalore, 2-4 June 2000.* Bangalore, India: SRELS; 2001. p. 43-50.

10. Davies, Roy. 1989. "The creation of new knowledge by information retrieval and classification," *Journal of Documentation* 45 (4): 273-301.

11. Jian Qin and M. Jay Norton, eds. 1999. "Knowledge discovery in bibliographic databases," *Library Trends* 48 (1): 1-281.

12. Neelameghan, A. and Prasad, K.N. 2002. "Digitized schemes for subject classification and thesauri: complementary roles," *Information Studies* 8(1): 25-42.

13. Garfield, Eugene. 1994a. Scientography: mapping the tracks of science. *The ISI essays.* Philadelphia: ISI.

14. _____. 1994b. Mapping the precursors of modern structural biology. *The ISI essays.* Philadelphia: ISI.

15. Neelameghan and Prasad, ibid.

16. as in 9.

17. as in 13, 14.

18. Buzan, Tony and Buzan, Barry. 1993. *The mind map book.* London: BBC Books.

19. Neelameghan, A. 2000. "Content organization as aid to knowledge discovery: case studies." In: *Content organization in the new millennium: Seminar on Content Organization in the New Millennium, Bangalore, 2-4 June 2000*; Bangalore, India. p. 39-42.

20. Rajashekar, T.B., Srinivasa, Ravi, A. and Neelameghan, A. 1998. "Designing a multimedia information service for the Internet and CD-ROM," *Information Studies* 4(3): 125-142.

21. Neelameghan, A. 1999. "An online glossary for a multilingual database," *Information Studies* 5(2): 83-94.

22. Ranganathan, S.R. 1964. "Design of depth classification methodology." *Library Science With a Slant to Documentation*, 1; Paper A: 1-43.

23. Neelameghan 1997. *S.R. Ranganathan's postulates and normative principles: applications in specialized database design, indexing and retrieval.* Bangalore, India: SRELS.

24. Neelameghan, A. 1996. "Geographical information system: an overview," *Information studies* 2(2): 85-127.

LINGUISTICS, TERMINOLOGY, AND NATURAL LANGUAGE PROCESSING

Human Language Technology and Its Role in Information Access and Management

Widad Mustafa el Hadi

SUMMARY. The role of linguistics in information access,[1] extraction and dissemination is essential. Radical changes in the techniques of information and communication at the end of the twentieth century have had a significant effect on the function of the linguistic paradigm and its applications in all forms of communication. The introduction of new technical means have deeply changed the possibilities for the distribution of information. In this situation, what is the role of the linguistic paradigm and its practical applications, i.e., natural language processing (NLP) techniques when ap-

Widad Mustafa el Hadi, PhD, is Maitre de Conferences, UFR IDST and CERSATES (CNRS UMR 8529), Université Charles De Gaulle, Lille 3, BP 149 F-59 653 Villeneuve D'Ascq, France (E-mail: Mustafa@univ-lille3.fr).

[Haworth co-indexing entry note]: "Human Language Technology and Its Role in Information Access and Management." Mustafa el Hadi, Widad. Co-published simultaneously in *Cataloging & Classification Quarterly* (The Haworth Information Press, an imprint of The Haworth Press, Inc.) Vol. 37, No. 1/2, 2003, pp. 131-151; and: *Knowledge Organization and Classification in International Information Retrieval* (ed: Nancy J. Williamson, and Clare Beghtol) The Haworth Information Press, an imprint of The Haworth Press, Inc., 2003, pp. 131-151. Single or multiple copies of this article are available for a fee from The Haworth Document Delivery Service [1-800-HAWORTH, 9:00 a.m. - 5:00 p.m. (EST). E-mail address: docdelivery@haworthpress.com].

http://www.haworthpress.com/store/product.asp?sku=J104

Digital Object Identifier: 10.1300/J104v37n01_10

plied to information access? What solutions can linguistics offer in human computer interaction, extraction and management? Many fields show the relevance of the linguistic paradigm through the various technologies that require NLP, such as document and message understanding, information detection, extraction, and retrieval, question and answer, cross-language information retrieval (CLIR), text summarization, filtering, and spoken document retrieval. This paper focuses on the central role of human language technologies in the information society, surveys the current situation, describes the benefits of the above mentioned applications, outlines successes and challenges, and discusses solutions. It reviews the resources and means needed to advance information access and dissemination across language boundaries in the twenty-first century. Multilingualism, which is a natural result of globalization, requires more effort in the direction of language technology. The scope of human language technology (HLT) is large, so we limit our review to applications that involve multilinguality.

KEYWORDS. Human language technology, natural language processing, multilinguality

BACKGROUND: HUMAN LANGUAGE TECHNOLOGY IN THE INFORMATION AGE

The globalization of the economy requires efficient communication, information management and dissemination across boundaries. Since we assume that information is primarily encoded as text, information retrieval (IR) can also be an application of NLP techniques: it is vital to understand the content of a document in order to decide whether it is relevant to a given information need. Some specialists point out the need for NLP technology to build the information systems of the future.[2] For these reasons, the last few years have seen a growing interest in HLT in general and its applications to information access and management in particular. This paper examines HLT's contribution to information access, extraction and dissemination across boundaries and provides an overview of the state-of-the-art of HLT applied to information access and management. The scope of this volume being "Knowledge Organization and Classification in International Information Retrieval," we will address more specifically applications and linguistic resources (i.e., terminologies and lexical resources and technologies) oriented towards multilingual applications. Multilinguality is not only limited to textual data but takes on spoken form when information services are to extend across language groups. Although multilingual speech recognition and understanding is in constant development (public service operators, police, telephone operators, multimodal information systems, etc.) this study is limited to written language processing. It examines the role of language technology in information access and how the contribution of language technology is crucial in the globalization era by focusing on the role of technology in multilingual environments.

THE ROLE OF NLP IN INFORMATION ACCESS

We are using the term "information access" in a wide sense since it involves multiple technologies: traditional IR techniques, monolingual CLIR, summarization, information extraction, automated question and answering, machine translation in IR environments, document understanding, and multimedia document and image retrieval. We first review a number of information access technologies.

IR and NLP

Standard IR procedures consist of a search among records in order to satisfy ordinary information needs. The major components of this process are the sets of records or documents, user's need, query, search strategy, retrieved set and its relevance. Most IR interfaces use documentary languages (a list of index terms or keywords, controlled vocabulary, etc.) where each index term is understood to describe the text contents. This process can be defined as the matching of a given user query against useful parts of free textual data or structured textual data. In most cases IR systems use exact pattern matching to compare the terms of queries with the terms in the texts. The extraction of adequate terms to retrieve information can either be done by a field specialist or automatically processed. Indexing is used for identifying suitable terms from a document, usually to facilitate IR. All of the different controlled vocabularies have about the same level of retrieval performance, and indexing with the words in the documents ("the bag of words" approach, also referred to as "automatic indexing") did as well as any of the controlled vocabularies.[3] This led to various efforts to use statistics to improve performance and to incorporate information about language into the retrieval model. In spite of intensive efforts, many of the experiments in using linguistic information have not resulted in an improvement over the bags of words representation. The vast majority of retrieval systems currently in use range from simple Boolean systems to systems using statistical or NLP.[4] Internet access created new search needs involving user-friendly interfaces, natural language interfaces and translation facilities. Substantial research in the area of document retrieval has been carried out for more than thirty years.[5] This period has been dominated by the use of statistical methods to automatically match natural language user queries against records. There has also been interest in using NLP to enhance single term matching by adding phrases or more precisely "noun-phrases."[6] Much work has been done in this direction within the framework of term recognition and extraction technology. NLP techniques, however have not significantly improved performance of document retrieval as Sparck Jones pointed out.[7] Most researchers in the IR community believe that retrieval effectiveness is easier to improve by means of statistical methods than by NLP-based approaches and this is established by results, although there are exceptions.[8]

Even though NLP in IR is much debated[9] some examples show the relevance of this technology in keyword extraction for IR.[10] Many authors including Sparck Jones agree, nevertheless, on the obvious role of NLP technology in information extraction, information management and knowledge management contexts.[11] Others think that the success of NLP technology depends on a more radical change of focus.[12]

Requirements for Improving the Capacity of Retrieval Systems: The Role of Linguistic Resources

NLP resources used in extracting information from text as described by Jacobs,[13] such as thesauri, lexicons, dictionaries, named entities, are used regularly in information retrieval research. It seems, therefore, according to Jacobs,[14] that NLP *resources* rather than NLP techniques are having more of an impact on document retrieval effectiveness at present.[15] Part of the reason for the limited success reported in many articles and books[16] is that NLP techniques are generally not designed to handle large amounts of text from many different domains.[17] The most successful directions in NLP applications are in information extraction, information and knowledge management, information filtering and text summarization.

Terminology: An Application for Natural Language Technology

As a result of the growing interest in automatic handling of terms, a number of products aimed at term recognition and extraction have been developed, mostly in the IR context. While this research can be traced back to the late 1950s, automatic term extraction aiming at building reference tools for translation, technical writing or knowledge-based systems and CLIR are more recent developments.

Term extraction deals with two main activities: term acquisition, i.e., covering of a domain, which includes discovering new terms,[18] and indexing. The purpose of term acquisition is the construction of terminological resources, such as controlled vocabularies. Thesauri are used for assisting information access through query expansion,[19] for cross-lingual information retrieval[20] or for thesaurus-based querying. In this domain, automatic thesaurus construction is a well established tradition and studies have focused either on the discovery of terms or on the discovery of semantic relations.[21] Bilingual term extraction tools[22] based on part-of-speech tagging and word alignment technologies to extract candidate terms and their translations can be used for both tasks. The monolingual part of this type of system can be used for indexing and for term extraction while the bilingual component can serve both for translation and for IR in multilingual text collections.[23] Although this type of system was initially created for term extraction and translation, it was later reused and adapted for indexing as well, as reported by Landauer.[24] Term extraction designers should keep in mind these new requirements (i.e., translation and IR in multilingual text collections) when designing such systems because the need for them is going to be increasingly evident.

Here we briefly account for some of the innovative techniques involving automatic terminology resources acquisition[25] which is a basic component of information access. Coarse extraction techniques, as Bourigault *et al.*[26] pointed out, tend to produce huge lists of undifferentiated terms that are of little use for efficient document indexing and retrieval. To be of use, these types of lists must be subject to structuring, which is an important step towards exploiting extraction results. Some efforts were undertaken to avoid the overproduction of terms. Peter[27] suggests selecting only faceted terms, i.e., terms that pertain to the domain of the query. Hongyan *et al.*[28] suggest solutions to terminological disambiguation in order to avoid conflating morphologically related terms with no semantic relationship. These two methods have allowed for accurate indexing and enhanced precision in document retrieval.[29]

In the same direction Jacquemin *et al.*[30] and Jacquemin[31] suggested an approach by automatic indexing over controlled vocabulary which accounts for term variation. The approach, considered by this author as rich indexing, combines a part of speech tagger, a generator of morphologically related forms and a shallow transformational parser. The FASTER system has been applied to the French language. Evaluation of this tool on indexing tasks has produced encouraging results[32] as far as improvement of indexing through variant extraction was concerned. Moreover, Jacquemin *et al.*[33] have pointed out the importance of exploiting lexical and terminological data as a key to success in such approaches.

From a general point of view the tools we have evaluated in our previous work, especially term extraction ones, have only a limited interest for indexing tasks, although this is not the case with other tools such as semantic relation extractors. Some of the semantic extraction tools have been adapted *inter alia* for indexing tasks.[34] Other techniques aim at improving term and environment extraction quality. Studies in this area deal with collocations and specialized verbs[35] and relational adjectives.[36] Other techniques are used in CLIR information retrieval.[37] One of the requirements is access to multilingual data with cross-language connections between terms and their equivalents in other languages. Akiko and Kageura[38] show how bilingual keyword lists frequently found in scientific journal articles can be used to build multilingual keyword clusters. Such clusters can be used for query expansion in cross-language information access and even for monolingual query expansion.[39] Other significant contributions in this area are Bisson, Hull and Gaussier.[40] From that point of view it might be interesting to design term extraction tools for generic bilingual production.

NLP-Based Ontologies

Ontologies have emerged as one of the most popular means of modeling the knowledge of a domain. They can act as an index to the memory of an organization and facilitate semantic searches and the retrieval of knowledge from the corporate memory as it is embodied in documents and other archives. Though ontologies are different from the concepts of lexicon, classification schemes and thesauri, their inter-relationship is still obvious. This is why we think that terminology resources are the basis for this type of organization.[41] We assume that a hybridized approach for ontology elaboration (a formal and linguistic one) is necessary (cf. relevant experiences below). Ontologies can be seen as "enriched" thesauri since they include definitions and semantic relations. Their role is to reduce conceptual and terminological ambiguities by identifying and properly defining a set of relevant concepts characterizing a domain. They can solve semantic ambiguity, a core problem in text understanding. In this respect, machine translation (MT) is increasingly seen as an important element of success in CLIR as it involves elements of both MT and IR. Many other uses are mentioned in the literature, but the most relevant ontology models for our approach and interest in this subject are *GALEN* (for its multilingual terminological module), *CYC* (especially for the levels enabling natural language understanding and generation) and *MIKROKOSMOS* (for MT application). Moreover, this type of ontology could be useful in MT environments and consequently in CLIR. This point will be examined intensively in the light of the research study we are currently conducting.

Most of the methods used in building ontologies are rather empirical. Two main research trends can be pointed out: the *linguistic approach* which is represented by the research done by terminology and artificial intelligence teams[42] and the *formal* one.[43] As far as the former approach is concerned, terminology acquisition tools can be used in building ontologies. The first step in building ontologies is to acquire terminological resources from corpora in different languages.[44] In our case, the idea is to use available terminology acquisition tools.[45]

Relevant Work and Similar Experiences in NLP-Based Ontologies

NLP-based ontologies are used to reduce the cost of ontology engineering. It follows in the path of comparable work in the field of NLP applications to MT such as the SENSUS-based ontology (for more details and relevant examples see Fenandez Lopèz[46] and TERMINAE,[47] a tool for generating ontologies from specialized corpora). Other efforts are oriented toward ontologies for knowledge management and knowledge sharing. *SymOntos*,[48] a symbolic ontology management system, is an example of this family of tools. The system uses *OPAL* (Object, Process, and Actor modeling language), a methodology for the modeling and management of a company knowledge base that enables the representation of semi-formal knowledge. *SymOntos* gathers terms denoting concepts, definitions (in natural language), the meaning of concepts and a set of relationships.

Recently we discussed how existing tools can be geared towards information and knowledge management applications, namely for building domain specific ontologies.[49] Our observations and suggestions are based on a series of research projects dealing with automated term and semantic relations extraction tools that we conducted over the last four years.[50] Techniques used for building ontologies used in the emerging discipline of knowledge management (KM) are also discussed.

Word Sense Disambiguation

Word sense disambiguation is one of the directions of future research in NLP. It can help to separate relevant from non-relevant documents. Ambiguity characterizes even a small domain specific collection of documents. The results indicate the potential for word sense disambiguation to improve IR. The importance of word sense disambiguation on the impact of lexical ambiguity on IR systems has been reported in experiments.[51]

INFORMATION EXTRACTION

Information extraction is the task of filling templates or tables from natural language input.[52] The proliferation of online text motivates most current work in text interpretation. Often, being able to make efficient use of information from text requires that the information be put in some sort of structured format (for example, in a relational database), or systematically indexed and linked. Currently, extracting the information required for a useful database or index is an expensive manual process; hence online text creates a need for automatic text processing methods to extract the information automatically.[53] Current methods generally start by identifying key artifacts in the text, such as proper names, dates, times, and locations, and then use a combination of linguistic constraints and domain knowledge to identify the important content of each relevant text. Currently, there have been rapid advances in the robustness and applicability of these methods. However, current systems are limited because they are reliant on domain knowledge. These problems are moderated by the availability of online resources, such as lexicons and corpora. Yet, the issue of how to develop a technology base that applies to many problems is still the major challenge, as reported in Jacobs.[54]

HLT IN INFORMATION MANAGEMENT[55]

There are a number of areas in which language technologies can improve and enable Information Management (IM). These have been identified as: input analysis, content-based IR, information extraction, question answering, translation, dialogue management, user modeling, summarization, and presentation.[56] More have also been identified: automatic tracking and detection of emerging topics from unstructured data (text mining), information filtering, knowledge mapping and access (lexical information, language modeling), text categorization.

Knowledge Management

Domain-specific information on WWW ontologies are used in knowledge portals in order to narrow the gap between finding knowledge in texts and providing it to the portals. HLT is used, moreover, to reduce the cost of ontology engineering, as mentioned above. Some applications show how language technology will help in creating new knowledge from large collections of textual information and in sharing knowledge across boundaries.[57] Some current work on HLT for KM applications is reported in Maybury.[58]

Knowledge Sharing

Sharing of knowledge/knowledge transfer is the "The process of disseminating individual experiences, information or knowledge throughout the organisation to those who (might) need it."[59] For this activity, HLT can provide the means for associating knowledge with the relevant decisions. The technology associated with this application is called automatic relational "hyper-linking." Relational hyperlinks are different from the simple HTML hyperlinks in that they are composed from a number of named links that can be selected from a menu. HLT is used to identify and disambiguate the concepts in the documents that need to be linked. To this end, specific techniques are used, such as named entity recognition. This method has been applied in the Hypercode system of DFKI Lab.[60]

TEXT SUMMARIZATION

The goal of summarization is to take information from a source, extract content from it, and present the most important content to the user in a condensed form and in a manner sensitive to the user's application need. Sparck Jones[61] traced back "automatic abstracting" which was first attempted in the 1950s, in the form of Luhn's auto-extracts.[62] The increasing volume of machine-readable text and advances in natural language processing have stimulated a new interest in automatic summarizing. In order to have efficient systems, Sparck Jones[63] points out the crucial need for "The *full text revolution*" which has effects on indexing. This implies a pressing need for automatic summarizing. NLP technology provides the basic resource for this revolution. In cross-language text summarization, several languages are processed from input, with summaries in different languages.[64]

NLP AND ITS ROLE IN THE GLOBALIZATION ERA

Multilingual Information Access and CLIR Technology

The problem of multilingual access to text databases can be seen as an extension of the general IR problem. The technology used to accomplish this specific type of IR is called CLIR. This field is at the crossroads of both MT and IR. It represents a real challenge to the IR community and will require a solid cooperation with the NLP community. The WWW, as a huge repository of multilingual information freely accessible through the various search engines, has certainly increased interest in CLIR. The use of MT, such as the "Translate" facility available on the Altavista web service and many other utilities, is now a necessity for users wishing to retrieve documents in various languages. But the quality of the translations provided is not satisfactory and a lot of work remains to be done.

The tools and linguistic resources to be developed to improve CLIR range from part-of-speech taggers, syntactic analyzers, monolingual dictionaries, bilingual dictionaries (for language pairs), to lexical databases, terminological databases, monolingual corpora and aligned corpora (for language pairs).

The ideal strategy is to enable the user to express his/her query in natural language and in his/her mother tongue so as to grant access to any textual information relevant to the query, independently of the language in which the needed information is presented. Most users can read documents written in a foreign language but have difficulty finding the appropriate words to express their query in an efficient way. The choice of an inaccurate term or expression can drastically affect a search process and lead to a poor performance. For these reasons it is preferable to give the user the opportunity to express the query in the language he/she knows best. Though CLIR functions largely as a traditional IR system, it has some specific problems not shared by monolingual text retrieval. A traditional IR system can work with words used in the initial user query. The more a document contains words appearing in a user's query the more likely it is that the document will be relevant to that query.[65]

A Review of Some Techniques Used in CLIR That Remain to Be Solved: Finding Translations, Pruning Translations, Weighting Translation

This review is far from being exhaustive. We give here a brief account of the most popular methods implemented and tested in CLIR environments. They can be classified in four categories: thesaurus-based, corpus-based, machine translation-based and latent semantic analysis-based.

Approaches Using Machine Translation

This approach is based on using existing MT systems to translate either the database or the queries. Even at a very poor quality level (Altavista Web translation service for instance), MT is becoming popular as it enables users to read documents in different languages. Many users are able to understand documents in another language, even if they are not fluent enough in that language to query a database.

a. Translating the complete database required for an information search task is quite a job because of the sheer quantity of translation required. The memory space required for storing language pairs translations prevents using this approach for large document collections. Moreover, the limitations of this technique are widely known: MT systems provide a word for word translation, incorrect translations for polysemous words, etc.

b. As for query translation, the idea is to leave the documents in their original languages and to transform each query into every language at run time.[66] Query translation is efficient when short queries are presented, but unsophisticated techniques based on simple word substitution will negatively affect retrieval efficiency when compared with monolingual IR scenarios. This adverse impact, as pointed out by Dorr *et al.*,[67] seems to derive from translation ambiguity, limited lexical coverage, and a failure to correctly translate non-compositional phrases. This second approach, is considered to be "faster and straightforward and has demonstrated retrieval performances comparable to the document translation approach."[68] It uses online bilingual and multilingual dictionaries to offer translations for queries.

Another MT technique which consists of using parallel corpora of texts (see later discussion), (i.e., naturally-occurring sets of documents that are not translations of each other), to generate necessary translations, is documented in Grefenstette[69] and Harmann.[70]

Automatic translation works best when domains are well defined and when the system is supplied with a specific terminology. What is particularly binding with CLIR is that IR is not limited to a specific domain, so that for the operation to be successful, we should have as many specialized terminologies as there are domains about which information is being sought.

Automatic CLIR Using Latent Semantic Indexing

The method has been reported in Littman *et al.*[71] It consists of document retrieval in which no query translation is required. This is accomplished by a method that automatically constructs a multi-lingual semantic space using latent semantic indexing (LSI). The method is based on an initial sample of translated documents. From these translations (either by machine or by humans), the authors produce a set of parallel texts or documents from both languages. These documents are used to "train" the system. An LSI analysis of these training documents results in a dual-language semantic space in which terms from both languages are represented. For a complete review of LSI methods see Littman *et al.*[72]

Another method relying upon LSI has been implemented in a Biomedical Information Communication Center.[73] It consists of mapping vocabularies using LSI. The idea is to map natural language into appropriate special terms as well as mapping one system's specialized terminology into another's. This mapping will depend on semantic equivalences among terms, not merely the superficial matching of words or phrases. The relevance of this method for CLIR is that other lexical items in several languages can be used side by side to represent the conceptual contents of terms. The resulting semantic space will locate terms on multilingual dimensions. This method has been tested on Spanish and English.[74]

Automatic Building of Cross-Language Thesaurus Using Comparable Corpus as Input

Harmann[75] described an experiment conducted by the Swiss Federal Institute of Technology in which they automatically built a cross-language thesaurus by using a comparable corpus as input. This corpus, consisting of Swiss news agency dispatches in three languages, was used as a naturally-occurring set of documents not being translations of each other (as in parallel corpora) and were independently-produced articles dealing with the same time period.[76] This experiment has been evaluated within the TREC6 cross-language track framework.[77] Hudon[78] has pointed out the relevance of multilingual thesauri as a potential solution to increasing communication difficulties.

Bilingual and Multilingual Reformulation

Another linguistic technique known as "reformulation" is used by SPIRIT.[79] It is a technique initially used in expanding the search to other parts of a database by using stemming and semantic relations. For CLIR, the approach consists of using a bilingual reformulation which tries every possible translation for each word. If there is an answer to the query, the ambiguities are then resolved by using relevant documents as a semantic filter to help in choosing the right translation.[80]

The purpose of the mechanisms developed in the EMIR[81] (European Multilingual Information Retrieval) is to match the terms expressed in the user's query with the terms used–eventually in another language–by the authors of the documents stored in the database. The matching procedure relies on the lexical semantic knowledge integrated into the reformulation tool. It is based on an automatic linguistic (morphological and syntactic) analysis of both the queries and the documents. A statistical treatment allows a comparison between the query and the documents linked to the proffered concepts. SPIRIT with its reformulation module exemplifies this type of technology.[82]

Use of Large Parallel Corpora

Parallel corpora are useful for disambiguating monolingual terms senses in limited tests.[83] They have also been used for training and as an effective methods-text model for translation. Davis[84] has also pointed out the implicit use of parallel corpora in CLIR by Landauer and Littman,[85] who generated query translation matrixes using LSI.

CLIR Using Comparable Corpus Querying

This method is somewhat comparable to the previous one (i.e., the use of large parallel corpora). It is related to the work accomplished in corpus linguistics. It has been implemented in a system that has been designed to process and query comparable text corpora, i.e., collections of texts from pairs or multiples of languages referring to the same domain. The system retrieves natural language equivalents from sets of sub-language texts in English and Italian. The authors think that if the system is provided with necessary morphological and lexical components it could be extended to other languages. The system has applications in the fields of bi- and multilingual terminology and in CLIR.[86] There are many other methods used in CLIR technology. For overviews and recent textbooks, see Grefenstette and LTREC Conference Proceedings.[87]

Drawbacks to CLIR

Grefenstette[88] gives a detailed account of the major problems facing CLIR in the light of papers presented in that volume. The author points out many linguistic and computational problems dealing with multilingual collections (properly treating multiple characters sets, separating languages via language recognition, language-specific stemming routines or morphological analysis) that should be solved. As we have all experienced, the present level of translation when using the AltaVista "Translate" facility is not adequate. The main shortcoming of this approach is that MT tools can provide only one translation for each word and that if the wrong translation is provided, something that is very likely in the case of polysemous words, the result is useless. Efforts have concentrated on query translation techniques. There are two ways of finding translation terms. The first and most common one is through the use of a bilingual dictionary listing the possible translation terms. The main issue in this type of application is the construction and development of bilingual resources (dictionaries, terminologies, etc.). Moreover, translation systems in general should be improved in terms of accuracy and usability.

The second one is based on alignment technology: word alignment, compound alignment, sentence alignment and whole corpora alignment. The whole spectrum can be used to improve query translations. There is a growing interest for such a resource, the quality of which is improving. Two important requirements for these bilingual dictionaries designed for CLIR are: (a) the coverage provided by the dictionary for domain independent corpora; and (b) the efficiency of the translations provided for finding relevant documents in the other language. There is, of course, an even more serious problem in properly understanding nuances that are more cross-cultural than cross-lingual.[89]

Besides the techniques we have reviewed, other techniques are now being tested. They have only given limited satisfaction so far. Among those are lexical conceptual structures (LCS).[90]

CONCLUSION AND FUTURE DIRECTIONS

We briefly sketched the crucial role of the linguistic paradigm in IR and its necessary adaptation to the multilingual information society. The emergence of NLP techniques will be a major factor leading to this adaptation. These techniques and tools try to adapt to current needs, i.e., retrieving information from documents written and indexed in a foreign language by using a native language query to express the information need. To meet the challenges in developing multilingual technology, multilingual research should involve collaborations on an international level. There is a need for common multilingual resources. Evaluation should be an essential activity to assess the systems performance. It is essential to adapt the output of current natural language technology and resources to improving IR and information extraction techniques. NLP techniques could be used directly to produce tools for these activities by creating linguistic resources (morph-syntactic resources, corpora), lexical databases, terminologies, thesauri, etc. The future of information extraction will also depend on these vital resources. NLP technology for building the information systems for the future "unlike today's relatively crude search engines that retrieve long lists of documents of often questionable relevance, the future systems will deliver the exact information that the user is seeking and will do so with the highest precision and reliability. To accomplish this will require the systems to 'understand' both user's information need, as well as the information they possess in their databases."[91] Many areas involving language technology in both monolingual and multilingual environments could not be covered in this overview for lack of space.

NOTES

1. We are using the term "information access" in a broad sense since it involves multiple technologies. See Section 2, The Role of NLP in Information Access.

2. Strzalkowski, T. (ed). *Natural Language Information Retrieval.* Kluwer Academic, 1999.

3. Sparck Jones, K. Summarization. In Cole, R., Mariani, J., Uszkoreit, H., Varile, G.B., Zaenen, A., Zampolli, A., Zue, V. (eds). *Survey of the State of the Art in Human Language Technology*, Cambridge University Press, 1997. Pp. 232-233. Sparck Jones, K. What is the Role of NLP in Text Retrieval. In Strzalkowski, T. (ed). *Natural Language Information Retrieval.* Kluwer Academic, 1999. Pp. 1-21.

4. Harman, D., Schäuble, P., and Smeaton, A. Document Retrieval. In Cole, R., Mariani, J., Uszkoreit, H., Varile, G.B., Zaenen, A., Zampolli, A., Zue, V. (eds). *Survey of the State of the Art in Human Language Technology*, Cambridge University Press, 1997. Pp. 226-229.

5. Belkin, N. J. and Croft, W. B. Retrieval techniques. In Williams, M., (ed). *Annual Review of Information Science and Technology*, Volume 22. Elsevier, New York, 1987. Pp. 109-145.

6. See our previous work: Mustafa El Hadi, W. Penser les Nouvelles Fonctionnalités du Thesaurus. In *Terminologies nouvelles*, Rint n° 21, 2001. Mustafa El Hadi, W., Timimi, I., Béguin, A. and Debrito, M. The ARC A Project: Terminology Acquisition Tools: Evaluation Method and Tasks. In *Evaluation Methodologies for Language ad Dialogue Systems Workshop, ACL/EACL*, Toulouse, 6-7 Juillet 2001, Pp. 41-50. Mustafa El Hadi, W. Automatic Term Recognition and Extraction Tools: Examining the New Interfaces and their Effective Communication Role in LSP Discourse. In *Structures and Relations in Knowledge Organization*. Mustafa El Hadi,W., Maniez, J., Pollitt, S. (eds). Proceedings of the 5th International ISKO Conference, Lille 25-29 August. Würzburg: Ergon, 1998. Pp. 204-212. Mustafa El Hadi, Widad. Terminology and Information Retrieval: New Tools for New Needs. In Lopez-Huertas, M. and Munoz-Fernanadez, F. (eds). *Challenges in Knowledge Representation and Organization. Proceedings of the 7th Int. ISKO Conference*, Granada, Spain, July 10-13. Würzburg: Ergon, 2002. Pp. 142-149.

7. Sparck Jones, K. What is the Role of NLP in Text Retrieval. In Strzalkowski, T. (ed). *Natural Language Information Retrieval*. Kluwer Academic, 1999. Pp. 1-21.

8. Sparck Jones, K. Summarization. In Cole, R., Mariani, J., Uszkoreit, H., Varile, G.B., Zaenen, A., Zampolli, A., Zue, V. (eds). *Survey of the State of the Art in Human Language Technology*, Cambridge University Press, 1997. Pp. 232-233. Strzalkowski, T. (ed). *Natural Language Information Retrieval*. Kluwer Academic, 1999. Jacquemin, Ch., and Tzoukermann, E. NLP for Term Variant Extraction: Synergy between Morphology, Lexicon and Syntax. In Strzalkowski, T. (ed). *Natural Language Information Retreival*. Kluwer Academic, 1999. Pp. 25-74.

9. Sparck Jones, K. What is the Role of NLP in Text Retrieval. In Strzalkowski, T. (ed). *Natural Language Information Retreival*. Kluwer Academic, 1999. Pp. 1-21.

10. Jacquemin, Ch., and Tzoukermann, E. NLP for Term Variant Extraction: Synergy between Morphology, Lexicon and Syntax. In Strzalkowski, T. (ed). *Natural Language Information Retrieval*. Kluwer Academic, 1999. Pp. 25-74. Jacquemin, Ch. *Spotting and Discovering Terms through Natural Language Processing*. Cambridge, MA: MIT Press, 2001.

11. Sparck Jones, K. What is the Role of NLP in Text Retrieval. In Strzalkowski, T. (ed). *Natural Language Information Retrieval*. Kluwer Academic, 1999. Pp. 1-21. Maybury, M. Human Language Technology for Knowledge Management. In *Proceedings of ACL 39th Annual Meeting. Proceedings of the workshop HLT and KM*, July 6th-7th, 2001. Bontcheva, K., Bewster, Ch., Ciravena, F., Cunningham, H., Gutherie, L., Gaizauskas, R., and Wilks, Y. Using HLT for Acquiring, Retrieving and Publishing Knowledge in AKT: Position Paper. In *Proceedings of ACL 39th Annual Meeting. Proceedings of the Workshop HLT and KM*, July 6th-7th, 2001.

12. Strzalkowski, T. (ed). *Natural Language Information Retrieval*. Kluwer Academic, 1999.

13. Jacobs, Paul. Text Interpretation: Extracting Information. In Cole, R., Mariani, J., Uszkoreit, H., Varile, G.B., Zaenen, A., Zampolli, A., Zue, V. (eds). *Sur-*

vey of the State of the Art in Human Language Technology. Cambridge University Press and Giardini, 1997. Pp. 230-231.

14. Ibid.

15. Krovetz, R. On the Importance of Word Sense Disambiguation for IR. In *LREC 2002, Workshop Proceedings; Using Semantics for Information Retrieval: State of the Art and Future Research,* 2nd June, 2002, Las Palmas de Gran Canaria, 2002.

16. Strzalkowski, T. (ed). *Natural Language Information Retrieval.* Kluwer Academic, 1999. Sparck Jones, K. What is the Role of NLP in Text Retrieval. In Strzalkowski, T. (ed). *Natural Language Information Retrieval.* Kluwer Academic, 1999. Pp. 1-21.

17. Harman, D., Schäuble, P., and Smeaton, A. Document Retrieval. In Cole, R., Mariani, J., Uszkoreit, H., Varile, G.B., Zaenen, A., Zampolli, A., Zue, V. (eds). *Survey of the State of the Art in Human Language Technology,* Cambridge University Press and Giardini, 1997. Pp. 226-229.

18. Cf. Jacquemin, Ch. Variation terminologique: Reconnaissance et Acquisition Automatique de Termes et de leurs Variantes en Corpus. Mémoire d'Habilitation à Diriger des Recherches en Informatique Fondamental, Université de Nantes,1997.

19. Salton, G., Lesk, M.E. Information Analysis and Dictionary Construction. In *The Smart Retrieval System–Experiments in Automatic Document Processing.* Englewood Cliffs, NJ, Prentice Hall, 1971. Pp.115-142. Voorhees, E. Using WordNet to Disambiguate Word Senses for Text Retrieval. In *Proceedings, 16th Annual International ACM SIGIR Conference on Research and development in IR* (SIGIR'93. Pittsburgh), 1993. Pp. 171-180.

20. Eichmann, D.A., Ruiz, M.E., and Srinivasan, P. Cross-language Information Retrieval with the UMLS Methathesaurus. In *Proceedings, 21st Annual International ACM SIGIR Conference on Research and Development in Information Retrieval* (SIGIR'98). Melbourne, 1998. Pp. 72-80.

21. For a detailed review, see Jacquemin, Ch. Variation Terminologique: Reconnaissance et Acquisition Automatique de Termes et de leurs Variantes en Corpus. Mémoire d'Habilitation à Diriger des Recherches en Informatique Fondamental, Université de Nantes,1997.

22. See Dagan, I. and Church, K. TERMIGHT: Identifying and Translating Technical Terminology. In *Proceedings of 4th Applied NLP Conference*, 1994. Pp. 34-40.

23. Ibid.

24. Landauer *et al.*, In Grefenstette, Gregory (ed). *Cross-Language Information Retrieval.* Kluwer Academic, 2000. Quoted in Dagan, I. and Church, K. TERMIGHT: Identifying and Translating Technical Terminology. In: *Proceedings of 4th Applied NLP Conference,* 1994. Pp. 34-40.

25. This activity covers term extraction, semantic relations, identification and extraction together with term classification. These distinctions go back to our early work on evaluating the relevant tools: term extractors, semantic relation extractors and classifiers. See Mustafa El Hadi, W. Penser les Nouvelles Fonctionnalités du Thesaurus. In *Terminologies nouvelles*, Rint n° 21, 2001. Mustafa El Hadi, W., Timimi, I., Béguin, A. and Debrito, M. The ARC A Project: Terminology Acquisition Tools: Evaluation Method and Tasks. In *Evaluation Methodologies for Language ad Dialogue Systems Workshop, ACL/EACL*, Toulouse, 6-7 Juillet 2001, Pp. 41-50. Mustafa El Hadi, W. Automatic Term Recognition and Extraction Tools: Examining the New Interfaces and their Effective Communication Role in LSP Discourse. *Structures and Relations in Knowledge Organization.* Mustafa El Hadi, W., Maniez, J., and Pollitt, S. (eds). Pro-

ceedings of the 5th International ISKO Conference, Lille 25-29 August. Würzburg: Ergon, 1998. Pp. 204-212.

26. Bourigault, D., Jacquemin Ch. and L'Homme, M.-Cl. (eds). *Recent Advances in Computational Terminology*. John Benjamins, 2001.

27. Peter, A. The Automatic Construction of Faceted Terminological Feedback for Interactive Document Retrieval. In Bourigault, D., Jacquemin, Ch., and L'Homme, M-Cl. (eds). *Recent Advances in Computational Terminology*. John Benjamins, 2001. Pp. 29-52.

28. Hongyan, J. and Tzoukermann, E. Determining Semantic Equivalence of Terms in Information Retrieval: An Approach Based on Context Distance and Morphology. In Bourigault, D., Jacquemin, Ch., and L'Homme, M-Cl. (eds). *Recent Advances in Computational Terminology*. John Benjamins, 2001. Pp. 245-260.

29. Cf. Bourigault, D., Jacquemin, Ch. and L'Homme, M.-Cl. (eds). *Recent Advances in Computational Terminology*. John Benjamins. 2001.

30. Jacquemin, Ch., and Tzoukermann, E. NLP for Term Variant Extraction: Synergy between Morphology, Lexicon and Syntax. In Strzalkowski, T. (ed). *Natural Language Information Retreival*. Kluwer Academic. 1999. Pp. 25-74. Jacquemin, Ch. *Spotting and Discovering Terms Through Natural Language Processing*. Cambridge, MA: MIT Press. 2001.

31. Rich indexing is opposed to simple indexing. The former means extraction of multi-word term occurrences and the latter means extraction of multi-word term occurrences without considering variations. Jacquemin, Ch., and Tzoukermann, E. NLP for Term Variant Extraction: Synergy between Morphology, Lexicon and Syntax. In Strzalkowski, T. (ed). *Natural Language Information Retreival*. Kluwer Academic. 1999. Pp. 25-74.

32. Cf. Jacquemin, Ch., and Tzoukermann, E. NLP for Term Variant Extraction: Synergy between Morphology, Lexicon and Syntax. In Strzalkowski, T. (ed). *Natural Language Information Retreival*. Kluwer Academic. 1999. Pp. 25-74.

33. Ibid.

34. *Iota* and *Loria*, for instance. Cf. Mustafa El Hadi, W., Timimi, I., Béguin, A. and Debrito, M. The ARC A Project: Terminology Acquisition Tools: Evaluation Method and Tasks. In *Evaluation Methodologies for Language ad Dialogue Systems Workshop, ACL/EACL*, Toulouse, 6-7 Juillet 2001. Pp. 41-50.

35. Collocations are opposed by L'Homme to specialized lexical combinations. The former comprise general combinations, the latter specialized ones. They can comprise specialized verbs and specialized adjectives. To improve term extraction and relevance especially in indexing, technical writing and translation tasks, the identification and retrieval of these elements are becoming increasingly popular in NLP applied to term and term extraction. L'Homme, M.-Cl. Understanding Specialized Lexical Combinations. *Terminology*, Vol. 6/1 (2000), 89-110.

36. As for relational adjectives included in noun compounds, an interesting study was carried out by Daille showing how these adjectives can be useful in several types of NLP applications. In the context of terminology resources for IR, the method suggested by Daille aims at grouping synonym forms referring to a unique concept. The method is used in updating thesauri. Daille, B. Qualitative Terminology Extraction: Identifying Relational Adjectives. In Bourigault, D. Jacquemin, Ch. and L'Homme, M.-Cl. *Recent Advances in Computational Terminology*. John Benjamins, 2001. Pp. 149-166.

37. We will deal with this activity in detail in Section 6 NLF and Its Role in the Globalization Era.

38. Akiko, A. and Kageura, K. The Automatic Construction of Faceted Terminological Feedback for Interactive Documental Retrieval. In Bourigault, D., Jacquemin, Ch. and L'Homme, M.-Cl. (eds). *Recent Advances in Computational Terminology.* John Benjamins, 2001. Pp. 1-28.

39. Bourigault, D., Jacquemin, Ch. and L'Homme, M.-Cl. (eds). *Recent Advances in Computational Terminology.* John Benjamins, 2001.

40. Bisson, F. and Fluhr, Ch. Sentence Alignment in Bilingual Corpora Based on Cross-lingual Querying. In *RIAO 2000 Conference Proceeding, Content-Based Multimedia Information Access.* Collège de France, Paris, April 12-14, 2000. Pp. 529-542. Hull, D. Extracting Useful Terms for Practical Expressions by Combination Simple Rules and Statistical Measures: A Comparative Evaluation of Bigram Statistics. In Bourigault, D., Jacquemin, Ch. and L'Homme, M.-Cl. (eds). *Recent Advances in Computational Terminology*, John Benjamins, 2001. Pp. 209-224. Gaussier, E. General Considerations on Bilingual Terminology Extraction. In Bourigault, D., Jacquemin, Ch. and L'Homme, M.-Cl. (eds). *Recent Advances in Computational Terminology.* John Benjamins, 2001. Pp. 167-184.

41. Mustafa El Hadi, W. Terminology and Information Retrieval: New Tools for New Needs. In Lopez-Huertas, M., and Munoz-Fernanadez, F. (eds). (2002). *Challenges in Knowledge Representation and Organization. Proceedings of the 7th Int. ISKO Conference*, Granada, Spain, July 10-13. Würzburg: Ergon, 2002. Pp. 142-149.

42. Biebow, B. and Sulman, S. *Terminae*, Une Approche Terminologique pour la Construction d'Ontologies à Partir de Textes. *Actes du Colloque de Reconnaissances de Formes et Intelligence Artificielle* (RIFA '2000), vol. 11. Pp. 81-90.

43. Gomez-Perez, A. Développements Récents en Matière de Conception, de Maintenance et d'Utilisation d'Ontologies. In *Terminologies Nouvelles.* Rint 19. Actes du Colloque Terminologie et Intelligence Artificielle. 1999.

44. Most of the tools we studied are monolingual extractors. Bilingual or multilingual resources can otherwise be acquired by alignment technology.

45. For a complete account of these tools see Mustafa El Hadi, W., Timimi, I., Béguin, A. and Debrito, M. The ARC A Project: Terminology Acquisition Tools: Evaluation Method and Tasks. In *Evaluation Methodologies for Language ad Dialogue Systems Workshop, ACL/EACL*, Toulouse, 6-7 Juillet 2001. Pp. 41-50.

46. Fernandez Lopèz, M. (1999). Overview of Methodologies for Building Ontologies. In *Proceedings of IJCAAI-99 Workshop on Ontologies and Problem Solving Methods*, Stockholm, Sweden, August 2, 1999. Pp. 4-1-4-13.

47. Biebow, B. and Sulman S. *Terminae*, Une Approche Terminologique pour la Construction d'Ontologies à Partir de Textes. *Actes du colloque de Reconnaissances de formes et intelligence artificielle,* (RIFA '2000), vol. 11, 2000. Pp. 81-90.

48. Verlardi, P., Missikoff, M. and Basili, R. Identification of Relevant Terms to Support the Construction of Domain Ontologies. In *Proceedings of ACL 39th Annual Meeting. Proceedings of the workshop HLT and KM*, July 6th-7th, 2001.

49. Mustafa El Hadi, W. Terminology and Information Retrieval: New Tools for New Needs. In Lopez-Huertas, M. and Munoz-Fernanadez, F. (eds). *Challenges in Knowledge Representation and Organization. Proceedings of the 7th Int. ISKO Conference*, Granada, Spain, July 10-13. Würzburg: Ergon, 2002. Pp. 142-149.

50. See Mustafa El Hadi, W. Penser les Nouvelles Fonctionnalités du Thesaurus. In *Terminologies nouvelles*, Rint n° 21, 2001. Mustafa El Hadi, W., Timimi, I., Béguin,

A. and Debrito, M. The ARC A Project: Terminology Acquisition Tools: Evaluation Method and Tasks. In *Evaluation Methodologies for Language ad Dialogue Systems Workshop, ACL/EACL*, Toulouse, 6-7 Juillet 2001, Pp. 41-50. Mustafa El Hadi, W. Automatic Term Recognition and Extraction Tools: Examining the New Interfaces and their Effective Communication Role in LSP Discourse. *Structures and Relations in Knowledge Organization.* Mustafa El Hadi, W., Maniez, J., Pollitt, S. (eds). *Proceedings of the 5th International ISKO Conference*, Lille 25-29 August. Würzburg: Ergon, 1998. Pp. 204-212.

51. Krovetz, R. On the Importance of Word Sense Disambiguation for IR. In *LREC 2002, Workshop Proceedings; Using Semantics for Information Retrieval: State of the Art and Future Research,* 2nd June, 2002, Las Palmas de Gran Canaria, 2002. Krovetz, R., Croft, W.B. Lexical Ambiguity and Information Retrieval. *ACM Transactions on Information Systems*, 1992. Pp 115-141.

52. Mani, Inderjeet. *Automatic Summarization.* John Benjamins, 2001.

53. Jacobs, P. Text Interpretation: Extracting Information. In Cole, R., Mariani, J., Uszkoreit, H., Varile, G.B., Zaenen, A., Zampolli, A., Zue, V. (eds). *Survey of the State of the Art in Human Language Technology,* Cambridge University Press, 1997. Pp. 230-231.

54. Ibid.

55. We prefer using "information management" (IM) rather than "knowledge management" (KM) even if the activities overlap, because the terminology is still not stable. Knowledge in this context is defined in the European KM Forum on the Web, as "an information transformed into capability for effective action." KM is defined in the same website as "the process through which firms create and use their institutional and collective knowledge. KM deals with organizing and controlling the operational processes in the knowledge value chain in the most efficient way. KM focuses on facilitating and managing knowledge related activities such as creation, capture, transformation and used KM is the systematic, explicit, and deliberate building, renewal, and application of knowledge to maximize an enterprise's knowledge-related effectiveness and returns from its knowledge assets." European KM Framework, European KM Forum IST-2000-2639305.08.01 D11extract_V03_2001-07-31_KM_Terminology_Approaches.doc. Page 11.

56. Maybury, M. Human Language Technology for Knowledge Management. In *Proceedings of ACL 39th Annual Meeting. Proceedings of the Workshop HLT and KM*, July 6th-7th, 2001.

57. Uszkoreit, H. Human Language Technology for Knowledge Management. In *Proceedings of ACL 39th Annual Meeting. Proceedings of the Workshop HLT and KM*, July 6th-7th, 2001.

58. Maybury, M. Human Language Technology for Knowledge Management. In *Proceedings of ACL 39th Annual Meeting. Proceedings of the Workshop HLT and KM*, July 6th-7th, 2001.

59. See European KM Framework, European KM Forum IST-2000-2639305.08.01 D11extract_V03_2001-07-31_KM_Terminology_Approaches.doc.

60. Uszkoreit, H. Human Language Technology for Knowledge Management. In *Proceedings of ACL 39th Annual Meeting. Proceedings of the Workshop HLT and KM*, July 6th-7th, 2001.

61. Sparck Jones, K. Summarization. In Cole, R., Mariani, J., Uszkoreit, H., Varile, G.B., Zaenen, A., Zampolli, A., Zue, V. (eds). *Survey of the State of the Art in Human Language Technology*, Cambridge University Press, 1997. Pp. 232-233.

62. Paice, C. D. Constructing Literature Abstracts by Computer. *Information Processing and Management*, 1990 26(1):171-186. Quoted in Sparck Jones, K. Summarization. In Cole, R., Mariani, J., Uszkoreit, H., Varile, G.B., Zaenen, A., Zampolli, A., Zue, V. (eds). *Survey of the State of the Art in Human Language Technology,* Cambridge University Press, 1997. Pp. 232-233.

63. Sparck Jones, K. Summarization. In Cole, R., Mariani, J., Uszkoreit, H., Varile, G.B., Zaenen, A., Zampolli, A., Zue, V. (eds). *Survey of the State of the Art in Human Language Technology,* Cambridge University Press, 1997. Pp. 232-233.

64. Mani, Inderjeet. *Automatic Summarization.* John Benjamins, 2001. P. 22.

65. Grefenstette, G. (ed). *Cross-Language Information Retrieval.* Kluwer Academic, 2000.

66. Dorr, B.J. and Oard, D. Evaluating Resources for Query Translation in Cross-Language Information Retrieval. In *Proceedings of the 1st International Conference on Language Resources and Evaluation.* Granada, Spain, 28-30 May 1998. Pp. 759-764.

67. Ibid.

68. Ibid.

69. Grefenstette, G. Evaluating the Adequacy of a Multilingual Transfer Dictionary for Cross-Language Information Retrieval. In *Proceedings of the 1st International Conference on Language Resources and Evaluation.* Granada, Spain, 28-30 May 1998. Pp. 523-524.

70. Harman, D. The Text Retrieval Conferences (TRECs) and the Cross-Language Track. In *Proceedings of the First International Conference on Language Resources and Evaluation,* Granada, Spain, 28-30 May 1998. Pp. 517-522.

71. Littman, M., Dumais, S., Landauer, T., and Thomas, K. Automatic CLIR Using Latent Semantic Indexing. In Grefenstette, G. (ed). *Cross-Language Information Retrieval.* Kluwer Academic, 2000. Pp. 51-62.

72. Ibid.

73. Evans, D., Handerson, A., Steve, K., Monarch, I., Pereiro, A., Javier, D., Laurent, H., Willliam, R. Mapping Vocabularies Using Latent Semantics. In Grefenstette, G. (ed). *Cross-Language Information Retrieval.* Kluwer Academic, 2000. Pp. 63-79.

74. Ibid.

75. Harman, D. The Text Retrieval Conferences (TRECs) and the Cross-Language Track. In *Proceedings of the First International Conference on Language Resources and Evaluation,* Granada, Spain 28-30 May 1998. Pp. 517-522.

76. Ibid.

77. For more detail, see Ibid.

78. Hudon, M. Multilingual Thesaurus construction: Integrating the Views of Different Cultures in One Gateway to Knowledge and Concepts. *Knowledge Organization,* 24(1997)N° 2, 84-91.

79. SPIRIT stands for "Syntactic and Probabilistic Indexing and Retrieval of Information in Texts."

80. Fluhr, Ch., Schmit, D., Andrieux, C., Ortet, Ph. and Combet, V. Cross-Lingual Interrogation for Multilingual Catalogs, presented for the *Third European Conference on Research and Advanced Technology for Digital Libraries*, Paris, France, September 22-24, 1999.

81. For a detailed account see Fluhr, Ch., EMIR, (European Multilingual Information Retrieval), Final Report, Project 5312, INSTN/TECHNOLOGIES/TRANSMODUL/UNIVERSITY of LIEGE. Revised Version October 1994. Bisson, F. and Fluhr, Ch. Sen-

tence Alignment in Bilingual Corpora Based on Cross-lingual Querying. In *RIAO 2000 Conference Proceeding, Content-Based Multimedia Information Access.* Collège de France, Paris, April 12-14, 2000. Pp. 529-542.

82. Bisson, F. and Fluhr, Ch. Sentence Alignment in Bilingual Corpora Based on Cross-lingual Querying. In *RIAO 2000 Conference Proceeding, Content-Based Multimedia Information Access.* Collège de France, Paris, April 12-14, 2000. Pp. 529-542.

83. Davis, W. M. On the Effective Use of Large Parallel Corpora in CL Text Retrieval. In Grefenstette, G. (ed). *Cross-Language Information Retrieval.* Kluwer Academic, 2000. Pp. 11-21.

84. Ibid.

85. Littman, M.L., Dumais, S., Landauer, T. and Thomas, K. Automatic CLIR Using Latent Semantic Indexing. In Grefenstette, G. (ed). *Cross-Language Information Retrieval.* Kluwer Academic, 2000, Pp. 51-62.

86. Picchi, E. and Peters, C. CLIR: A System for Comparable Corpus Querying. In Grefenstette, G. (ed). *Cross-Language Information Retrieval.* Kluwer Academic, 2000, Pp. 81-90.

87. Grefenstette, G. (ed). *Cross-Language Information Retrieval.* Kluwer Academic, 2000.

88. Ibid.

89. Harman, D. The Text Retrieval Conferences (TRECs) and the Cross-Language Track. In *Proceedings of the First International Conference on Language Resources and Evaluation,* Granada, Spain, 28-30 May 1998. Pp. 517-522. Hudon, M. Multilingual Thesaurus construction: Integrating the Views of Different Cultures in One Gateway to Knowledge and Concepts. *Knowledge Organization,* 24(1997)N° 2. Pp. 84-91.

90. For a detailed description of this method, see Dorr, B.J. and Oard, D. Evaluating Resources for Query Translation in Cross-Language Information Retrieval. In *Proceedings of the 1st International Conference on Language Resources and Evaluation.* Granada, Spain, 28-30 May 1998. Pp. 759-764.

91. Strzalkowski, T. (ed). *Natural Language Information Retrieval.* Kluwer Academic, 1999. Pp. 15.

Lexical Knowledge Patterns, Semantic Relations, and Language Varieties: Exploring the Possibilities for Refining Information Retrieval in an International Context

Lynne Bowker

SUMMARY. As part of their work, terminologists need to find "knowledge-rich contexts," which are contexts that provide information about semantic relations between concepts in specialized domains. One way of finding these contexts is to search for lexical patterns that have the potential to reveal underlying semantic relations. Consequently, terminology researchers are in the process of compiling inventories of useful lexical patterns so that these can be programmed into specialized information retrieval tools. However, one factor that has not yet been addressed is the impact that different language varieties can have on these lexical patterns. This paper provides an overview of the research done to date on lexical patterns, presents a pilot study investigating the impact of language varieties, and considers applications of this work outside the discipline of terminology. *[Article copies available for a fee from The Haworth Document Delivery Service: 1-800-HAWORTH. E-mail address: <docdelivery@haworthpress.com> Website: <http://www.HaworthPress.com> © 2003 by The Haworth Press, Inc. All rights reserved.]*

Lynne Bowker, PhD, is Assistant Professor, School of Translation and Interpretation, University of Ottawa, P.O. Box 450, Station A, Ottawa, Ontario K1N 6N5, Canada (E-mail: lbowker@uottawa.ca).

[Haworth co-indexing entry note]: "Lexical Knowledge Patterns, Semantic Relations, and Language Varieties: Exploring the Possibilities for Refining Information Retrieval in an International Context." Bowker, Lynne. Co-published simultaneously in *Cataloging & Classification Quarterly* (The Haworth Information Press, an imprint of The Haworth Press, Inc.) Vol. 37, No. 1/2, 2003, pp. 153-171; and: *Knowledge Organization and Classification in International Information Retrieval* (ed: Nancy J. Williamson, and Clare Beghtol) The Haworth Information Press, an imprint of The Haworth Press, Inc., 2003, pp. 153-171. Single or multiple copies of this article are available for a fee from The Haworth Document Delivery Service [1-800-HAWORTH, 9:00 a.m. - 5:00 p.m. (EST). E-mail address: docdelivery@haworthpress.com].

http://www.haworthpress.com/store/product.asp?sku=J104

Digital Object Identifier: 10.1300/J104v37n01_11

KEYWORDS. Lexical knowledge patterns, semantic relations, terminology, knowledge-rich contexts, knowledge extraction, language varieties, communicative settings, information retrieval

INTRODUCTION

One of the principal ways of organizing (and thus understanding) knowledge is on the basis of semantic relations. Concepts can hold a variety of semantic relations with one another (e.g., hypernymic or generic-specific relations, meronymic or part-whole relations). There are a number of disciplines concerned with organizing knowledge on the basis of semantic relations, including the discipline of terminology. Terminology focuses on the collection and description of concepts–which are designated by terms (i.e., lexical items)–in specialized domains. The product of terminology research is usually a resource such as a specialized dictionary or glossary that contains definitions of the terms used in specialized domains. These resources can be monolingual or multilingual. Terminologists engage in concept analysis in order to determine the semantic relations that hold between the concepts designated by terms. An understanding of the semantic relations is necessary for terminologists to achieve an understanding of the domain, which is in turn essential for enabling them to construct accurate definitions of the terms.

When researching a specialized domain, terminologists aim to acquire as complete an understanding of this domain as possible. Sager[1] provides the following explanation of the difference between passive and full understanding: "We understand 'passively' when we have only a vague idea of the place of a concept in the knowledge space. We understand 'fully' when we know the precise place of a concept in relation to others."

Semantic relations are important to terminologists for two main reasons. Firstly, they help terminologists to create a "map" of the subject field by enabling them to create a sort of classification in which each concept is situated in relation to others in the domain. Some of these classifications are hierarchical in nature (e.g., based on generic-specific relations), while others are non-hierarchical (e.g., based on functional relations). This map can be used as the basis for creating a thematically-organized dictionary or glossary (as opposed to an alphabetically-organized volume), which allows the users to get a good overall picture of the specialized domain and its composite subdomains.

Secondly, semantic relations can be used to help terminologists create a definition for each concept since a common way of defining a specialized concept is by explaining it in terms of its relation to another concept. For example:

- an X *is a* Y that has characteristics A, B and C (hypernymic or generic-specific relation)
- an X *has the parts* A, B and C (meroynymic or part-whole relation)
- an X *is used to* A, B and C (functional relation)
- X *is the result of* A, B and C (causal relation).

Traditionally, the work of identifying semantic relations was done manually. Terminologists would gather together collections of texts (referred to as corpora) and they would read through these texts trying to identify "knowledge-rich contexts."[2] Typically a knowledge-rich context is one that provides important information about the concepts in the specialized domain. Important components of a knowledge-rich context include conceptual attributes (e.g., the properties of X are A, B and C), and semantic relations. While it is important for terminologists to identify both conceptual attributes and semantic relations, the focus of this article will be on semantic relations. Table 1 provides some examples of knowledge-rich contexts that reveal important semantic relations between concepts in the specialized domain of infertility.

Clearly, the manual identification of knowledge-rich contexts is a time-consuming process, and in the 21st century, terminologists are faced with a double challenge. Firstly, in this information age, users of terminology products (e.g., translators, students learning a specialized domain, and in some cases, even the general public) are clamoring for terminology resources to help them keep up with the rapidly expanding body of knowledge. Related to this pressure is the fact that the body of knowledge that terminologists must consult in order to create glossaries and dictionaries is growing at a phenomenal rate. Consider, for example, resources such as the World Wide Web and online databases, which have contributed to an information explosion. Taken together, these two factors mean that terminologists are under pressure to sift through a huge volume of data (often in the order of millions of words) in a relatively short period

TABLE 1. Examples of knowledge-rich contexts containing semantic relations.

Hypernymic relation	A 'poor responder' is a woman whose ovaries do not release multiple mature egg follicles following a course of hormone injections.
Meroynymic relation	The contractions are also stimulated by prostaglandins, a component of the seminal fluid which carries the sperm.
Functional relation	Women with blocked or missing fallopian tubes, which are used to carry the eggs from the ovaries to the womb, can now benefit from in vitro fertilization.
Causal relation	Low progesterone levels lead to luteal-phase deficiency.

of time–all without sacrificing the quality of their work. To help them achieve this goal, many terminologists are turning towards computerized tools.

Now that texts are more easily available in electronic form (e.g., WWW, databases), tools known as corpus analysis tools can be used to help terminologists search through these texts. The corpus analysis tools that are currently available are typically limited to allowing a keyword search. In other words, if a terminologist is interested in finding contexts relating to a specific term (e.g., "GIFT"), then he or she can enter that term as a keyword and the corpus analysis tool will retrieve all occurrences of that term, whether or not it appears in a knowledge-rich context (see Table 2 for an example[3]). The terminologist must then manually peruse the retrieved contexts and identify those which are knowledge-rich. While this is certainly an improvement over manually reading the entire text, it is still a labour-intensive process. Therefore, one area of research that is currently attracting a great deal of interest is the development of knowledge extraction tools for terminologists which go beyond a simple keyword search. If tools could be created to help terminologists focus indirectly on knowledge- rich contexts without having to wade through those portions of a text that are terminologically uninteresting, terminologists would be able to work more quickly and process a larger volume of text.

As noted above, one of the features of a knowledge-rich context is that it provides information about semantic relations. It has long been suggested (e.g., Lyons;[4] Cruse;[5] Ahmed and Fulford[6]) that certain lexical patterns[7] have the potential to reveal underlying semantic relations. As seen in the example above, "is a" is a lexical knowledge pattern that can reveal a hypernymic relation, but it is not the only lexical knowledge pattern used to express this relation. Other possible patterns include "kind of," "sort of," "type of," etc. Clearly, it is not reasonable to assume that terminologists will be able to spontaneously think of all possible knowledge patterns that may indicate a particular type of semantic relation. This is particularly true for those who are conducting a search in a foreign language or language variant since they may not be aware of all the possible synonyms or constructions that can be used to express a given conceptual relation.

TABLE 2. A search on the keyword "GIFT" that has retrieved all occurrences of this term, whether or not it appears in a knowledge-rich context.

```
dequately all the clinics offering GIFT. This is a simpler procedure th
ncy rate of almost 25 per cent for GIFT compared with 22 per cent for I
 IVF delivery and 6.3 ova for each GIFT delivery. Since 1987, the ILA's
gies of in vitro fertilisation and GIFT (gamete intrafallopian transfer
le pregnancies in women treated by GIFT. The figures from 1987 show a m
eption' techniques such as IVF and GIFT also increases the risk of a mu
ncies after the transfer by IVF of GIFT of three or four eggs or embryo
ward and the increased use of IVF, GIFT and associated procedures. The
rtility treatments such as IVF and GIFT. A new study reveals the costs
The VLA has gathered figures about GIFT (gamete intrafallopian transfer
```

Nor is it realistic to think that terminologists will have the time or patience to conduct consecutive searches using all these possible patterns as key words. Therefore, what is needed is (1) an inventory of lexical knowledge patterns signaling different types of semantic relations, and (2) a tool that encodes these lexical knowledge patterns and allows users to conduct searches on the basis of both keywords and semantic relations when these two elements occur within a given proximity (e.g., within 5 words of each other). This would allow the terminologist to specify both a search term and a relation type and to effectively say to the search tool "Find me contexts about the *parts* of X" or "Find me contexts showing the *function* of Y." The result of this search would be a list of knowledge-rich contexts for the terms X and Y, rather than all contexts simply containing instances of X or Y.

Recently, a number of terminology researchers (e.g., Davidson,[8] Pearson,[9] Morgan,[10] Condamines and Rebeyrolle,[11] Marshman,[12,13] Marshman et al.,[14] Feliu and Cabré[15]) have begun to explore the possibility of establishing detailed inventories of such lexical knowledge patterns in the hopes that they can be encoded into knowledge extraction tools where they could act as probes that would identify knowledge-rich contexts. Terminologists could then take these contexts and use them to help map out the overall conceptual classification of the domain and to construct definitions of the specialized concepts within the domain.

The overall aim of this article is to explore the state-of-the art in knowledge extraction for terminology, and to suggest ways in which this research might be extended, both within the domain of terminology as well as to other types of information retrieval. To this end, the article will be divided into 3 main parts. Section 1 provides an overview of research done to date in the area of lexical knowledge pattern identification, including an examination of difficulties that have been encountered. Section 2 presents a pilot study that constitutes a preliminary investigation into the impact of language varieties–specifically French and Canadian French–on lexical knowledge pattern identification. This is an area that has been largely unexplored in terminology knowledge extraction research undertaken thus far, but it is an important consideration if these tools are to be truly useful in an international context. Finally, Section 3 will briefly consider how this work could be usefully applied outside the field of terminology to help with other types of information retrieval.

LEXICAL PATTERNS FOR KNOWLEDGE EXTRACTION IN TERMINOLOGY

Meyer[16] outlines the following general methodology for developing knowledge extraction tools for terminology. The first step consists of identifying an initial set of lexical knowledge patterns for each semantic relation that the system will handle. These patterns should be tested and the output should be analyzed in order to identify additional patterns as well as restrictions that may need to be applied to existing patterns. These changes should be programmed into the system, and further testing should be carried out.

Two different approaches–both of which are largely manual[17]–have been used to help with the initial identification of lexical knowledge patterns. Davidson,[18] for example, examined the definitions contained in existing terminological resources in order to identify the lexical patterns that had been used to convey semantic relations in these definitions. In contrast, Morgan[19] and Marshman[20] used corpus analysis tools to generate lists of contexts for specific terms, and they then examined these contexts manually in order to identify relevant semantic relations that indicated knowledge-rich contexts. Some studies, such as Marshman et al.,[21] have combined both approaches.

As noted by Meyer,[22] simply providing an extraction tool with an initial set of patterns, no matter how scrupulously they have been collected and analyzed, is not the end of the development process. Rather, the process is an iterative one, and the output of a search should be further analyzed to identify problems such as noise and silence.

Noise and silence are not unique to knowledge extraction for terminology; they are problems associated with information retrieval in general and are tied to the concepts of recall and precision. Noise is the term used to refer to hits that are retrieved, but that turn out not to be relevant. For example, in searching for a knowledge-rich context for the term "IVF," the lexical knowledge pattern "is a" might return an irrelevant context such as "*IVF is a* touchy subject." Although this context contains both the search term and the lexical knowledge pattern, it is not a knowledge-rich context and is therefore considered to be noise. In contrast, silence refers to the situation where a useful knowledge-rich context exists in the corpus, but it is not retrieved. This may happen because a relevant lexical knowledge pattern has not yet been identified and programmed into the system. Identifying silences is a labour-intensive process as it requires further manual analysis of contexts in order to find the relevant patterns. Furthermore, the process of adding new patterns that result from analyzing silences can create another problem: while every addition to the knowledge patterns has the potential to increase the number of possible hits, it may also increase the noise. In other words, as observed by numerous researchers (e.g., Davidson,[23] Meyer[24]), any gain in recall can lead to a reduction in precision.[25]

DIFFICULTIES ENCOUNTERED WHEN WORKING WITH LEXICAL KNOWLEDGE PATTERNS

While the use of lexical knowledge patterns seems promising, it is not always straightforward. Researchers working in this area have observed a number of challenges, some of which are summarized here.

Search Window Horizon

A pattern-based approach to knowledge extraction relies on finding patterns located within a number of words/characters to the left or right of a search term–a distance known as the horizon. An effective horizon is one that does not generate too much noise, but at the same time does not exclude valid knowledge-rich contexts. The wider the search window horizon, the greater the potential for noise; however, if the horizon is too small, the system may eliminate useful contexts such as the following, where the search term "binding" is a considerable distance from the lexical knowledge pattern "is an":

> *Binding*–the process whereby the sperm attaches itself to the oocyte's protective coat, known as the zona pellucida–*is an* essential first step in fertilization.

Noisy Patterns

As mentioned previously, some lexical knowledge patterns can generate noise. In other words, a given pattern may retrieve hits that are not relevant to the search at hand. For example, the pattern "kind of" could retrieve a useful context, such as "A *car* can be described as a *kind of* motorized vehicle," but it could also retrieve an irrelevant context, such as "It was *kind of* you to lend me your *car*," where "kind" is being used in an adjectival rather than a nominal sense. Because the search tool is simply matching a lexical pattern without considering syntactic or semantic information, this type of noise can occur. Therefore, before deciding whether or not to include a particular pattern, consideration must be given to how much noise it will generate.

Pattern Variation

The very nature of language means that a lexical pattern may come in various forms. For instance, a pattern may change depending on whether it is written in the active or passive voice (e.g., "causes" vs. "is caused by"). Another type of variation may result from a grammatical requirement (e.g., "is a" vs. "is an"). Similarly, verbs may appear in different inflected forms, so that the meronymic pattern "contains" may also need to be considered in its plural form "contain" as well as in the past tense "contained." It is important to keep in mind, however, that relevant pattern variation does not necessarily extend to all lexical items including the core string as this may generate noise. For instance, "containment" includes the string "contain," but it does not reflect a semantic relation and would not be a good indicator of a knowledge-rich context.

Although inflection-related variation is an issue that must be considered when working with a language such as English (which has minimal inflection), this becomes even more important when working with highly inflected languages such as French and Spanish, where there are a greater number variations in verb conjugation and agreement, and where diacritics may also introduce variation. For example, the causal pattern "générer" in French can also occur in forms such as "génère," "génèrent," "généré," "générés," "générée," "générées" and "générant."

Non-Contiguous Patterns

Non-contiguous patterns are patterns that may be broken up by intervening words (e.g., modifiers). For example, when appearing in a text, the causal pattern "result in" could be interrupted by an adverb as in the context "IVF treatment could *result* initially *in* pregnancy, but may not end with a live birth." Non-contiguity can present an added challenge to the automatic identification and extraction of knowledge-rich contexts because an optimal horizon for the search window must be established. As noted above, if the horizon is too large, this may lead to noise, but if it is too small, or if the pattern form is too restricted, silence may result.

Anaphoric Reference

As noted above, when using a pattern-based approach to knowledge extraction, a tool attempts to identify a given pattern when it occurs within a certain distance of a search term. However, the nature of language can sometimes make this difficult because the search term itself may not necessarily be repeated over and over again in a text; instead, it may be replaced by a pronoun or another term (e.g., synonym, abbreviation). This is known as anaphoric reference. For instance, consider the following two sentences:

> A *blastocyst* develops after approximately five days of growth in a specialized culture. It *is a* ball of cells no bigger than the period at the end of this sentence.

The search term "blastocyst" is present in the first sentence, but in the second sentence (which also contains the lexical knowledge pattern "is a"), the term "blastocyst" has been replaced by the pronoun "it." Because of the large number of characters that occur between the search term and the lexical knowledge pattern, the knowledge extraction tool may not retrieve this context.

Hedges and Modals

Two linguistic devices that are often used to moderate the strength of a statement are hedges (e.g., possibly, perhaps) and modals (e.g., might, may, could). For example, consider the following sentence:

Most cases of *male infertility* could be *caused by* a deficiency in a protein that is normally found on the surface of sperm cells.

While this sentence does contain information of interest to a terminologist, it cannot be considered as good an example of a knowledge-rich context as one that does not contain hedges or modals.

Generic vs. Domain-Dependent Patterns

Researchers such as Morgan,[26] Meyer,[27] and Marshman[28] have observed that there are two broad categories of lexical knowledge patterns: generic patterns and domain-specific patterns. Generic patterns are those that seem to be independent of a given subject field and which therefore occur in a wide variety of domains (e.g., "is a"). Although the majority of lexical knowledge patterns appear to be generic, many specialized domains also seem to have at least a few patterns that tend be limited to that domain (or to closely related domains). Meyer[29] gives the examples of "shade of" (e.g., maroon is a shade of red), which is a pattern that is used when describing colour terms, and "species of," which is typical in the biological sciences. It is interesting to note that domain-specific patterns do not necessarily produce more accurate results than generic patterns since the former can also can generate noise.

Language Dependency

Work on establishing inventories of lexical knowledge patterns has convincingly demonstrated that such inventories must be drawn up independently for different languages. In other words, it would not be useful to draw up an inventory in a language such as English and then simply assume that the closest translations of those patterns could be used to effectively retrieve knowledge in French or Spanish, etc.

As pointed out by Morgan,[30] some lexical knowledge patterns may have no literal equivalent in another language. For example, the French patterns "dont" and "il s'agit de" cannot be easily translated into English. Furthermore, Marshman[31] points that commonality of form rarely guarantees usefulness for the purposes of knowledge extraction because the recall potential of a given form often differs greatly in different languages. For instance, the French patterns "constituer" and "désigner" have proven to be more effective at retrieving knowledge-rich contexts than their English cognates "constitute" and "designate." Similarly, the English form "include" seems more reliable than the French form "inclure."

This means that while it may be interesting to investigate cognates or translations of previously identified patterns in another language, the patterns must be identified within their own language in order for their true usefulness to be discovered. For this reason, research is currently being carried out independently in languages such as English (e.g., Meyer[32]), French (Condamines and Rebeyrolle,[33] Marshman et al.[34]) and Spanish (Feliu and Cabré[35]), to name just a few.

LANGUAGE VARIETIES AND LEXICAL KNOWLEDGE PATTERNS

While researchers have made important progress in establishing inventories of lexical knowledge patterns and in identifying problematic issues that must be addressed if these patterns are to be used effectively, one area that has been virtually unexplored to date is the impact of language varieties on lexical knowledge patterns. By language varieties I mean the different "versions" of a language that are spoken in different geographic regions, such as the different varieties of English that are spoken in America, Britain, Canada, Ireland, Jamaica, New Zealand and Australia, or the different varieties of German that are spoken in Germany, Austria and Switzerland.

Terminologists have long realized that, even when people speak the same basic language, speakers from different parts of the world may use different terms to refer to the same concept. Examples of the type "truck" (American English) vs. "lorry" (British English) and "navigateur" (French from France) vs. "fureteur" (Canadian French) are plentiful. For this reason, terminologists are careful to include geographic or regional labels in their specialized dictionaries and glossaries in order to help users (e.g., translators) pick the most appropriate term for their intended audience (Sager,[36] Dubuc,[37] Pavel and Nolet[38]).

Although it is clear that speakers from different regions may have different preferences when it comes to using specialized terms, it has not yet been established whether they also have different preferences when it comes to using lexical knowledge patterns. If speakers from different geographical locations do in fact use different knowledge patterns, this may have an impact on the establishment of pattern inventories and the implementation of knowledge extraction tools. In the 21st century, software localization is a booming industry. Software localization refers to the process of adapting a software product to the linguistic and cultural needs of the target users.[39] "Foreign" users (both English speakers and non-English speakers) are no longer willing to accept products produced only in American English,[40] and companies who refuse to localize their software stand to lose a lot of business. For more information on software localization, see Esselink[41] and Sprung.[42] Therefore, developers of knowledge extraction tools may well need to take into account the lexical knowledge patterns used in different regions in order to localize their products.

With this in mind, I have undertaken a preliminary investigation to determine whether or not language varieties have an impact on lexical knowledge patterns. This pilot study is presented in the following section.

Pilot Study

The aim of this pilot study is to see whether the lexical knowledge patterns used by speakers of "French from France" (hereafter referred to simply as French) differ from those used by speakers of Canadian French. To carry out this study, I compiled two different yet comparable corpora (i.e., collections of text). Both of the corpora deal with the specialized domain of infertility. The first corpus contains 16 articles totalling 28,024 words that were taken from the popular science magazine *Science et Vie*, which is published in France. These articles were written between 1987 and 1998. The second corpus contains 18 articles totalling 26,586 words that were taken from a comparable popular science magazine called *Québec Science*, which is published in Canada. These articles were written between 1987 and 1997.

Next, I consulted the inventories of French-language lexical knowledge patterns compiled by Morgan[43] (hypernymic patterns), Davidson[44] (meronymic and functional patterns) and Marshman[45] (causal patterns). Each of these researchers has drawn up an extensive list of knowledge patterns, and from these lists I selected 10 patterns for each type of semantic relation. I tried to choose the patterns that the researchers had noted as being (1) generic rather than domain dependent, and (2) productive (i.e., helpful for locating knowledge-rich contexts).

Using the corpus analysis software package WordSmith Tools,[46] I entered each of the lexical knowledge patterns and analyzed all of the contexts that were retrieved in order to identify which of these could be considered knowledge-rich contexts. I then counted the total number of knowledge-rich contexts (KRCs) retrieved from each corpus for each of the patterns. The results are shown in Tables 3 to 6.[47]

DISCUSSION

The data reveal that, overall, there were a greater number of knowledge-rich contexts retrieved from the French corpus (172) than from the Canadian French corpus (132) when using the lexical knowledge patterns identified by Morgan,[48] Davidson[49] and Marshman.[50] Some possible explanations for this may include the following.

Firstly, it is possible that speakers of Canadian French use other types of patterns to mark knowledge-rich contexts. As pointed out by Meyer[51] in addition to lexical knowledge patterns, grammatical knowledge patterns and paralinguistic

TABLE 3. Lexical knowledge patterns for hypernymic relations that were used to retrieve knowledge-rich contexts (KRCs).

Lexical knowledge patterns for hypernymic relations (Morgan 2000, 34-38)	**KRCs in *Science et Vie* corpus (French)**	**KRCs in *Québec Science* corpus (Canadian French)**
type* de /d'	7	6
est un(e) / sont des	23	11
(s') appel*	15	5
est le(la, l') / sont les	10	16
comme	17	12
(se) nomm*	1	0
tel(le(s)) (que, qu')	7	1
sorte*	1	0
par exemple	7	3
forme* d*	1	2

TABLE 4. Lexical knowledge patterns for meronymic relations that were used to retrieve knowledge-rich contexts (KRCs).

Lexical knowledge patterns for meronymic relations (Davidson 1998, 64)	**KRCs in *Science et Vie* corpus (French)**	**KRCs in *Québec Science* corpus (Canadian French)**
constitu*	4	1
conten* / contien*	10	4
compos*	6	3
compren*	0	1
chargé* d*	0	0
présentant	2	0
pourvu* d*	0	0
incluant	0	0
trouv* dans	0	0
à base d*	0	1

knowledge patterns may also be used. Grammatical knowledge patterns such as NOUN + VERB have proven useful for identifying functional relations, for example. Meanwhile, paralinguistic patterns could include punctuation marks, such as parentheses, dashes or commas that are used to set off explanatory material, or even formatting features, such as bold or italics.

Another possible explanation for the limited number of knowledge-rich contexts retrieved in the Canadian French corpus could be linked to the cor-

TABLE 5. Lexical knowledge patterns for functional relations that were used to retrieve knowledge-rich contexts (KRCs).

Lexical knowledge patterns for functional relations (Davidson 1998, 65)	**KRCs in *Science et Vie* corpus (French)**	**KRCs in *Québec Science* corpus (Canadian French)**
utilis*	8	3
sert*/serv* à / au	4	3
permet*	3	19
joue* un rôle	5	1
fonction*	1	2
employ*	2	3
nécessaire à	3	2
a pour objet	1	0
affect* à / au	0	0
essentiel à / au	3	2

TABLE 6. Lexical knowledge patterns for causal relations that were used to retrieve knowledge-rich contexts (KRCs).

Lexical knowledge patterns for causal relations (Marshman 2002a, 71)	**KRCs in *Science et Vie* corpus (French)**	**KRCs in *Québec Science* corpus (Canadian French)**
provoc* / provoq*	9	0
parce qu*	13	1
grâce à / au	2	9
abouti* à / au	1	0
suscit*	2	4
de façon à	1	2
incit* à	1	2
génèr*	0	0
entraîn*	0	6
car	3	7

pora that were used to compile the initial inventories of lexical knowledge patterns. All three researchers (Morgan,[52] Davidson,[53] Marshman[54]) acknowledged that they used the World Wide Web as their principal source of texts, and they all followed the same basic procedure of conducting keyword searches in search engines and subject directories in order to find texts dealing with their respective specialized domains.[55] None of the three gave any indication that language variety was a factor in their choice of texts–they all appeared to make their choices based primarily on the basis of the subject matter of the text. It is therefore possible that the corpora were unbalanced in terms of the language varieties they contained. If, for example, the corpora contained mainly French texts, with relatively few Canadian French texts, this could help to explain why the lexical knowledge patterns drawn from these corpora retrieved a greater number of knowledge-rich contexts from the French corpus than from the Canadian French corpus. Of course, it is not possible to know this for certain without knowing the precise linguistic make-up of the original corpora from which the lexical knowledge patterns were identified. Nevertheless, based on the results of the pilot study, it would appear that it could be worthwhile to conduct an independent analysis of the two corpora to see if additional knowledge patterns can be identified that appear to be specific to (or more prevalent in) one or the other of the two language varieties.

The data from the pilot study also reveal that, while for many of the lexical knowledge patterns, a relatively comparable number of knowledge-rich contexts were retrieved, there were also some instances where the number of contexts differed significantly, and some of these are summarized in Table 7.

The fact that, in some cases, the same lexical knowledge patterns retrieved a significantly different number of knowledge-rich contexts would seem to indicate that, just as speakers from different geographical regions have some different preferences for specialized terminology, so too do they appear to have some different preferences for lexical knowledge patterns that indicate semantic relations. This would seem to parallel the observation made in the section on *language dependency* about language-dependent patterns, where it was noted that a form that was particularly productive in one language may not be productive in another language

TABLE 7. A selection of patterns that resulted in a significantly different number of knowledge-rich contexts being retrieved from the two corpora.

Lexical knowledge patterns	**KRCs in *Science et Vie* corpus (French)**	**KRCs in *Québec Science* corpus (Canadian French)**
est un(e) / sont des	23	11
(s') appel*	15	5
tel(le(s)) (que, qu')	7	1
conten* / contien*	10	4
utilis*	8	3
parce qu*	13	1
est le(la, l') / sont les	10	16
permet*	3	19
grâce à / au	2	9
Car	3	7

(e.g., cognates such as "inclure" in French and "include" in English). Similarly, a form that is productive in one language variety (e.g., French) may not be equally productive in another language variety (e.g., Canadian French).

Although this pilot study was limited in a number of ways (i.e., small corpora, two language varieties, one subject field, one text type), I feel that the preliminary results do indicate that language variety may be a relevant factor in the identification of lexical knowledge patterns, and that a more extensive study of this phenomenon would be worthwhile. Future studies could include identifying lexical knowledge patterns that are specific to a particular language variety, as well as ranking the relative productivity of those patterns that appear to be generic across multiple varieties.

APPLICATIONS BEYOND TERMINOLOGICAL KNOWLEDGE EXTRACTION

The focus of this paper has been on the potential of lexical knowledge patterns to help terminologists retrieve knowledge-rich contexts, but in addition to being useful for terminologists, I believe that research into knowledge patterns also has the potential to be adapted for use in the broader context of information retrieval. Indeed, recent publications by Bean and Green[56] and Green et al.[57] clearly demonstrate that semantic relations are an important factor for knowledge organization in many different disciplines. It is well known that there is no single correct way of classifying a document. The fact that a single document can be classified in a number of ways presents a challenge to both the classifier, who may have trouble deciding where to place the document within the classification system, and to the user, who may be unsure of where to look for this document.

In this electronic age, the challenge of knowing precisely where to look for information has been alleviated somewhat by the possibility of conducting keyword searches (e.g., in databases or on the World Wide Web). For instance, if a patient is looking for documents on a particular fertility drug–let's call it medication X–she does not need to worry about whether these documents are grouped with documents on "prescription drugs" or with documents on "infertility treatments." She can simply do a full-text search using the keyword "medication X" and documents dealing with this subject will be retrieved.

Imagine, however, that the patient does not want to retrieve *all* documents dealing with "medication X" (which may include very technical texts, research-oriented texts, advertising material, etc.). Instead, suppose that she only wishes to see those documents describing the side effects of "medication X." In this case, she may decide to conduct a search on the World Wide Web for documents containing both the search terms "medication X" AND "side effects." This search may indeed retrieve some relevant documents, since it is possible that the desired information can be expressed using lexical patterns such as "Medication X has the following side effects: A, B, C" and "A, B, C are common side effects of medication X."

However, it is also possible that this information could be expressed without using the term "side effects," in which case some relevant documents may be unintentionally overlooked. For example, consider the expressions:

- Medication X may cause A, B, C.
- Reactions to medication X include A, B, C.
- A, B, C may result from taking medication X.
- Medication X may inhibit A.
- Medication X may affect A.

The organizational basis for the knowledge contained in each of the above expressions is the *causal relation* between "medication X" and "side effects," even though this relation has been expressed using a variety of lexical knowledge patterns ("side effects," "cause," "reactions," "result from," "inhibit," "affect").

As was the case with terminologists, it would not be reasonable to expect any user to spontaneously think of all possible knowledge patterns that may indicate a particular type of semantic relation. The situation is further exacerbated when using an international resource such as the World Wide Web because users may be not be aware of all the possible constructions that can be used to express a knowledge pattern in another language or language variety. An Internet or database search tool that allows searches to be conducted using a combination of keywords and lexical knowledge patterns could help users achieve a better balance between recall and precision with regard to the documents they retrieve. However, for such a tool to be truly useful in an international context, it will be necessary to pursue efforts that are currently underway to inventory the lexical knowledge patterns that exist for various languages, as well as for different language varieties.

NOTES

1. Sager, Jan C. 1994. *Language Engineering and Translation: Consequences of Automation.* Amsterdam/Philadelphia: John Benjamins, 43.

2. Meyer, Ingrid. 2001. "Extracting Knowledge-Rich Contexts for Terminography: A Conceptual and Methodological Framework," in *Recent Advances in Computational Terminology,* Didier Bourigault, Christian Jacquemin and Marie-Claude L'Homme (eds.). Amsterdam/Philadelphia: John Benjamins, 280.

3. This type of display shown in Table 2 is known as a KWIC (keyword in context) display, which typically shows each occurrence in a single line of text; however, the display can be easily expanded to show multiple lines of context for each occurrence.

4. Lyons, John. 1977. *Semantics: Volume 1*. Cambridge: Cambridge University Press.

5. Cruse, D.A. 1986. *Lexical Semantics*. Cambridge: Cambridge University Press.

6. Ahmad, Khurshid and Heather Fulford. 1992. "Knowledge Processing: 4. Semantic Relations and their Use in Elaborating Terminology" (Computing Sciences Report CS-92-07). Guildford: University of Surrey.

7. As observed by Meyer (in 3, p. 290), in addition to lexical patterns, other types of patterns, such as grammatical patterns (e.g., NOUN + VERB) are paralinguistic patterns (e.g., various types of punctuation, formatting), can also be used to identify underlying semantic relations. The scope of the present paper, however, is limited to lexical patterns.

8. Davidson, Laura. 1998. *Knowledge Extraction Technology for Terminology*. MA Thesis, University of Ottawa, Canada.

9. Pearson, Jennifer. 1998. *Terms in Context*. Amsterdam/Philadelphia: John Benjamins.

10. Morgan, Tricia. 2000. *A Comparative Study of Hypernymic Patterns for Knowledge Extraction*. MA Thesis, University of Ottawa, Canada.

11. Condamines, Anne and Josette Rebeyrolle. 2001. Searching for and identifying conceptual relationships via a corpus-based approach to a Terminological Knowledge Base. In *Recent Advances in Computational Terminology*, Didier Bourigault, Christian Jacquemin and Marie-Claude L'Homme (eds.). Amsterdam/Philadelphia: John Benjamins, 127-148.

12. Marshman, Elizabeth. 2002a. *The Cause Relation in Biopharmaceutical Corpora: English and French Patterns for Knowledge Extraction*. MA Thesis, University of Ottawa, Canada.

13. Marshman, Elizabeth. 2002b. "The Cause-Effect Relation in a Biopharmaceutical Corpus: English Knowledge Patterns," in *Proceedings of the 6th International Conference on Terminology and Knowledge Engineering* (Nancy, France, 28-30 August 2002).

14. Marshman, Elizabeth, Tricia Morgan and Ingrid Meyer. 2002. "French Patterns for Expressing Concept Relations." *Terminology* 8:1.

15. Feliu, Judit and M. Teresa Cabré. 2002. "Conceptual Relations in Specialized Texts: New Typology and an Extraction System Proposal," in *Proceedings of the 6th International Conference on Terminology and Knowledge Engineering* (Nancy, France, 28-30 August 2002).

16. as 3, p. 292.

17. Both approaches are therefore very labour intensive–something which unfortunately cannot be avoided during the establishment of an inventory of lexical knowledge patterns–but once identified, these patterns will prove useful for the semi-automatic extraction of knowledge-rich contexts from future corpora.

18. as in 9.

19. as in 11.

20. as in 13.

21. as in 15.

22. as in 3, p. 293.
23. as in 9, p. 76.
24. as in 3, p. 294.
25. (Recall = hits/(hits + silences); precision = hits/(hits + noise).
26. as in 11, p. 49.
27. as in 3, p. 296.
28. as in 13, p. 23.
29. as in 3, p. 296.
30. as in 11, p. 77.
31. as in 13, p. 96.
32. as in 3.
33. as in 12.
34. as in 15.
35. as in 16.
36. Sager, Juan C. 1990. *A Practical Course in Terminology Processing.* Amsterdam/Philadelphia: John Benjamins, 148.
37. Dubuc, Robert. 1997. *Terminology: A Practical Approach.* Adapted by Elaine Kennedy. Brossard, Quebec: Linguatech.
38. Pavel, Sylvia and Diane Nolet. 2001. *Handbook of Terminology.* Ottawa: Minister of Public Works and Government Services Canada.
39. This includes translating the on-screen displays (e.g., menus, error messages, dialog boxes), help files and accompanying documentation. It may also include the adaptation of graphics, data formats, currencies or any other cultural references. For more information on software localization see Esselink[41] and Sprung.[42]
40. Clearly, software products are also developed in countries other than the United States, and these too can be localized for other target audiences. However, at the present time, the United States is the largest developer and exporter of software products.
41. Esselink, Bert. 2000. *A Practical Guide to Localization.* Rev. ed. Amsterdam/Philadelphia: John Benjamins.
42. Sprung, Robert C., (ed.). 2000. *Translating into Success: Cutting-Edge Strategies for Going Multilingual in a Global Age.* Amsterdam/Philadelphia: John Benjamins.
43. as in 11.
44. as in 9.
45. as in 13.
46. WordSmith Tools was developed by Mike Scott of the University of Liverpool and is available from Oxford University Press.
47. The asterisk (*) that appears in some of the lexical knowledge patterns is known as a wildcard, which means that during a search, it can represent any string of characters. In a way, a search using the pattern "type*" would find occurrences of both "type" and "types."
48. as in 11.
49. as in 9.
50. as in 13.
51. as in 3, p. 290.
52. as in 11, p. 24.
53. as in 9, p. 51.
54. as in 13, p. 37.

55. Morgan worked in the domains of computing and genetics, Davidson worked in the domain of composting and Marshman worked in the domain of biopharmaceuticals.

56. Bean, Carol A. and Rebecca Green (eds.). 2001. *Relationships in the Organization of Knowledge*. Dordrecht: Kluwer Academic Publishers.

57. Green, Rebecca, Carol A. Bean and Sung Hyon Myaeng (eds.). 2002. *The Semantics of Relationships: An Interdisciplinary Perspective*. Dordrecht: Kluwer Academic Publishers.

Designing a Common Namespace for Searching Metadata-Enabled Knowledge Repositories: An International Perspective

Lynne C. Howarth

SUMMARY. With the proliferation of digitized resources accessible internationally via Internet and Intranet knowledge bases and a pressing need to develop more sophisticated tools for the identification and retrieval of electronic resources, both general purpose and domain-specific metadata schemes have assumed a particular prominence. This has resulted in a growing number of online repositories that must be accessed using terminology that would be considered unfamiliar to most searchers. Assuming that a natural language "gateway" requiring no prior knowledge of specific metadata tagging could facilitate cross-repository searching, end-users were engaged

---

Lynne C. Howarth, BA, MLS, PhD, is Associate Professor and Dean, Faculty of Information Studies, University of Toronto, 140 St. George Street, Toronto, Ontario M5S 3G6, Canada (E-mail: howarth@fis.utoronto.ca).

The author gratefully acknowledges the financial assistance provided by the Social Sciences and Humanities Research Council of Canada in funding this research project (SSHRC SRG # 410-99-1287), and extends particular thanks to Julie Hannaford and Christopher Cronin who have provided invaluable research assistance throughout the study.

[Haworth co-indexing entry note]: "Designing a Common Namespace for Searching Metadata-Enabled Knowledge Repositories: An International Perspective." Howarth, Lynne C. Co-published simultaneously in *Cataloging & Classification Quarterly* (The Haworth Information Press, an imprint of The Haworth Press, Inc.) Vol. 37, No. 1/2, 2003, pp. 173-185; and: *Knowledge Organization and Classification in International Information Retrieval* (ed: Nancy J. Williamson, and Clare Beghtol) The Haworth Information Press, an imprint of The Haworth Press, Inc., 2003, pp. 173-185. Single or multiple copies of this article are available for a fee from The Haworth Document Delivery Service [1-800-HAWORTH, 9:00 a.m. - 5:00 p.m. (EST). E-mail address: docdelivery@haworthpress.com].

http://www.haworthpress.com/store/product.asp?sku=J104

Digital Object Identifier: 10.1300/J104v37n01_12

in focus group testing of a "namespace" of common categories derived from nine metadata schemes. Findings and their implications within an international context are presented.

KEYWORDS. Metadata schemas, metadata crosswalks, metadata mapping, knowledge repositories, terminology gateways

INTRODUCTION

Within an international context, having tools that facilitate transparent, readily understood search vocabulary access to a diversity of web-enabled repositories has assumed an importance, if not an urgency. Yet, while the number of digital libraries, enterprise portals, and metadata-enabled knowledge repositories continues to proliferate, much of the work to date has focused on developing or refining media- or domain-specific schemas for indexing, categorizing, or otherwise organizing digital objects for access. Even broad application metadata schemes, such as the Dublin Core, have undergone extensive modifications to accommodate unique requirements of a field or discipline.[1] As Buckland et al. note, " . . . the number and proportion of network accessible repositories with unfamiliar metadata vocabularies are rapidly growing. The amount of searching can be expected to rise, but diminishing search effectiveness is the predictable result."[2] The design of a common, natural language "gateway" for end-users to access resources without having to know the underlying metadata tagging, or domain-specific vocabularies would seem an important step towards facilitating cross-repository searching.

Recognizing the potential utility of a common "gateway," a study was undertaken to derive and design a "namespace," or set of labelled categories, based on the analyses and mapping of nine metadata schemes (i.e., EAD; Dublin Core; GILS; TEI; VRA; CIMI; CSDGM; ONIX; MARC).[3] The methods used for, and the particular problems encountered with, developing a multi-domain source-to-target (baseline) crosswalk[4] provided context for the subsequent determination of a natural language "namespace" comprised of seventeen elements or labelled fields. Specific challenges encountered in determining semantic commonalities across diverse metadata schemes, in resolving semantic ambiguities and term-to-term mapping anomalies, and in creating the category names and definitions comprising the final natural language, cross-domain "namespace" have been described previously.[5] This paper summarizes findings from focus group studies undertaken to determine the clarity and potential usefulness of the common language terminology, and discusses implications from an international perspective.

EVALUATING THE "NAMESPACE"

As Stephen DeRose noted in 1997, ". . . navigation requires naming, as does access whether by database, catalog, finding aid, or hypertext link. Choosing the right names for information units is perhaps the most crucial issue facing the electronic document community."[6] At the same time, simplifying access to repositories of metadata-enabled electronic resources through a search interface powered by natural language query boxes can open a world of separate, yet potentially related knowledge bases to novice or expert information seekers, alike. But what natural language (i.e., the searcher's own language) constitutes "the right name"?

The seventeen categories and accompanying definitions derived from the iterative cross-schema comparison (see Table 1), completed during an earlier phase of related research,[7] were designed to be descriptive and inclusive of many of the tags comprising the nine metadata standards selected for initial analysis. As such, the resulting model of common categories represented an overarching framework where semantically related concepts and relationships were brought together under a common "label" or "namespace." The categories, however, were derived and assigned both "labels" (names) and definitions based on the researchers' interpretation of, and mental models of, categorization. Yet to be determined was how, and how well prospective end-users would make the cognitive match between what the researchers had suggested as being relevant or useful to the searcher's query terminology, and what individuals would consider appropriate. As a consequence, focus group methodology was employed to obtain end-user responses to, and an evaluation of, the seventeen categories, their labels or element names, and their corresponding definitions. The study was designed to test the following two hypotheses:

- Hypothesis #1–The category names provided are readily understandable to end-users.
- Hypothesis #2–The definitions provided are useful for clarifying the meaning of the category names.

Analyses and findings would assist, first in evaluating the categorization model (or "namespace") being proposed as a gateway for end-users to access cultural repositories without having to know the underlying metadata tagging or domain-specific vocabularies, and, second, in assessing the potential for the

TABLE 1. Element Label and Definitions

Element Label	Definition
Contact Information	Information on how to communicate with someone about a work, i.e., names, phone numbers, etc.
Rights/Restrictions on Use	Legal limitations/rules that affect how you can *use* a work *after* you have been given access to it
Edition	Information on a work's version
Roles	The function of an individual or organization associated with a work
Summary & Description	Details about a work that illustrate its main points
Identifiers	Unique names or numbers assigned to a work so that it can be distinguished from others, for example, its ISBN
Sources, References & Related Works	Other works that are related to the work you are seeking or were used to develop the work you are looking for
Language	The language or dialect of a work
Physical Format	The physical appearance of a work
Subject	The topic of a work; its intellectual content
Date & Time Period	Dates associated with a work, as well as time period information regarding a work's content can be obtained through this category
Terms of Access & Availability	The legal limitations/rules that affect your ability to access a work. This relates to privacy or intellectual property concerns
Methodology	The procedures/techniques used to make or change a work
Genre Type	The nature or style of a work's intellectual content
Names	Names of individuals or organizations associated with a work, such as creators, publishers, sponsors, etc.
Title	The name or phrase assigned to a work for identification purposes
Place	Locations associated with a work, for example, where a work was created, published, is housed, etc.

"namespace" to serve as a linguistic baseline for capturing similar concepts in other languages and thus to support cross-language searching.

METHODOLOGY AND ANALYSIS OF DATA

Quantitative data were gathered by means of questionnaires, a terminology matching exercise, and three post-activity statements using a Likert scale to measure degree of response. Qualitative data were obtained through focus group discussions based on the matching activities and three follow-up statements. Participants were recruited from a convenience sample of current students at the Faculty of Information Studies, University of Toronto, and professional librarians working within University of Toronto libraries. In response to electronic notices and paper posters, a total of nineteen (n = 19) self-selected volunteers engaged in the study. Of these, twelve (n = 12) were designated as having some formal knowledge of search systems (i.e., librarians with a graduate degree in library science/information science/information studies and currently working in the field), and seven (n = 7) were considered to have little or no formal knowledge of search systems (i.e., first year Master of Information Studies [MISt] degree students, with undergraduate degrees in the Social Sciences or Humanities, and no completed courses in information retrieval/search strategies, or cataloguing). This sample was intended to ensure a balance of "novice" and "experienced" feedback, in response to both the matching activities and the subsequent focus group discussions.

Activity One: Matching Element Labels and Definitions

In both the pilot study and subsequent formal focus group sessions, participants were instructed to match category names (n = 17) with the definition(s) they considered most appropriate to that particular label (see also Table 1). While there was, in fact, only one definition per element name, participants were told they could match as many definitions as they considered appropriate to the label. A total of four (n = 4) participants correctly matched all elements to their respective definitions (23.5% accuracy rate), while all nineteen participants matched (only) three elements correctly, and without additional qualifiers. These included:

- Physical format: "physical appearance of the work"
- Language: "the language or dialect of the work"
- Date & Time period: "Dates associated with a work, as well as the time period information regarding a work's content can be obtained through this category."

Comments emanating from subsequent focus group discussions regarding the matching exercise confirmed that all participants found both "physical format" and "language" to have representative definitions that could be readily matched to the category label. This was largely attributable to the content of the definition for each element that, in including the words, "physical" and "language," referred to the label name, per se. "Date & Time period," on the other hand, was described by some as being easy to match, while others commented that the category name was "fuzzy" and difficult to link with its definition.

Table 2 summarizes the number of participants who correctly matched a definition to its respective element label, and shows where there was some level of ambiguity requiring an *additional* definition or definitions to clarify the meaning of the label. Linking the corresponding definition–"legal limitations/rules that affect how you can use a work after you have been given access to it"–for the element "Rights/Restrictions on Use" proved most problematic among the seventeen element/definition combinations included in the activity. Seven participants incorrectly chose the definition for "Terms of Access & Availability"–"the legal limitations/rules that affect your ability to access a work. This relates to privacy or intellectual property concerns"–as either the sole or an additional match. In subsequent focus group discussions, participants commented that it was difficult to disentangle the respective category labels when parts of the definitions for each applied just as well for the other. The terms "Rights/Restrictions on Use" and "Terms of Access & Availability" need to be distinguished more clearly, one from the other, through more precise definition.

In addition to the three elements, "Physical format," "Language," and "Date & Time" period, noted previously, all participants also correctly linked definitions corresponding to the following element labels:

- Sources, References & Related Works
- Roles
- Contact Information
- Identifiers.

That the former two attracted one additional definition, while the latter two merited two supplementary qualifiers, suggested some level of semantic ambiguity with each of the terms, and the possible inadequacy of a sole definition in those instances. In focus group discussions, participants recommended "Sources and References" and "Related Works" as distinct, separate element labels. The term "Roles" was described as "not difficult–just odd," and perhaps more representatively rendered as "Roles & Responsibilities." While the *definition* attached to "Contact Information" was described as "fuzzy," participants agreed that the *category label*, "Identifiers," was itself problematic, and alternately described as "cryptic," or "nebulous." In focus group discussions, many individuals commented that they had narrowed this category down to two options–the definition for "Identifiers" and the definition for "Title"–before deciding on the correct or final definition. For some, confusion was underscored by the fact that the definition for "Title" included the phrase "for *identification* purposes"–interpreted as a logical derivative of the term "identifier."

A higher degree of terminological ambiguity was suggested where at least one mismatch of definition to element label occurred, and/or where participants connected one or more *additional* definitions to the named element. This apparent lack of clarity occurred with the following:

- Edition (definition incorrectly matched)
- Subject
- Summary & Description
- Genre Type
- Names.

TABLE 2. Outcomes from Definition-to-Element Label Matching Activity

Element Label	Number of Participants Matching Correct Definition to Element Label	Number of Participants Matching Additional or Other Definition(s) to Element Label [specified by element label corresponding to additional or other definition(s) matched]
Sources, References & Related Works	19	1 = [Methodology]
Roles	19	1 = [Names]
Contact Information	19	2 = [Place] 1 = [Names]
Identifiers	19	1 = [Edition] 1 = [Title]
Place	18	1 = No match made for this category
Edition	18	1 = [Methodology]
Subject	18	1 = [Summary & Description] 3 = [Genre Type]
Summary & Description	18	2 = [Genre Type] 2 = [Subject]
Genre Type	17	4 = [Subject] 1 = [Edition]
Names	17	2 = [Roles] 1 = [Title]
Methodology	17	2 = No match made for this category 1 = [Genre Type]
Title	16	2 = No match made for this category 1 = [Subject]
Rights/Restrictions on Use	15	7 = [Terms of Access & Availability] 1 = [Methodology]

While most participants described the definition-to-element label match for "Edition" as "easy," some suggested differentiating between numerical versions (i.e., 1st edition, 2nd edition, etc.) and language editions. Focus group discussions highlighted the potential overlap of the respective definitions for "Subject" and "Genre Type" because of the inclusion of the phrase "intellectual content" in both. The definitions for "Subject," "Summary & Description," and "Genre Type" were also viewed as variously interchangeable by some, with the latter proving especially confusing. In focus group discussions, the phrase "nature or style" used in the definition for "Genre Type" posed its own semantic challenges, eliciting a comment that, while participants knew the meaning of "genre" as a concept, the definition itself was not readily understandable. In contrast, the definition for "Names" was judged as easy to match with its element label because it directly and self-referentially incorporated the word "names." But while the description was clear the category *per se* was viewed as "fuzzy" and "meaningless." One focus group participant took exception to the extensive coverage of the term, exclaiming,

". . . creator, a publisher, a sponsor . . . there's a dizillion ways you could be associated with a work–and that's all under 'Name'?"

More problematic from the perspective of clarity in definition were elements where no match was made by one or more participants, suggesting a high level of ambiguity ascribing to the element label. For two of the three instances that follow, at least one participant either effected a mismatch or linked an additional definition to the element label, further underscoring problems with understanding the terminology:

- Place
- Methodology (addition of definition for "Genre Type")
- Title (addition of definition for "Subject").

Focus group participants noted that, while use of the word "locations" was a verbal clue to linking the definition to the element name for "Place," it was considered by some to be *situationally* ambiguous. As one individual observed, "[It's] hard to think of 'Place' as where the thing is housed . . . I always think of 'Place' as where it's coming from, so where it was published, where it originated. I would have used 'Location' for where it's housed." Others suggested that the category, "covered too many things," and could benefit from being more focused in scope and coverage. The inclusion of a category labelled as "Methodology" merited extensive focus group discussion, and was judged universally to be problematic. "Put a big star next to 'Methodology,' " quipped one individual. While some participants agreed that an example might help to clarify the definition and to facilitate a successful match to its element name, others questioned the overall relevance and applicability of the concept. One wondered, "What the heck is this supposed to mean? I can't imagine where you would use this term, why you would need a definition for it?" The definition for the element label "Title" was sufficiently ambiguous to dissuade two individuals from effecting a match and one to assign a mismatch of the definition for "Subject." Focus group participants found the inclusion of the word "name" in the definition to be misleading, and disliked the word "assigned" as it seemed to imply that the title of the work was "an afterthought" and made up by someone other than the author/creator. One commented that, "[title] is actually the meaning to the book [sic] in many cases–more than something that's just stuck in afterwards."

To summarize outcomes from the definition-to-element label matching activity, while over seventeen percent (n = 17.6%) of elements required no additional definition to clarify their meaning, just over twenty-nine percent (n = 29.4%) of elements required one additional definition to clarify their meaning for at least one participant in the study, and slightly more than forty-one percent (n = 41.2%) of elements required two additional definitions to clarify their meaning for one or more research participants. Over seventeen percent (n = 17.6%) of elements were not matched to any category by 26.3% of participants.

Activity Two: Assessing Opinions

Individuals were then asked to respond to three statements of opinion using a 5-point Likert scale from 1 = strongly agree to 5 = strongly disagree, with 3 = neither agree nor disagree (the "neutral" opinion). The three statements assessed (1) perceived ease in making the matches, (2) how representative participants considered the names of the categories relative to the definitions, and (3) whether the definitions helped participants to understand the categories. As with the previous activity, the focus group facilitator asked participants to add to their responses in a detailed discussion immediately following completion of activity two, thus augmenting quantitative data with valuable qualitative commentary.

In response to the first statement, "In general, I found it easy to make the match between this category name and the definitions," the highest level of agreement, and the perceived ease of match resided with the following (with mean score):

- Language (score = 1)
- Sources, References & Related works (score = 1.17)
- Physical format (score = 1.17)
- Contact information (score = 1.67)
- Identifiers (score = 1.83)
- Subject (score = 1.83)
- Time and Date period (score = 1.83).

Least agreement with the statement was registered for "Methodology" (score = 3.17), and "Roles" (score = 3.17).

Responses to the second statement, "In general, this category name represents what is described in the definition," elicited most agreement on:

- "Language" (score = 1)
- "Sources, References & Related works" (score = 1.33)
- "Physical format" (score = 1.33)
- "Edition" (score = 1.67)
- "Contact information" (score = 1.83).

Least agreement for the statement was registered for "Genre Type" (score = 3.0), and "Methodology" (score = 3.33).

Participant reactions to the third statement, "In general, I found the definition I selected for this category name helpful in clarifying the meaning of this category," showed greatest concurrence for the following (with mean score):

- Language (score = 1.17)
- Sources, References & Related works (score = 1.17)
- Identifiers (score = 1.33)
- Physical format (score = 1.5)
- Edition (score = 1.5)
- Contact information (score = 1.67)
- Terms of Access/Availability (score = 1.67).

"Time and Date period" (score = 3.0), "Genre Type" (score = 3.17), and "Methodology" (score = 3.3) elicited the least agreement regarding the relative usefulness of respective definitions for clarifying the meaning of the category.

OVERALL FINDINGS AND IMPLICATIONS

The study was designed to test two hypotheses relative to the common language "namespace"–or model set of categories–of seventeen elements that had been derived from analyzing crosswalks mapped across nine metadata schemes. In using the matching exercise, the follow-up three Likert-scale statements and focus group discussions with participants, the first hypothesis, that the category names provided are readily understandable to end-users, was only partially supported. Based on the matching exercise, category names "Language," "Physical format," and "Date & Time Period" are most readily understood; all others (n = 14) appeared to require additional definition for clarity. Based on Likert-scale responses to the three follow-up statements, participants appeared to agree that, with the exception of "Methodology," "Genre Type," and "Roles," the category names or labels are readily understandable to end-users.

Testing the second hypothesis, namely, that definitions provided are useful for clarifying the meaning of the category names or labels, also yielded mixed results. Based on the matching exercise, fully 70.6% of elements required some additional definition to clarify their meaning, and 17.6% of elements were not matched to any category by over one quarter (n = 26.3%) of the participants. These results would suggest that the definitions were not uniformly helpful in clarifying the meaning of the element names. In response to the Likert-scale statements, however, participants generally concurred that, with the exception of the definitions for "Methodology," "Genre Type," and "Date

& Time Period," definitions were helpful in clarifying the meaning of the category names.

Overall, findings suggested that, while certain categories were readily interpreted and understood, others–namely, "Methodology," "Genre Type," and "Roles"– proved ambiguous, confusing, or even misleading. Definitions for namespace elements (e.g., "Title") that contained words (e.g., "the name . . .") also used as category labels (i.e., "Name"), were identified as problematic. Self-referential labels and definitions (e.g., "Language" defined as "the *language* or dialect of the work") were most transparent, if seemingly redundant. Focus group participants expressed a preference for mutually exclusive terms, suggesting that "Date & Time period" be separated out into its component parts. Finally, while the activity of matching category names and definitions was largely straightforward for search and subject experts alike, all agreed that "context" is vital to constructing meaning. Confusion occurs when a category cannot readily be placed within a familiar context, such as occurred for one participant who situated the term "Roles" within a theatrical context, but could not relate it to a bibliographic setting. The provision of brief, simple definitions devoid of topical or other perspective was insufficient to clearly and unequivocally identify all elements. In short, how the category "fit" within a specific or a broader context was seen as being essential to uniquely understanding each term.

CONCLUSIONS: THE INTERNATIONAL PERSPECTIVE

The aim of creating a "gateway" to cross-domain knowledge repositories using a set of common terms that represent, but are independent of, a particular metadata scheme, may be a valuable one. As the research findings have suggested, however, extracting a model "namespace" with elements assigned familiar labels, carefully defined, exhibits semantic challenges that can only be exacerbated as one moves from a uniform linguistic and cultural environment to a multilingual, multicultural international setting. Capturing the fundamental attributes of English language metadata schemes, derived from and for largely Anglo-American digital resources and repositories, is an achievable, though painstaking process. Nonetheless, the interpretation of terminology, even given a relatively homogenous group of individuals working in one language and operating within a largely uniform cultural and educational environment, was not straightforward. Individuals come to labels and definitions with different mental models, particularly when they are given no contextual reference points. Thus simple English language terms, such as "Roles" or "Methodology," can be expected to take on different meanings depending on how, where, or by whom they are being used, while other labels, such as "Language" seem self-referential and more readily understood quite apart from any context.

The focus group activities and discussions underscore not only the need to revisit and refine both terminology and definition, but also the potential pitfalls of carrying over linguistic and cultural assumptions into the international arena. Until "what's in a name" can be more accurately captured, and represented as unambiguously as possible–perhaps independent of language–the goal of a "universal gateway" to combinations of cross-domain, cross-language, and/or cross-cultural digital knowledge repositories may remain elusive, if not unrealistic.

NOTES

1. Consider, for example, the Dublin Core Metadata Initiative (DCMI) working groups for refining the basic fifteen element Dublin Core metadata set for applications in education, libraries, government, etc.

2. Buckland, M.K. et al. 1999. "Mapping Entry Vocabulary to Unfamiliar Metadata Vocabularies." *D-Lib Magazine*, 5 (1), January 1999. p. 1. URL: http://www.dlib.org/dlib/january99/buckland/01buckland.html. Accessed 27/12/2002.

3. The nine metadata schemes analysed and mapped included the Encoded Archival Description (EAD), the Dublin Core (DC), the Government Information Locator Services (GILS) metadata scheme, the Text Encoding Initiative (TEI) Header, the Visual Resources Association (VRA) Visual Document Description Categories, the Consortium for the Interchange of Museum Information (CIMI) metadata set, the Content Standard for Digital Geospatial Metadata (CSDGM), the ONIX publishing standard, and the standard for encoding and exchanging bibliographic records, Machine-Readable Cataloging (MARC21).

4. Cromwell-Kessler, W. (1998). Crosswalks, metadata mapping and interoperability: What does it all mean? In Murtha Baca (ed.), *Introduction to Metadata: Pathways to Digital Information.* Los Angeles: Getty Information Institute. pp.19-22. St. Pierre, Margaret, and LaPlant, William P. (1998). Content Metadata. In *NISO Standards: Issues in Crosswalking*. [http://www.niso.org/press/whitepapers/crsswalk.html]. Accessed 30/12/02.

5. Howarth, L.C., Cronin, C., and Hannaford, J. 2002. "Designing a Metadata-Enabled Namespace for Accessing Resources Across Domains." In *Advancing Knowledge: Expanding Horizons for Information Science: Proceedings of the 30th Annual Conference of the Canadian Association for Information Science/Association canadienne des sciences de l'information–held with the Congress for the Social Sciences and Humanities of Canada, University of Toronto, Toronto, Canada, 30 May-1 June, 2002.* Edited by L.C. Howarth, A. Slawek, and C. Arsenault. pp. 223-232. Howarth, L.C. 2001. "Designing a Metadata-Enabled Namespace for Enhancing Resource Discovery in Knowledge Bases." In *International Conference on Electronic Resources: Definition, Selection, and Cataloguing, Rome, Italy, 24-29 November, 2001.* [http://w3.uniromal.it/ssab/er/relazioni/ howarth_eng.pdf] Accessed 04/12/02.

6. DeRose, Stephen J. (1997). Navigation, access, and control using structured information. *American Archivist,* 60: 298-309. p. 301.

7. Howarth, L.C. 2000. "Designing a 'Human-Understandable' Metalevel Ontology for Enhancing Resource Discovery in Knowledge Bases." In *Dynamism and Sta-*

bility in Knowledge Organization: Proceedings of the Sixth International Conference of the International Society of Knowledge Organization, University of Toronto, Toronto, Canada, 10-13 July, 2000. Edited by N.J. Williamson, C. Beghtol, and L.C. Howarth. Würzburg: Ergon Verlag. pp. 391-397. Howarth, L.C. 1999. "Modelling a 'Human-Understandable' Metalevel Ontology for Enhancing Information Seeking on the World Wide Web." In *Information Science: Where Has it Been, Where is it Going?: Proceedings of the 27th Annual Conference of the Canadian Association for Information Science, Congress of the Social Sciences and Humanities, Université de Sherbrooke, Sherbrooke, Québec, 9-11 June, 1999.* Edited by J. Turner. Toronto: CAIS. pp. 115-124.

The IFF Foundation for Ontological Knowledge Organization

Robert E. Kent

SUMMARY. This paper discusses an axiomatic approach for the semantic integration of ontologies, an approach that extends to first order logic, a previous approach[1] based on information flow. This axiomatic approach is represented in the Information Flow Framework (IFF), a metalevel framework for organizing the information that appears in digital libraries, distributed databases and ontologies.[2] The paper argues that the semantic integration of ontologies is the two-step process of alignment and unification. Ontological alignment consists of the sharing of common terminology and semantics through a mediating ontology. Ontological unification, concentrated in a virtual ontology of community connections, is fusion of the alignment diagram of participant community ontologies–the quotient of the sum of the participant portals modulo the ontological alignment structure. *[Article copies available for a fee from The Haworth Document Deliv-*

Robert E. Kent, BA, MA, PhD, is a voting member of the Standard Upper Ontology (SUO) working group, where he has authored the starter documents for the Information Flow Framework (IFF). He currently resides in Pullman, WA, 99163 USA (E-mail: rekemt@ontologos.org).

[Haworth co-indexing entry note]: "The IFF Foundation for Ontological Knowledge Organization." Kent, Robert E. Co-published simultaneously in *Cataloging & Classification Quarterly* (The Haworth Information Press, an imprint of The Haworth Press, Inc.) Vol. 37, No. 1/2, 2003, pp. 187-203; and: *Knowledge Organization and Classification in International Information Retrieval* (ed: Nancy J. Williamson, and Clare Beghtol) The Haworth Information Press, an imprint of The Haworth Press, Inc., 2003, pp. 187-203. Single or multiple copies of this article are available for a fee from The Haworth Document Delivery Service [1-800-HAWORTH, 9:00 a.m. - 5:00 p.m. (EST). E-mail address: docdelivery@haworthpress.com].

http://www.haworthpress.com/store/product.asp?sku=J104

Digital Object Identifier: 10.1300/J104v37n01_13

KEYWORDS. Knowledge organization, information flow, ontology, semantic integration, alignment, unification, semantics, classification, model, theory, logic

INTRODUCTION

The library organizes portions of the bibliography universe.[3] The bibliographic universe consists of all information-bearing entities,[4] whether written, printed, digitized, taped, painted, etc. The library organizes both knowledge and materials. The organization of knowledge and the organization of materials are distinct, but with important interconnections. Knowledge organization underlies most modern library classifications. It involves the registration, evaluation, and classification of "thoughts, ideas, and concepts" in order to adequately represent universal knowledge.[5]

Many people believe[6] that a new library idea is emerging, a shift from the public space phenomenon of the modern library to a private space phenomenon. New information technologies are transforming the modern library into an emerging library in the same way that earlier libraries were transformed in the 19th century into the modern library. Although knowledge organization has been important in the modern library, it will be even more important in the emerging library. And ontology, a core concept of knowledge organization, will be vitally important in the emerging library. The ontologies of the emerging library will be organized in ontological frameworks. However, the emerging library will eschew a monolithic approach to ontological frameworks, and instead will advocate a modular approach.

The IFF, an ontological framework that supports modularity in a principled fashion, will organize the ontologies of the emerging library by means of a "concept lattice of theories." Because the emerging library is a private space library,[7] the semantic integration of ontologies will also be an important concept. Semantic integration uses the paradigm of participant community ontologies formalized as IFF logics, communities interacting through portal logics, a common shared extensible ontology formalized as an IFF theory, participant community alignment links formalizable as IFF theory morphisms, and the free lifting of alignment links from the theoretical context to the logical context. Figure 1 schematically presents the architecture for semantic integration. By using the techniques, principles and terminology of the IFF, this architecture can be constructed through the two-step process of alignment and unification.

It is the goal of this paper to explain how ontologies and the process of semantic integration are represented with the concepts and terminology of the IFF. This paper extends semantic integration from the theory of information flow (Kent 2000)

to first order logic. The paper has seven sections. Sections 2 and 3 provide background information about ontologies and the IFF. Section 4 explains how standard ideas of semantic integration are represented in the IFF. Section 5 presents the two-step process of semantic integration. As a complement to the theoretical approach in the main part of the paper, section 6 gives a related practical approach. Section 7 gives a summary of the study. The Reference section presents the ideas of semantic integration and explains important concepts of the IFF.

ONTOLOGIES

Ontology is a branch of metaphysics concerned with the nature and relations of being and the categorical structure of reality. Categories are the most fundamental things that exist or may exist in a domain of discourse. Ontology studies such categories. The word *ontology* comes from the Greek–it is constructed from the prefix *ontos* that means "being" or "existence" and the base *logos* that means "to reason." The expressions in an ontology use a language containing the relevant predications (entity and relation types). Ontological languages are modeled here with the concept of an IFF *type language*.[8] Ontologies and ontology sharing traditionally reside within the field of knowledge representation.[9] Knowledge representation applies logic and ontology to knowledge organization. Logic supplies the form, consisting of framework and inferencing capabilities, whereas ontology supplies the content, consisting of the entities, relations, and constraints in the application domain.

FIGURE 1. Ontological Integration Process–Schema

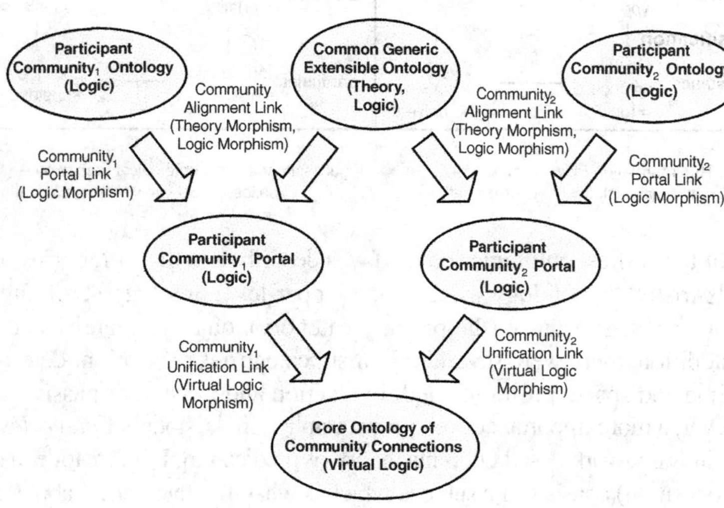

The use of ontologies for knowledge organization is both old and new.[10] In the far past, Aristotle effectively used ontological ideas in his study of predication and his system of classification (his categories). In the near past, Ranganathan effectively used dynamic ontological organizing principles (now understandable as ideas of conceptual and relational knowledge organization) in his development of the Colon faceted classification system for organizing large research libraries. In the emerging library, generic knowledge-organizing frameworks, such as the IFF, advocate the use of ontologies for domains such as e-commerce, bio-informatics, etc. The theory and practice of semantic integration developed in this paper will facilitate interoperability between the knowledge organizations in the emerging library.

Ontologies fall along a formal spectrum. The terminological ontologies or taxonomies, located at the informal end of the spectrum, axiomatize the hierarchy of categories by utilizing the meta-relations of subtyping and disjointness. The WordNet system, developed at Princeton and widely used for natural language processing, is a large example of a terminological ontology. The axiomatized ontologies are located at the formal end of the spectrum. The Cyc project, whose avowed purpose is to model common-sense knowledge and reasoning, is a large example of an axiomatized ontology.

FIGURE 2

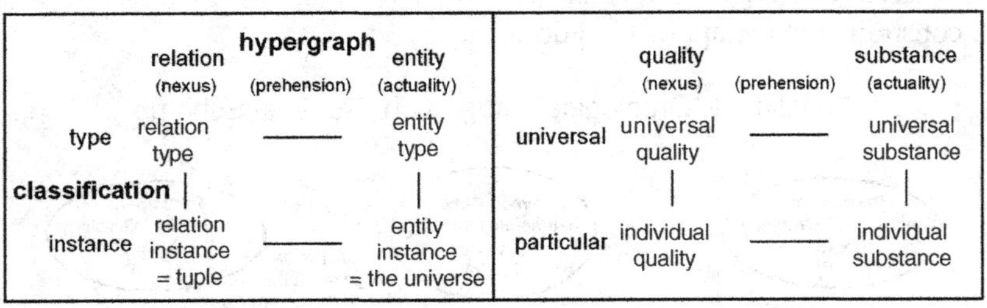

Figure 2a: The Information Flow Framework–mathematical knowledge organization

Figure 2b: Aristotle's ontological framework–philosophical knowledge organization

One of the earliest ontologies created was described in the *Categories* of Aristotle.[11] Aristotle's ontology was a simple upper-level ontology involving four major categories: substance (the primary category), quality, quantity and relation; in addition, there were several minor subcategories of relation: determination in time and space, position, condition, action and passion or passivity.

However, a more important development implicit in Aristotle's *Categories* is an ontological framework based upon his theory of predication. For Aristotle, a statement (proposition) consists of a subject, which is what the statement is about, and a predicate, which is what the statement says about its subject. For Aristotle there are two kinds of predication: essential predication and accidental predication.

- An essential predication is something that is said-of a subject. This is the relation of ontological classification between a thing and a natural kind. Essential predication is represented with the concept of an IFF *classification*.[12]
- An accidental predication is something that is being-in a subject. This is the relation of ontological dependence between a substance and a quality. Accidental predication is represented with the concept of an IFF *hypergraph*.[13]

Essential predication divides things into universals (types) and particulars (instances). Accidental predication divides things into substances (entities) and qualities (relations). The mathematical knowledge organization used in this paper is represented by the semantic architecture of the IFF (Figure 2a) and concentrated in the concept of an IFF *model*.[14] An IFF model represents "interpretative semantics." This semantic architecture is comparable to the structure of Aristotle's ontological framework (Figure 2b). The two distinctions in Aristotle's ontological framework of "universal versus particular" and of "quality versus substance" are analogous to the two distinctions in the semantic architecture of the IFF between "type versus instance" and "relation versus entity."

THE INFORMATION FLOW FRAMEWORK

The Information Flow Framework (IFF) is designed to realize the goal of interoperability between distributed software applications, database applications and knowledge bases. It provides an approach for representing distributed logic, ontologies, and knowledge representation. The IFF is a metalogic that uses modularity to support semantic interoperability among object-level ontologies. The IFF takes a building blocks approach towards the development and utilization of object-level ontological structure. This rather elaborate categorical approach uses insights from the theory of information flow[15] and the theory of formal concept analysis.[16] In this paper, we show how the IFF provides a foundation for the semantic integration of ontologies in a zdistributed setting. In turn, the idea of semantic integration illustrates the intuitions behind the IFF foundation for ontological knowledge organization.

The IFF provides a principled foundation for sharing, manipulating, relating, partitioning, composing, and discussing ontologies. The IFF represents metalogic, and as such operates at the structural level of ontologies. In the IFF, there is a precise boundary between the metalevel and the object level. The terminology and axiomatics of the IFF are located in various meta-ontologies. The IFF is partitioned into three metalevels: top, upper and lower. These metalevels correspond to the set-theoretic distinction in foundations between the generic, the large and the small.

- The top metalevel of the IFF is used to represent and axiomatize the upper metalevel. It does this by providing an interface between the Knowledge Interchange Format (KIF) logical language and the upper metalevel of the IFF. The top metalevel contains the basic KIF meta-ontology.
- The upper metalevel of the IFF is used to represent and axiomatize the lower metalevel. It does this by representing category theory, information flow and formal concept analysis. The upper metalevel contains the core, classification and category theory meta-ontologies.
- The lower metalevel of the IFF is used to represent and axiomatize the object metalevel. It represents the structural aspect of the Standard Upper Ontology (SUO) using a categorical expression. The lower metalevel contains the core, classification, model theory, algebraic theory and ontology meta-ontologies. The model theory meta-ontology (IFF-MT) represents a somewhat novel version of model theory, whereas the closely related algebraic theory meta-ontology (IFF-AT) represents universal algebra. However, the ontology meta-ontology (IFF-ONT) is the central ontology in the lower metalevel. It provides a metalevel axiomatic framework for the semantics of object-level ontologies, by adding the new notions of theory and logic to the notions of language and model previously axiomatized in the IFF-MT. In support of the IFF-MT, IFF-AT and IFF-ONT are the classification and core meta-ontologies.

In order to formulate the semantic integration of object-level ontologies in terms of the IFF, this paper uses the terminology and semantics of the IFF-ONT. In this paper, we represent an ontology as an IFF *theory*[17] and we represent a populated ontology as an IFF *logic.*[18] An ontology *O* is represented as a theory ***T*** if it has no instances. A theory represents formal or axiomatic semantics. Otherwise, an ontology *O* is represented as a logic ***L***. A logic represents a combined semantics, both the formal semantics of its theory component and the interpretative semantics of its model component.

THE NATURE OF SEMANTIC INTEGRATION

In this section, we formulate various notions of semantic integration[19] in terms of the IFF. In the following, reference is made to the endnotes where John Sowa's glossary definitions[20] for semantic integration are paraphrased with respect to two participant community ontologies (Figure 3). These glossary definitions define the terminology of methods and techniques for defining, sharing, and merging ontologies. According to Sowa, this terminology and these notions

FIGURE 3. Integration

originated from a working group of the International Committee for the Information Technology Standards (NCITS).

This section represents these notions with concepts from the IFF: refinement is represented as appropriate morphisms in the theoretical or logical context; alignment is represented by the creation of a span of morphisms over representations for the community ontologies; and aligned unification is represented as a pushout of the alignment span.

FIGURE 4

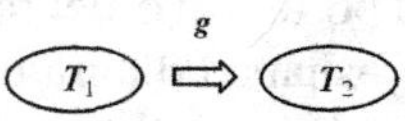

Figure 4a: Refinement–abstract

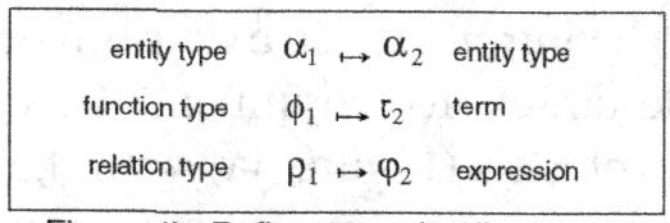

Figure 4b: Refinement–details

First, we represent the refinement operator. This representation is key, since alignment and unification are expressed in terms of refinement. A primitive type is represented as an IFF type–an entity type, a function type or a relation type. A composite type is represented as an IFF term or an IFF expression. A composite type generalizes a primitive type–terms generalize function types and expressions generalize relation types. Entity types are not composite. The general notion of refinement[21] maps the entity types of the first ontology to entity types of the second ontology, but maps the function or relation types of the first ontology to terms and expressions of the second ontology, respectively (Figure 4b). From this original formal viewpoint, an ontology is represented as an IFF theory, a refinement is represented as an IFF theory interpretation (Figure 4a), and the partial ordering of refinements is represented as composition of IFF theory interpretations. From an extended composite viewpoint, an ontology is represented as an IFF logic, a refinement is represented as an IFF logic interpretation, and the partial ordering of refinements is represented as composition of IFF logic interpretations.

FIGURE 5

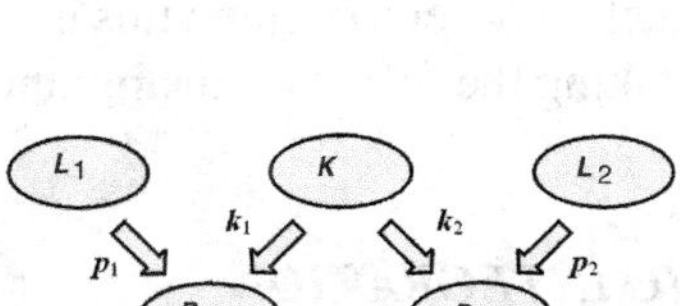

Figure 5a: Alignment Diagram–abstract

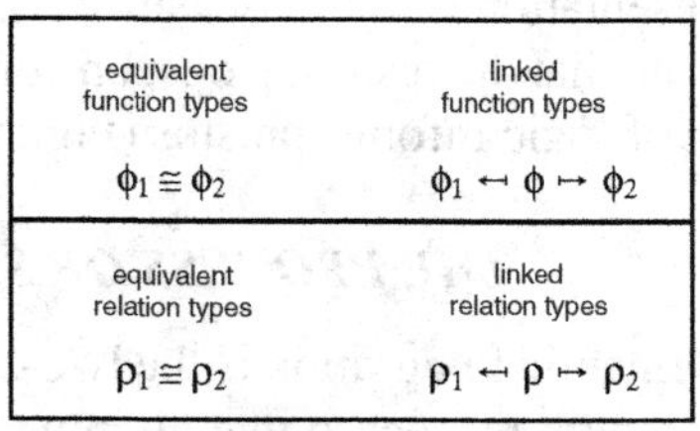

Figure 5b: Alignment or Partial Compatibility–details

Next, we represent alignment and partial compatibility.[22] The intent of alignment is that mapped categories are equivalent. To appropriately formalize this, we represent an equivalence pair of types as a single type in a mediating ontology, with two mappings from this new type back to the participant community types (Figure 5b). This implies that alignment and partial compatibility can be represented as a kernel span of theory morphisms (Figure 5a). The mediating ontology $\boldsymbol{K}$ represents both the equivalenced categories and the axiomatization needed for the degree of compatibility, partial or complete. Since the theoretical alignment links $\boldsymbol{k}_1$ and $\boldsymbol{k}_2$ preserve this axiomatization, compatibility will be enforced. However, new subtypes or supertypes may need to be introduced in extension ontologies called portals in order to provide suitable targets for alignment. This results in a 'W'-shaped diagram of logic infomorphisms (Figure 5a) with the logical portal links $\boldsymbol{p}_1$ and $\boldsymbol{p}_2$ connecting the participant community ontologies to their portal logics $\boldsymbol{P}_1$ and $\boldsymbol{P}_2$. The direction of the portal links is compatible with the unification diagram below.

FIGURE 6

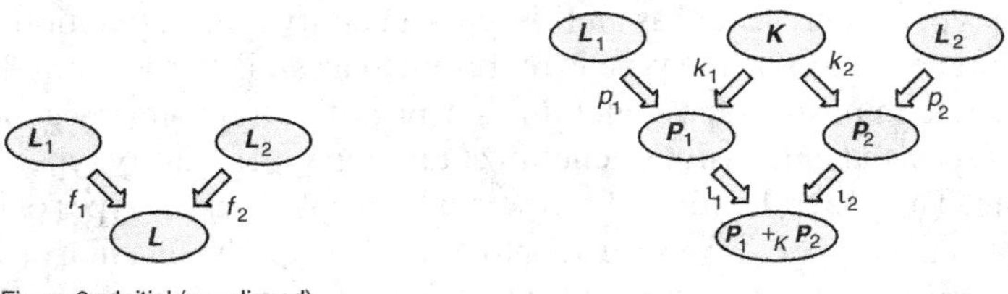

Figure 6a: Initial (nonaligned) Unification Diagram

Figure 6b: Aligned Unification Diagram

Finally, we represent unification.[23] In the usual approach to unification, the refinements are represented by logic infomorphisms from the two participant community ontologies to refined ontologies, where the latter are isomorphic. Because of this isomorphism, we can replace these refinements with a single logic $\boldsymbol{L}$. We end up with an opspan of logic infomorphisms (Figure 6a) consisting of two infomorphisms $\boldsymbol{f}_1$ and $\boldsymbol{f}_2$ with common target logic. However, although we have a representation in terms of the IFF, we feel that this opspan representation is too loose, since it is not aligned. In order to tighten this up we assume that the resulting opspan comes from taking the fusion of an alignment span of logic infomorphisms (Figure 6b).

THE PROCESS OF SEMANTIC INTEGRATION

Semantic integration is the two-step process of (1) alignment and (2) unification with respect to that alignment. Unification is the automatic process of fusion in the theoretical/logical context. However, alignment is not automatic.

We start (Figure 7) with two participant community ontologies represented as logics $\boldsymbol{L}_1$ and $\boldsymbol{L}_2$. We end, after alignment and unification, with an opspan of logic infomorphisms

$$f_1 : \boldsymbol{L}_1 \rightleftarrows \boldsymbol{L} \text{ and } f_2 : \boldsymbol{L}_2 \rightleftarrows \boldsymbol{L}$$

that represents the semantic integration of the participant community ontologies through a mediating ontology $\boldsymbol{K}$. The following discusses the process.

Alignment

Alignment is the process of specifying a diagram (Figure 7) in the theoretical/logical context that connects the participant community ontologies through common agreement. This alignment diagram is used for unification. Four questions need to be asked and answered for ontological alignment: where, what, who and a duplicate how–a how for where and a how for what.

Where do we want to interact with the other community and **how** is this place of interaction related to our community ontology? Where is the locus of integration? The question of "where" refers to the local *portal*, the logic we use for interaction. The question of "how" refers to the *portal link* for our community. Each community ontology involved in integration needs to localize its activities vis-à-vis integration. This locus of integration is called a portal–a portal is a communicating part or area of a system. The portals are represented by logics $\boldsymbol{P}_1$ and $\boldsymbol{P}_2$ and the portal links are represented by logic infomorphisms

FIGURE 7. Ontological Integration Process–Details

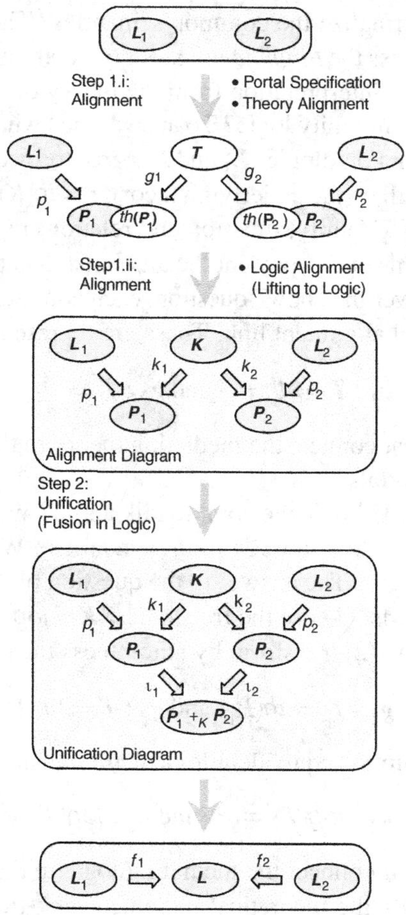

$$p_1 : L_1 \rightleftarrows P_1 \text{ and } p_2 : L_2 \rightleftarrows P_2$$

that connect the participants with their locus of integration (Figure 7). One reason for a portal is the incorporation into community ontologies of new subtypes or supertypes necessary for alignment. This incorporation extends the type aspect of the participant community ontology.

What do we want to say? What is the common semantics? What common meaning do we want to express? What is the expression for the *mediating ontology*? What is the language and theory of the mediating logic? The question about "what" refers to the mediating ontology–what is the language and theory of the mediating ontology? **How** do we say it in our own terms? How is this common semantics expressed in our own world? How does our community formalize the common semantics? The "how" question refers to how we express the *alignment link* for our community; that is, how do we specify the theory interpretation from the theory of the mediating logic to the theory of our community logic? To answer the "what" question, we assume that the participant ontologies L_1 and L_2 agree to specify their interaction via a theory T. This will be the underlying theory $T = th(K)$ of the mediating ontology K. The types of T (entity, function and relation) represent the aligned categories. The axioms of T represent the amount and nature of the desired compatibility. To answer the "how" question, each community ontology specifies its own theoretical alignment link. These are represented as theory morphisms

$$g_1 : T \Rightarrow th(P_1) \text{ and } g_2 : T \Rightarrow th(P_2)$$

that connect the mediating theory to the underlying theories of the participant portals.

Who do we want to talk about? What universe of discourse can serve as a base for the common semantics? What is the universe for the mediating logic? The answer to the question of "who" do we want to talk about has two parts: (1) use the free logic[24] $K = log(T)$ over the mediating theory $T = th(K)$, and (2) transform by adjointness the theoretical alignment links

$$g_1 : T \Rightarrow th(P_1) \text{ and } g_2 : T \Rightarrow th(P_2)$$

into the equivalent logical alignment links

$$k_1 : log(T) \rightleftarrows P_1 \text{ and } k_2 : log(T) \rightleftarrows P_2$$

that connect the mediating logic to the participant portals. Logical alignment lifts the theoretical alignment link to the free logic $L = log(T)$. The logical alignment links are the composition of the application of the logic operator to the theoretical alignment links

$$\mathsf{log}(\boldsymbol{g}_1) : \mathsf{log}(\boldsymbol{T}) \rightleftarrows \mathsf{log}(\mathsf{th}(\boldsymbol{P}_1)) \text{ and } \mathsf{log}(\boldsymbol{g}_2) : \mathsf{log}(\boldsymbol{T}) \rightleftarrows \mathsf{log}(\mathsf{th}(\boldsymbol{P}_2)),$$

followed by the canonical intent logic infomorphisms (counit components)

$$\varepsilon_{L1} : \mathsf{log}(\mathsf{th}(\boldsymbol{P}_1)) \rightleftarrows \boldsymbol{P}_1 \text{ and } \varepsilon_{L2} : \mathsf{log}(\mathsf{th}(\boldsymbol{P}_2)) \rightleftarrows \boldsymbol{P}_2,$$

which are the identity on types and the intent classification infomorphisms on entities and relations. The use of free logics has been successfully used in information flow (Kent 2000). This paper extends that technique to first order logic.[25]

Unification

The process of unification is fusion of the alignment diagram. We use the logic alignment diagram to specify a logic invariant: we use the type aspect to specify an equivalence relation on the types (entity, function and relation) of the sum logic, and we use the instance aspect to specify an appropriate subset of the instances (entity, function and relation) of the sum[26] logic $\boldsymbol{P}_1 + \boldsymbol{P}_2$. This logic invariant[27] induces a quotient logic[28] $\boldsymbol{P}_1 +_{\boldsymbol{K}} \boldsymbol{P}_2$ over the sum logic: types are the quotient classes of the corresponding equivalence relation, whereas instances are the members of the instance subsets of the logic invariant. This virtual ontology is a fusion[29] of the community portals with respect to the alignment diagram. It represents the complete system of semantic integration. A canonical logic infomorphism

$$\boldsymbol{q} : \boldsymbol{P}_1 + \boldsymbol{P}_2 \rightleftarrows \boldsymbol{P}_1 +_{\boldsymbol{K}} \boldsymbol{P}_2$$

links the sum logic to the quotient logic–its type component maps sum types to their equivalence class, and its instance component is subset inclusion. The fusion injections

$$\tilde{\iota}_1 = \iota_1 \cdot \boldsymbol{q} : \boldsymbol{P}_1 \rightleftarrows \boldsymbol{P}_1 + \boldsymbol{P}_2 \rightleftarrows \boldsymbol{P}_1 +_{\boldsymbol{K}} \boldsymbol{P}_2 \text{ and } \tilde{\iota}_2 = \iota_2 \cdot \boldsymbol{q} : \boldsymbol{P}_2 \rightleftarrows \boldsymbol{P}_1 + \boldsymbol{P}_2 \rightleftarrows \boldsymbol{P}_1 +_{\boldsymbol{K}} \boldsymbol{P}_2.$$

are the composition of the sum injections ι_1 and ι_2 with the canonical logic infomorphism $\boldsymbol{q}$. In Figure 7, the final semantic integration opspan defined the compositions $\boldsymbol{f}_1 = \boldsymbol{p}_1 \cdot \tilde{\iota}_1$ and $\boldsymbol{f}_2 = \boldsymbol{p}_2 \cdot \tilde{\iota}_2$. There are two extremes of semantic integration–nothing or everything. Any two logics can be vacuously integrated by forming the binary sum logic. This has no (empty) alignment and hence represents the trivial integration. Any logic can be completely integrated with a copy of itself. This has full (identity) alignment and complete integration.

A PRACTICAL ALTERNATIVE

The main part of this paper has discussed a theoretical approach to semantic integration. However, a practical approach also may be of interest. In both the theoretical and practical approaches, the participant community ontologies need to specify and interpret a mediating theory for semantic integration. Beyond this, the two approaches differ. To answer the question of "who" in the practical approach, we assume that the logics $\boldsymbol{L}_1$ and $\boldsymbol{L}_2$ of the two community ontologies agree to restrict their attention to a common part of both worlds called C. This means that the universes of the two community ontologies intersect and that $C \subseteq \mathsf{univ}(\boldsymbol{L}_1) \cap \mathsf{univ}(\boldsymbol{L}_2)$ is a subset of this intersection. Define the portals $\boldsymbol{P}_1 = \boldsymbol{L}_1@\mathrm{C}$ and $\boldsymbol{P}_2 = \boldsymbol{L}_2@\mathrm{C}$ to be the restriction of the full community logics to the sub-universe C, and define the portal links

$$\boldsymbol{p}_1 : \boldsymbol{L}_1 \Rightarrow \boldsymbol{L}_1@C \text{ and } \boldsymbol{p}_1 : \boldsymbol{L}_1 \Rightarrow \boldsymbol{L}_1@C$$

to be the restriction logic infomorphisms which are the identity on types and the inclusion on instances. The practical approach must answer the additional question: **Can** communities agree? Can all communities agree upon the meaning of the theory of the mediating ontology? The interpretative semantics that a participant community ontology gives to the mediating theory is specified by its theoretical alignment link. Do the interpretative semantics for all communities agree? In the practical approach, to answer the question of "can," the logic fiber operators $\boldsymbol{g}_1{}^{-1}$ and $\boldsymbol{g}_2{}^{-1}$ of the theoretical alignment links are applied to the portal logics $\boldsymbol{L}_1@\mathrm{C}$ and $\boldsymbol{L}_2@\mathrm{C}$, respectively. In order for alignment to succeed, the two logics that result must be the same: $\boldsymbol{g}_1{}^{-1}(\boldsymbol{L}_1@C) = \boldsymbol{L}@C = \boldsymbol{g}_2{}^{-1}(\boldsymbol{L}_2@C)$. This is defined to be the logic $\boldsymbol{K} = \boldsymbol{L}@C$ of the mediating ontology. This is not the free logic $\mathsf{log}(T)$, but there is a logic infomorphism

$$\mathsf{log}(T) \rightleftarrows \boldsymbol{L}@C$$

that connects the free logic to this mediating logic: it is the identity on types and maps an instance in C, whether entity or relation, to its intent. Then the fusion logic $\boldsymbol{L}_1{}^@C +_{\boldsymbol{L}@C} \boldsymbol{L}_2{}^@C$ has the fusion theory $\mathsf{th}(\boldsymbol{L}_1) +_T \mathsf{th}(\boldsymbol{L}_2)$ as its underlying theory and has C as its universe. There is a logic infomorphism

$$(\boldsymbol{L}_1{}^@C +_{\mathsf{log}(T)} \boldsymbol{L}_2{}^@C) \rightleftarrows (\boldsymbol{L}_1{}^@C +_{\boldsymbol{L}@C} \boldsymbol{L}_2{}^@C)$$

from the free fusion to the fusion at C: it is the identity on types and the diagonal function on instances in C.

In summary, in the practical approach to alignment there are three agreements between communities: the universe of the mediating ontology is the first agreement: $univ(\boldsymbol{K}) = C$; the theory of the mediating ontology is the second agreement: $th(\boldsymbol{K}) = \boldsymbol{T}$; and the identification of the mediating ontology with the fiber image of the portals along the theoretical alignment links is the third agreement.

CONCLUSION

The modern library is being transformed, and a new library is emerging.[30] Ontologies and the semantic integration of ontologies in a distributed environment[31] will be important and necessary concepts in the knowledge organization of the emerging library. This paper has discussed how the modular approach to ontologies and semantic integration needed in the emerging library can be represented in the metalogic of the Information Flow Framework.[32] This first order logic representation is an extension of the information flow representation for ontology sharing.[33]

REFERENCES

1. Kent, Robert E. 2000. The information flow foundation for conceptual knowledge organization. In *Dynamism and Stability in Knowledge Organization: Proceedings of the 6th International Conference of the International Society for Knowledge Organization (ISKO)*, (10-13 July 2000), Toronto, Canada. Würzburg, DE: Ergon Verlag.

2. ______. 2001. The Information Flow Framework. Starter document for IEEE P1600.1, the IEEE Standard Upper Ontology Working Group, http://suo.ieee.org/IFF/.

3. Wynar, Bodan S. and Arlene G. Taylor. 1992. *Introduction to Cataloging and Classification*, eighth edition. Englewood, Colorado: Libraries Unlimited, Inc.

4. Miksa, Francis L. 1996. The cultural legacy of the "modern library" for the future. Address given to the annual meeting of the Association for Library and Information Science Education (ALISE) in San Antonio, Texas, 17 January 1996. http://fiat.gslis.utexas.edu/faculty/modlib.html.

5. as 4.

6. as 5.

7. Ibid.

8. It has been the opinion of many that the best way to handle the multivalent relations in ontologies is with hypergraphs. A first order IFF *type language* is equivalent to the notion of a hypergraph. It consists of sets for variables, entity types corresponding to hypergraph nodes, and relation types corresponding to hyperedges, and functions for defining the signature and arity of relation types. The set of entity types linked by a relation type is called its signature. Type languages are related through type lan-

guage morphisms. A type language morphism from source type language to target type language maps source entity (relation) types to target entity (relation) types, preserving signature and arity.

In contrast to the notion of a hypergraph, any type language is extended to a type language of expressions, which has the same sets for variables and entity types, but has expressions as its relation types. The set of expressions is defined recursively and is the disjoint union of atomic expression, negation conjunction, disjunction, implication, existential and universal quantifications, and substitutions. There is an embedding type language morphism from any type language to its expression type language.

9. Sowa, John F. 2000. *Knowledge representation: logical, philosophical, and computional foundations*. Pacific Grove, CA: Brooks/Cole.

10. as 2.

11. Aristotle. 350 B.C.E. *Categories*. http://classics.mit.edu/Aristotle/categories.html. Translated by E. M. Edghill.

12. as 2.

13. A hypergraph is similar to a graph but allows edges that link more than two nodes. The set of nodes linked by a hyperedge is called its tuple. An IFF *hypergraph* consists of sets for names, nodes, and hyperedges, and functions for defining the tuple and arity of hyperedges. Hypergraphs are related through hypergraph morphisms. A hypergraph morphism from source hypergraph to target hypergraph maps source nodes (hyperedges) to target nodes (hyperedges), preserving tuple and arity.

14. The IFF gives a (somewhat novel) category-theoretic axiomatization for first-order model theory based upon the two fundamental ideas of classification and hypergraph (see the two dimensional structure in Figure 2a formed out of classifications along one dimension and hypergraphs along the other dimension). In one sense, an IFF *model* is a hypergraph of classifications. In place of nodes, there is a classification of entities, and in place of hyperedges, there is a classification of relations. The set of entity instances is called the universe of discourse, and the set of relation instances is called the tuple space. In another sense, an IFF model is a classification of hypergraphs–the instance aspect of a model forms an instance hypergraph, and dually the type aspect of a model forms a type language. IFF models are equivalent to the models of traditional many-sorted logic. In this equivalence, the extent functions of the entity, relation and expression classifications are regarded as interpretation functions.

The IFF has a lax notion of satisfaction for tuples. For a tuple to satisfy an expression, or that expression to hold for the tuple, we only require that the arity of the expression be a subset of the arity of the tuple and that the restriction of the tuple to that subset satisfy the expression in the usual sense. There is an expression classification, where an expression classifies a tuple when the expression holds for that tuple. A model satisfies an expression in its type language when that expression holds for all tuples; i.e., has maximal extent in the expression classification. A model for a theory is a model that satisfies every axiom of that theory. Satisfaction is defined recursively. Models are related through model infomorphisms. A model infomorphism is a classification infomorphism along the classification dimension and a hypergraph morphism along the hypergraph dimension. Models and model infomorphisms form the **Model** context.

15. Barwise, Jon and Jerry Seligman. 1997. Information flow: the logic of distributed systems. Cambridge University Tracts in Theoretical Computer Science 44. Cambridge: Cambridge University Press.

16. Bernhard Ganter and Rudolf Wille. Formal concept analysis: mathematical foundations. Heidelberg: Springer, 1999.

17. An IFF *theory* is a pair consisting of a base type language and a set of expressions of that language called axioms. A theory logically entails an expression of its base language when every model of the theory is also a model of the expression. Obviously, all axioms are entailed by a theory. The closure of a theory is the theory with the same base whose axioms consist of all expressions entailed by the original theory. An axiom of the closure is called a theorem of the original theory. Any axiom is a theorem. A theory is closed when it is its own closure. Every model generates a theory, whose base language is the type language of the model, and whose axioms are all expressions satisfied by the model. The theory of a model is closed, and is the maximal theory satisfied by that model. Theories are related through theory morphisms. A theory morphism from source theory to target theory is a language morphism that maps source axioms to target theorems. Theories and theory morphisms form the **Theory** context.

18. An IFF *prologic* is an inclusive idea combining the notions of model and theory into a (not necessarily sound) whole. It consists of a theory of types and a model of instances that share a common type language. The theory provides the formal semantics and the model provides the interpretative semantics. In addition, two special subsets are highlighted: there is a subset of the universe of discourse called the normal entities and a subset of the tuple space called the normal tuples, where the components of normal tuples are normal entities and normal entities and normal tuples satisfy the axioms of the theory. A prologic is sound, and is called a logic, when every instance of the universe and every tuple is normal. For any prologic, the sound part of the prologic is obtained by restriction–throwing away all abnormal instances and restricting the entity and relation classifications to normal instances. In this paper, we limit ourselves to logics, since these enable semantic integration. A logic infomorphism from source logic to target logic is a theory morphism along the theory aspect and a model infomorphism along the model aspect that share a common type language morphism. Logics and logic infomorphisms form the **Logic** context.

19. *Semantic integration* is the process of finding commonalities between two community ontologies O_1 and O_2 and deriving a new ontology O that facilitates interoperability between computational systems that are based on the O_1 and O_2 ontologies. The new ontology O may replace O_1 or O_2, or it may be used only as an intermediary between a system based on O_1 and a system based on O_2. Depending on the amount of change necessary to derive O from O_1 and O_2, different levels of integration can be distinguished: alignment, partial compatibility, and unification.

20. as in 10, Appendix B.

21. One ontology O_2 is a refinement of another ontology O_1 when there is an alignment of every type of O_1 to some type of O_2. Every type in O_1 must correspond to an equivalent type in O_2, but some primitive types (functions or relations) of O_1 might be equivalent to nonprimitives types (terms or expressions) in O_2. Refinement defines a partial ordering of ontologies. If O_2 is a refinement of O_1, and O_3 is a refinement of O_2, then O_3 is a refinement of O_1; if two ontologies are refinements of each other, then they are isomorphic.

22. An *alignment* of two ontologies O_1 and O_2 is a mapping of types (entity, function and/or relation) between two ontologies O_1 and O_2 that preserves the partial ordering by subtypes in both O_1 and O_2. If an alignment maps an entity ε_1, function ϕ_1 or relation ρ_1 in ontology O_1 to an entity ε_2, function ϕ_2 or relation ρ_2 in ontology O_2, then ε_1 and ε_2 are said to be equivalent, ϕ_1 and ϕ_2 are said to be equivalent, and ρ_1 and ρ_2 are said to be equivalent. The mapping may be partial–many types (entities, function or relations) in O_1 or O_2 may have no equivalents in the other ontology. Before two ontologies

O_1 and O_2 can be aligned, it may be necessary to introduce new subtypes or supertypes of concepts or relations in either O_1 or O_2 in order to provide suitable targets for alignment. No other changes to the axioms, definitions, proofs, or computations in either O_1 or O_2 are made during the process of alignment. A partial compatibility of two ontologies O_1 and O_2 is an alignment that supports equivalent inferences and computations on all equivalent types. If O_1 and O_2 are partially compatible, then any inference or computation, that is expressible in one ontology using only aligned types, can be translated to an equivalent inference or computation in the other ontology.

23. *Unification* or total compatibility may require extensive changes or major reorganizations of O_1 and O_2, but it can result in the most complete interoperability: everything that can be done with one can be done in an exactly equivalent way with the other. A unification is a one-to-one alignment of all entities and relations in two ontologies O_1 and O_2 that allows any inference or computation expressed in one to be mapped to an equivalent inference or computation in the other. The usual way of unifying two ontologies O_1 and O_2 is to refine each to more refined ontologies $\tilde{O}_1$ and $\tilde{O}_2$ whose categories are one-to-one equivalent.

24. For any theory ***T***, the free logic ***log(T)*** is defined as follows. Its component theory is ***T***. Its component model is the initial model over ***T***, whose entity classification is the power classification over the entity types of ***T*** and whose relation classification is a modification of the power classification over the relation types of ***T***. Instead of the power set of relation types, the tuples in ***log(T)*** consist of the subsets of relation types whose arity is a subset of a particular indexing arity. This is a kind of power classification over the arity function of ***T***. The instance arity function maps such a subset of relation types to their indexing arity. The instance signature function maps such a subset of relation types to the signature with indexing arity whose coordinate at any variable in that arity is the set of same coordinates for the signatures of all relation types whose arity contains that variable; that is, for any subset of variables X and any arity fiber subset R of relation types and any variable $x \in X$, define the instance signature function $\partial_0(R)_x = \{\partial_L(\rho)_x \mid \rho \in R, x \in \mathit{arity}(L)(\rho)\}$.

25. A *free logic* ***log(T)*** over a theory ***T*** has the following meaning: any theory morphism g from a theory ***T*** to the component theory ***th(L)*** is equivalent to a logic infomorphism $\hat{g}$ from the free logic ***log(T)*** to the logic ***L***. This adjoint logic infomorphism can be computed as the composition $\hat{g} = \log(g) \cdot \varepsilon_L$, where $_{\varepsilon L}$: ***log(th(L))*** □ ***L***, the ***L***th component of the counit called intent, is the identity on types, maps entity instances to their entity extents, and maps relation instances (tuples) to their relation extents consisting of all relation types (with possibly smaller arities) that classify that tuple. In Information Flow, the notion of power logic was used in the first step (**Lifting** to Logic) of the two-step process for ontology sharing (Kent 2000). That **Lifting** to Logic step corresponds to the logical alignment substep (Figure 7) of first order logics.

When free logics are investigated with respect to the lax IFF notion of satisfaction, there is a question about the relationship between unary relation types (unary predicates) and entity types (sorts). The IFF adopts a laissez-faire attitude: use the least constraints needed. It defines its basic logic using the constraint that every unary predicate have a particular sort (the single sort in its signature): the relational extent of the unary predicate is contained in the entity extent of its sort. However, the free logic construction seems to require some tightening up. The logic notion needed for the free logic construction further requires that every sort be the sort of some unary predicate that is extensionally equivalent to it.

26. Given two models $\boldsymbol{A}_0$ and $\boldsymbol{A}_1$, the sum $\boldsymbol{A}_0+\boldsymbol{A}_1$ is the model, whose instance hypergraph is the product of the component instance hypergraphs, whose type language is the sum of the component type languages, and whose entity (relation) classification is the sum of the component entity (relation) classifications. Each sum model comes equipped with two injection model infomorphisms from component models to sum. These are defined to be the sum injection on types and the product projection on instances. The sum model is a binary coproduct in Model, the model-theoretic context. Given two theories $\boldsymbol{T}_0$ and $\boldsymbol{T}_1$, the ***sum*** $\boldsymbol{T}_0+\boldsymbol{T}_1$ is the theory, whose base type language is the sum of the component languages, and whose axiom set is the union of the component axiom sets. The two base type language sum injection morphisms are theory sum injection morphisms. The theory sum is a coproduct in Theory, the theoretical context. Given two logics $\boldsymbol{L}_0$ and $\boldsymbol{L}_1$, the sum $\boldsymbol{L}_0+\boldsymbol{L}_1$ is the logic, whose component model is the sum of the component models, and whose component theory is the sum of the component theories. The component model sum injections are logic sum injections–the type language morphisms are also theory morphisms. The logic sum is a coproduct in Logic, the logical context.

27. For any model ***A***, a *dual invariant* is a pair ***J = (inst(J), typ(J)***) consisting of a sub-hypergraph ***inst(J)*** of the instance hypergraph ***inst(A)*** and an endorelation ***typ(J)*** on the type language ***typ(A)***. For any theory ***T***, *a theory endorelation* ***J*** is a type language endorelation on its base type language. For any logic ***L***, *a dual invariant* is a pair ***J = (mod(J), th(J))*** consisting of a dual invariant ***mod(J)*** on the component model ***mod(L)*** and an endorelation ***th(J)*** on the component theory ***th(L),*** where the type language endorelation of the model dual invariant is the same as the type language endorelation of the theory endorelation: ***typ(mod(J)) = lang(th(J))***.

28. The *dual quotient* of ***A*** by a model dual invariant ***J*** is the model ***A/J***, whose instance hypergraph is *inst*(***J***), whose type language is the quotient *typ(A)/typ*(***J***), whose entity classification is the quotient classification ***ent(A)/ent(J)***, and whose relation classification is the quotient classification ***rel(A)/rel(J)***. The quotient of ***T*** by a theory endorelation ***J***, written ***T/J***, is the theory whose base type language is the quotient type language ***lang(T)/lang(J)***, and whose axiom set consists of all "equivalence images" $[\varphi]_{\mathrm{lang(J)}}$ for all $\varphi\in$ ***axm(T)***. The *dual quotient* of ***L*** by a logic dual invariant ***J***, written ***L/J***, is the logic whose component model is ***mod(L)/mod(J)*** and whose component theory is ***th(L)/th(J)***. This is well-defined, since any relation instance *t* in ***inst(mod(L))*** satisfies any constraint $[\varphi]_{th(J)}\in$ ***axm(th(L)/th(J))***.

29. For any two logic infomorphisms f_0 : ***L*** □ $\boldsymbol{L}_0$ and f_1 : ***L*** □ $\boldsymbol{L}_1$ that share a common source logic ***L***, we define a dual invariant ***J*** = (***A, R***) on the sum $\boldsymbol{L}_0+\boldsymbol{L}_1$. Let ***A*** be the pairs of instances on which the instance functions of f_0 and f_1 agree, and let R be the binary relation between types of $\boldsymbol{L}_0$ and $\boldsymbol{L}_1$ that are linked by a type of ***L*** through the type functions of f_0 and f_1. The *fusion* logic is the dual quotient $\boldsymbol{L}_0+_L\boldsymbol{L}_1 = (\boldsymbol{L}_0+\boldsymbol{L}_1)/\boldsymbol{J}$. With the injection logic infomorphisms, the fusion logic is a pushout in Logic, the logical context.

30. as 5.
31. as 10.
32. as 3.
33. as 2.

Perspectives on Managing Knowledge in Organizations

Chun Wei Choo

SUMMARY. This paper compares two influential attempts at presenting a comprehensive framework of knowledge management. For each perspective the author examines theoretical foundations, highlights conceptual elements and themes, and discusses the role of information and information management. Ikujiro Nonaka and Hirotaka Takeuchi analyze the dynamics of knowledge creation, particularly the importance of tacit knowledge and its conversion into explicit knowledge. Thomas H. Davenport and Lawrence Prusak focus on the design of organizational processes that enable knowledge generation, codification, and transfer. It is suggested that, to a degree, the concepts and practices of each model reflect the national cultures of their authors–Japan and the United States. *[Article copies available for a fee from The Haworth Document Delivery Service: 1-800-HAWORTH. E-mail address: <docdelivery@ haworthpress.com> Website: <http://www.HaworthPress.com> © 2003 by The Haworth Press, Inc. All rights reserved.]*

KEYWORDS. Knowledge management frameworks, national cultures, knowledge creation, knowledge codification

---

Chun Wei Choo, PhD, is Associate Professor, Faculty of Information Studies, University of Toronto, 140 St. George Street, Toronto, Ontario M5S 3G6, Canada (E-mail: choo@fis.utoronto.ca).

[Haworth co-indexing entry note]: "Perspectives on Managing Knowledge in Organizations." Choo, Chun Wei. Co-published simultaneously in *Cataloging & Classification Quarterly* (The Haworth Information Press, an imprint of The Haworth Press, Inc.) Vol. 37, No. 1/2, 2003, pp. 205-220; and: *Knowledge Organization and Classification in International Information Retrieval* (ed: Nancy J. Williamson, and Clare Beghtol) The Haworth Information Press, an imprint of The Haworth Press, Inc., 2003, pp. 205-220. Single or multiple copies of this article are available for a fee from The Haworth Document Delivery Service [1-800-HAWORTH, 9:00 a.m. - 5:00 p.m. (EST). E-mail address: docdelivery@haworthpress.com].

http://www.haworthpress.com/store/product.asp?sku=J104

Digital Object Identifier: 10.1300/J104v37n01_14

INTRODUCTION

The objectives of this paper are to compare two influential models of knowledge management, and to explore how differences in their approaches might be related to national culture dimensions. In order to identify influential works on knowledge management, the Social Science Citation Index database was searched for articles with a primary focus on knowledge management. Cited authors were ranked. The five most frequently cited authors and cited references were as follows:

RANK No.	Items	Cited Author
1	197	NONAKA IKUJIRO
2	111	DAVENPORT THOMAS
3	76	POLANYI MICHAEL
4	67	BROWN JOHN SEELY
5	62	LEONARD-BARTON DOROTHY

RANK No.	Items	Cited Reference
1	126	NONAKA I, 1995, KNOWLEDGE CREATING COMPANY
2	48	NONAKA I, 1994, V5, P14, ORGANIZATION SCIENCE
3	43	DAVENPORT TH, 1998, WORKING KNOWLEDGE
4	39	LEONARDBARTON D, 1995, WELLSPRINGS OF KNOWLEDGE
5	39	POLANYI M, 1966, TACIT DIMENSION

The data suggest that Ikujiro Nonaka and Thomas Davenport are the two most often cited authors. Each of their books, *The Knowledge Creating Company* by Nonaka and Takeuchi[1] and *Working Knowledge* by Davenport and Prusak[2] offers a comprehensive framework on how organizations should manage their knowledge. The first two sections of the paper present the two frameworks. The third section compares the two perspectives, while the final section looks at the approaches in terms of national culture dimensions.

THE KNOWLEDGE CREATING COMPANY

The highly cited work of Nonaka and Takeuchi[3] emphasizes "management by creating *new* knowledge *continuously*" (*chishiki keiei*). The central idea is that knowledge creation in organizations is accomplished through knowledge conversion: existing knowledge is "converted" into new knowledge. Nonaka and Takeuchi adopt the traditional definition of knowledge as "justified true belief," but point out that where Western epistemology has focused on "truthfulness" as the essential attribute of knowledge, they stress the nature of knowledge as "justified belief":

> While traditional epistemology emphasizes the absolute, static, and non-human nature of knowledge, typically expressed in propositions and formal logic, we consider knowledge as *a dynamic human process of justifying personal belief toward the "truth."*[4]

The basis of organizational knowledge creation is the conversion of tacit knowledge into explicit knowledge and back again. Explicit knowledge is knowledge that "can be expressed in words and numbers, and easily communicated and shared in the form of hard data, scientific formulae, codified procedures, or universal principles."[5] Examples of explicit knowledge include chemical formulae, market forecasts, operations procedures, product specifications, software codes, and technical standards. Nonaka and Takeuchi do not view tacit knowledge and explicit knowledge as mutually exclusive but as complementary entities. Over time, human knowledge shifts between the tacit and the explicit through a process of social interaction between individuals that also produces new knowledge and expands its use.

Nonaka and Takeuchi suggest that the production of new knowledge involves "a process that 'organizationally' amplifies the knowledge created by individuals and crystallizes it as a part of the knowledge network of the organization."[6] Two sets of activities drive the process of knowledge amplification: (1) converting tacit knowledge into explicit knowledge; and (2) moving knowledge from the individual level to the group, organizational, and inter-organizational levels. The process grows like a spiral as the dance between tacit and explicit knowledge takes place at higher and higher levels of the organization.

There are four modes in which organizational knowledge is created through the interaction and conversion between tacit and explicit knowledge: socialization, externalization, combination, and internalization.[7] We outline these processes, using examples from Nonaka and Takeuchi's discussion of how Matushita developed an automatic home bakery product.

Socialization is a process of acquiring tacit knowledge through sharing experiences. As apprentices learn the craft of their masters through observation, imitation, and practice, so do employees of a firm learn new skills through on-the-job training. When Matsushita started developing its automatic home bread-making machine in 1985, an early problem was how to mechanize the dough-kneading process, a process that takes a master baker years of practice to perfect. To learn this tacit knowledge, a member of the software development team, Ikuko Tanaka, decided to volunteer herself as an apprentice to the head baker of the Osaka International Hotel, who was reputed to produce the area's best bread. After a period of imitation and practice, one day she observed that the baker was not only stretching but also twisting the dough in a particular fashion ("twisting stretch"), which turned out to be the secret for making tasty bread.

Externalization is a process of converting tacit knowledge into explicit concepts through the use of abstractions, metaphors, analogies, or models. The externalization of tacit knowledge is the quintessential knowledge-creation activity and is most often seen during the concept creation phase of new product development. Externalization can also be triggered by dialogue or collective reflection. Returning to the Matsushita case, Tanaka could not specify in engineering terms the "twisting stretch" motion she had learned from the master baker. Nevertheless she was able to communicate this tacit knowledge to the engineers by creating the mental concept of "twisting stretch," and by indicating the power and speed of the kneading propeller in order to imitate this motion. For example, Tanaka would say, "make the propeller move stronger," or "move it faster," and the engineers would make the necessary adjustments through trial-and-error.

Combination is a process of creating explicit knowledge by bringing together explicit knowledge from a number of sources. Thus, individuals exchange and combine their explicit knowledge through telephone conversations, meetings, memos, and so on. Existing information in computerized databases may be categorized, collated, and sorted in a number of ways to produce new explicit knowledge. The Matsushita home bakery team drew together eleven members from completely different specializations and cultures: product planning, mechanical engineering, control systems, and software development. The "twisting stretch" motion was finally materialized in a prototype after a year of iterative experimentation by the engineers and team members working closely together, combining their explicit knowledge. For example, the engineers added ribs to the inside of the dough case in order to hold the dough better as it is being churned. Another team member suggested a method (later patented) to add yeast at a later stage in the process, thereby saving the cost of a cooler otherwise needed to prevent the yeast from over-fermenting in high temperatures.

Finally, *internalization* is a process of embodying explicit knowledge into tacit knowledge, internalizing the experiences gained through the other modes of knowledge creation into individuals' tacit knowledge bases in the form of shared mental models or work practices. Internalization is facilitated if the knowledge is captured in documents or conveyed in the form of stories, so that individuals may re-experience indirectly the experience of others. Matsushita's home bakery product was a great success. It sold a record 536,000 units in its first year, topped the list of Mother's Day gifts, and was featured in a 1987 issue of Fortune magazine. The success story was disseminated throughout Matsushita by word of mouth and in-house publications, changing employees' perceptions about the potential of home appliances and inspiring them to develop other innovative products. The new tacit knowledge being internalized was that Matsushita could develop a product by interfacing directly with customers and by pursuing quality without compromise.

WORKING KNOWLEDGE

In their well-known book, Davenport and Prusak define knowledge as "a fluid mix of framed experience, values, contextual information, and expert insight that provides a framework for evaluating and incorporating new experiences and information. It originates and is applied in the minds of knowers. In organizations, it often becomes embedded not only in documents or repositories but also in organizational routines, process, practices, and norms."[8] In their view, organizations behave as knowledge markets, with buyers (people seeking knowledge to resolve an issue), sellers (people with an internal market reputation for having substantial knowledge about a process or subject), and brokers (people who make connections between people who need knowledge and those who have it: gatekeepers, boundary spanners, corporate librarians).

Markets work by having pricing and payment mechanisms. In knowledge markets, three kinds of payments operate: reciprocity, reputation, and altruism. A knowledgeable employee will take the time and effort to share knowledge if she expects the favor to be returned when it is her turn to seek or buy knowledge. An employee sharing knowledge may also be rewarded by gaining a reputation for being knowledgeable and being willing to share knowledge. Some individuals enjoy helping others, and share knowledge altruistically. Whatever the reason or incentive for sharing, knowledge markets require an environment of trust in order to function.

Any organization that wants to excel at managing knowledge will need to perform three KM processes well: generation, codification, and transfer of knowledge.

Knowledge generation refers to activities that increase the stock of organizational knowledge. Five modes of knowledge generation are discussed: acquisition; dedicating resources; fusion; adaptation; and building knowledge networks. Organizations may acquire knowledge by hiring individuals, buying another organization, or renting/leasing external knowledge. They may also dedicate resources to the generation of knowledge by establishing units that undertake research and development. The authors note that some corporate libraries function like R&D departments, developing and providing new knowledge to the organization. Knowledge generation through fusion can occur when different individuals and groups with different specializations and perspectives are brought together to work on a problem or project. Adaptation takes place when the organization responds to new conditions in its external environment. Here, knowledge generation is a result of organizations adapting to significant competitive, economic, or technological changes; and the most important adaptive resources are employees who can acquire new knowledge quickly and who have the openness to learn new skills. Knowledge is also generated in networks of people in an organization who share common work interests, face common work problems, and are motivated to exchange their knowledge. Organizations may attempt to formalize these informal, self-organizing networks over time.

Knowledge codification. Davenport and Prusak offer four principles that should guide the codification of organizational knowledge.

1. Managers must decide what business goals the codified knowledge will serve.
2. Managers must be able to identify knowledge existing in various forms appropriate to reaching these goals.
3. Knowledge managers must evaluate knowledge for usefulness and appropriateness for codification.
4. Codifiers must identify an appropriate medium for codification and distribution.[9]

Codification of tacit knowledge is generally limited to locating someone with the knowledge, pointing the seeker to it, and encouraging them to interact. For example, a knowledge map (an actual map, a Yellow Pages, a directory database) can be constructed to point to knowledge but does not contain it. Trying to turn knowledge into a "code" can sometimes seem to defeat the purpose of communicating it. The challenge is to codify knowledge and still leave its distinctive attributes intact, putting in place codification structures that can change as rapidly and flexibly as the knowledge itself. Davenport and Prusak suggest that stories, in their ability to embody and extend experience, and to combine feeling and thought, may be a way of capturing knowledge without removing its richness.

Knowledge transfer. Since organizations behave as knowledge markets, they should create market spaces and places where this trading and sharing of knowledge can happen. Much of knowledge transfer occurs through personal conversations, so places such as water coolers, talk rooms, knowledge fairs, and open forums become important venues for sharing information. A major theme in Davenport and Prusak's discussion is that the sharing of knowledge between people and groups in an organization may be the most daunting task in knowledge management. Most of the impediments are related to the culture of the organization. Davenport and Prusak identify seven barriers: lack of trust; different cultures, vocabularies, and frames of reference; lack of time and meeting places; status and rewards going to knowledge owners; lack of absorptive capacity in recipients; belief that knowledge is the prerogative of particular groups; the "not-invented-here" syndrome; and intolerance for mistakes or need for help.

Davenport and Prusak distinguish between formal and informal knowledge transfer, and point out that: "Informal knowledge transfer is endangered by a particularly American sense of what is and isn't 'real' work . . . an employee who reads a book at his desk–arguably an effective approach to knowledge acquisition–is looked at with suspicion . . . A company that claims to value knowledge but discourages reading and talking on company time sends mixed messages. The more convincing message is that knowledge is not much valued after all. Managers need to recognize that the availability of 'slack' time for learning and thinking may be one of the best metrics of a firm's knowledge orientation."[10]

TWO PERSPECTIVES COMPARED

Tacit Knowledge and Knowledge Creation

Nonaka and Takeuchi contrast Western and Eastern epistemological traditions, and conceptualize the importance of tacit knowledge. For them, the tacit knowledge of individuals lies at the heart and is the prime mover of knowledge creation in organizations. Davenport and Prusak develop a more pragmatic definition of organizational knowledge, and a more operational view of managing knowledge. They focus on how organizations can capture, codify and transfer knowledge, with a particular emphasis on knowledge sharing. Nonaka and Takeuchi concentrate on knowledge creation, and explain why organizational knowledge creation as a phenomenon has not been examined before in management research:

> There is a reason why Western observers tend not to address the issue of organizational knowledge creation. They take for granted a view of the organization as a machine for 'information processing.'[11]

This view is deeply ingrained in the traditions of Western management, from Frederick Taylor to Herbert Simon. And it is a view of knowledge as necessarily "explicit"–something formal and systematic . . . Japanese companies have a very different understanding of knowledge. They recognize that the knowledge expressed in words and numbers represents only the tip of the iceberg. They view knowledge as being primarily "tacit"–something not easily visible and expressible. Tacit knowledge is highly personal and hard to formalize, making it difficult to communicate or to share with others.

Organizational Design

Although both models recognize the complex, dynamic nature of creating, sharing, and using knowledge, each recommends a different structural approach to managing this complexity. Nonaka and Takeuchi believe that organizations need to be designed and managed as multilayered, "hypertext organizations." Davenport and Prusak believe that organizations need to function as knowledge markets and marketplaces where knowledge can be traded and transacted efficiently between buyers, sellers, and brokers. Nonaka and Takeuchi's hypertext organization consists of three layers: the knowledge base, business system, and project team. The knowledge base includes both tacit knowledge associated with organizational culture and procedures, and explicit knowledge in the form of documents, filing systems, databases. This layer "functions as an archive, or corporate university for the knowledge creation of the company."[12] The second layer is the business system where normal, routine operations are carried out by "a formal, hierarchical, bureaucratic organization." The topmost layer, the project team, is where multiple, loosely interlinked self-organizing project teams share in the joint creation of knowledge through a common corporate vision. In this hypertext organization, the agent of knowledge creation is the self-organizing team led by middle managers as team leaders who translate top management visions into more concrete concepts, which are to be realized in the field. Nonaka and Takeuchi call this "middle-up-down management."

Organizational Enablers

For Nonaka and Takeuchi, knowledge management requires the development of enabling conditions that promote or stimulate knowledge creation. For Davenport and Prusak, knowledge management in practice consists of identifiable activities and planned projects. Nonaka and Takeuchi[13] discuss five enabling conditions as being particularly important. First, since the knowledge spiral is driven by *organizational intention* or aspirations, the organization needs to clearly conceptualize a vision about what kind of knowledge would be most valuable to realizing the organizational intention, and to apply this vision as the principal yardstick for judging the usefulness of new knowledge. Second, organizational members, either on their own or in self-organizing teams, should be given the freedom to act with *autonomy* so that they would motivate themselves to experiment and discover new knowledge. Third, the organization can stimulate the knowledge creation process by inducing *fluctuation and creative chaos* by, for example, introducing breakdowns of set routines or habitual frameworks, evoking a sense of crisis, and stating ambiguous visions and goals. Fourth, information should be made available to organizational members, which goes beyond their immediate operational requirements. *Information redundancy* promotes the sharing of tacit knowledge, and the exchanging of ideas. Fifth, according to the principle of *requisite variety*, an organization's internal diversity must match the variety and complexity of its external environment. This implies that organizational members should have prompt access to a wide range of information so they can cope with fast-changing contingencies. Davenport and Prusak expand on the pragmatics of managing knowledge, and elaborate on the different types of projects that an organization might pursue. They distinguish between three types of projects.

1. Knowledge repositories that are aimed at capturing knowledge in documents and organizing them in a repository where it can be retrieved easily.
2. Knowledge access and transfer projects that link up people who possess knowledge and people who are prospective users of this knowledge.
3. Knowledge environment projects that include attempts to measure the value of knowledge capital, raising awareness and cultural receptivity, and changing behaviors that relate to knowledge.

NATIONAL CULTURE DIFFERENCES

This section applies the national cultural dimensions developed by Hofstede and his associates[14,15] to explore possible interactions between national cultural traits and the knowledge management concepts and practices presented in the models. Hofstede's ideas were first based on a large research project into national culture differences across subsidiaries of a multinational corporation (IBM) in 64 countries. Subsequent studies by others covered students in 23 countries, elites in 19 countries, commercial airline pilots in 23 countries, up-market consumers in 15 countries, and civil service managers in 14 countries.[16,17] These studies together identified and validated five independent dimensions of national culture differences: power distance, individualism versus collectivism, masculinity versus femininity, uncertainty avoidance, and long-term versus short-term orientation. (Scores on the first four dimensions were obtained for 50 countries and 3 regions on the basis of the IBM study, and on the fifth dimension for 23 countries on the basis of student data collected by Bond.)[18]

Power distance is defined as "the extent to which the less powerful members of institutions and organizations within a country expect and accept that power is distributed unequally."[19] This represents inequality as perceived by the members, and suggests that a society's level of inequality is endorsed by the followers as much as by the leaders. In the field studies, power distance scores were found to be higher for Latin, Asian and African countries and lower for Germanic countries.

Nonaka and Takeuchi do not examine organizational power in detail. However, they suggest that a formal, bureaucratic hierarchy is an effective way of managing routine operations, and this hierarchy should be one of the three layers in their "hypertext organization." Moreover, they write that it is the responsibility of top management to develop strategic visions (aspirations), and the task of middle management to translate these visions into attainable goals. Davenport and Prusak discuss the politics underlying the identification of employees who have knowledge valuable to the organization. They see the mapping of knowledge as being inherently political:

> Organizational knowledge maps are political documents too. Questions about who has the most useful knowledge are open to interpretation. If knowledge is genuinely important to an organization and those who have it are recognized and rewarded, then the knowledge map will be a picture of status and success as well as a locator.[20]

In an earlier analysis of more than 25 organizations, Davenport, Eccles and Prusak[21] observed five models of information politics: technological utopianism, anarchy, feudalism, monarchy, and federalism. The most common political model of information management was a form of *information feudalism*, in which individual managers and their departments control information acquisition, storage, distribution, and analysis. This fragmentation of information undermines efforts to consolidate knowledge assets so that the organization as a whole can learn and adapt. Instead of feudalism, Davenport et al. recommend a form of *information federalism* as being the most appropriate model in today's environment. Federalism recognizes that politics is a necessary and legitimate activity for people with divergent interests to work out a collective purpose and the means for realizing it. Under federalism, managers negotiate among themselves in order to produce a larger pool of knowledge that they can tap into and exploit to advantage.

Individualism versus collectivism. Individualism pertains to societies in which the ties between individuals are loose: everyone is expected to look after himself or herself and his or her immediate family. Collectivism pertains to societies in which people from birth onwards are integrated into strong, cohesive in-groups, which throughout people's lifetime continue to protect them in exchange for unquestioning loyalty.[22] The word "collectivism" in this sense has no political meaning: it refers to the group, not to the state. Individualism prevails in developed and Western countries, while collectivism prevails in less developed and Eastern countries; Japan takes a middle position on this dimension.

In Nonaka and Takeuchi's model, while the seed of new knowledge is individual (tacit) knowledge, this knowledge increases in utility when it becomes available to others in the organization. Thus, the externalization of tacit knowledge is a quintessential process in the knowledge conversion cycle, and this typically requires a group's members to interact and reflect collectively on a problem or an idea. Nonaka and Takeuchi[23] also contrast the Western view of human relationships as "atomistic and mechanistic" with the Japanese view that they are "collective and organic." For the Japanese, to work for others means to work for oneself: employees realize themselves in their relationship to others. Bhagat et al.[24] propose that people in individualist cultures emphasize explicit knowledge, preferring knowledge independent of its context, whereas those in collectivist cultures emphasize tacit knowledge, preferring systemic or contextually relevant knowledge. They note that Nonaka and Takeuchi discuss the relative superiority of collectivist cultures (i.e., Japan) in being able to convert tacit types of knowledge into explicit forms.

In examining organizations as knowledge markets, Davenport and Prusak identify several factors that can prevent the market from working efficiently. Generally, a strong sense of individualism can stymie the sharing and use of knowledge. Davenport and Prusak identify at least two cultural barriers that can exacerbate this effect: organizations reward and raise the status of people who own knowledge; and groups developed the belief that knowledge is their special right and privilege that should be preserved.

Both models recognize that the creation, sharing, and utilization of knowledge is a group phenomenon. Nonaka and Takeuchi describe self-organizing teams that emerge to work on problems. Davenport and Prusak discuss communities of practice that also self organize around shared interests and work practices in order to exchange knowledge. Indeed, the concept of communities of practice is one of the more enduring ideas to have emerged from knowledge management practice. Communities of practice, initially written about by Wenger,[25] are groups whose members face common work tasks and interests, who can see the benefit of sharing knowledge, and who share norms of trust and reciprocity. In a related vein, Nonaka and Takeuchi introduce the idea of "ba" as a shared space (physical, mental or virtual) where knowledge conversion and creation can unfold. Although "ba" appears similar to a community of practice, Nonaka, Toyama and Boysiere[26] underline some differences: "ba" is a place where new knowledge is created; participation in a "ba" is fluid and ad hoc; participants relate to a "ba" but do not belong as members.

Masculinity versus femininity refers to the distribution of roles between the genders. Masculinity refers to societies in which social gender roles are clearly distinct, i.e., men are supposed to be assertive, tough, and focused on material success whereas women are supposed to be more modest, tender, and concerned with the quality of life. Femininity refers to societies in which social gender roles overlap, i.e., both men and women are supposed to be modest, tender, and concerned with the quality of life.[27] The IBM studies revealed that (a) women's values differ less among societies than men's values; (b) men's values from one country to another contain a dimension from very assertive and competitive and maximally different from women's values on the one side, to modest and caring and similar to women's values on the other. The assertive pole has been called "masculine" and the modest, caring pole "feminine." Masculinity is high in Japan, in some European countries like Germany, Austria and Switzerland, and moderately high in Anglo countries; it is low in Nordic countries and in the Netherlands and moderately low in some Latin and Asian countries like France, Spain and Thailand.

Analyzing gender roles in the context of knowledge management has not been an active area of research. Recently, Nonaka and his associates highlight the importance of caring and care in enabling knowledge creation:

> to care for others is to help them to learn; to increase their awareness of important events and consequences; to nurture their personal knowledge while sharing their insights . . . the concept of care matters most in an organization when those in charge provide a context in which knowledge is created and shared freely . . . we have found that the concept of care quite satisfactorily describes relations that have a positive impact on knowledge creation . . . More recently, many American researchers and commentators have studied the increasing number of female executives, along with the overall rise in the number of women in the workforce . . . For these writers, women managers naturally have a more cooperative style, excelling at networking, team-building, mentoring–all hallmarks of a caring organization and an enabling context. [28]

Davenport and Prusak[29] appear to be relatively silent on the differentiation of gender roles in knowledge management in their book.

Uncertainty avoidance is defined as "the extent to which the members of a culture feel threatened by uncertain or unknown situations. This feeling is, among other things, expressed through nervous stress and in a need for predictability: a need for written and unwritten rules"[30] It indicates to what extent a culture programs its members to feel either uncomfortable or comfortable in unstructured situations. Unstructured situations are novel, unknown, surprising, and different from usual. Uncertainty-avoiding cultures try to minimize the possibility of such situations by laws and rules, safety and security measures, and on the philosophical and religious level by a belief in an absolute Truth. People in uncertainty-accepting cultures are more tolerant of opinions different from what they are used to; they minimize the need for rules, and they allow many philosophical and religious currents to co-exist. People within these cultures are more phlegmatic and contemplative, and not expected by their environment to express emotions. Uncertainty avoidance scores are higher in Latin countries, in Japan, and in German speaking countries, lower in Anglo, Nordic, and Chinese culture countries.

As noted earlier, Nonaka and Takeuchi recommend that organizations stimulate the knowledge creation process by deliberately introducing tension and chaos. This can be done by, for example, inducing breakdowns of set routines or habitual frameworks, evoking a sense of crisis, and stating ambiguous visions and goals. Organizations should also recognize the inherent complexity and uncertainty of the external environment they are operating in, and develop structures and information resources internally so that their internal information diversity matches the external complexity of the environment (the principle of "requisite variety" in systems theory). Compared with Nonaka and Takeuchi, Davenport and Prusak do not emphasize as much the chaotic or uncertainty aspects of knowledge-based initiatives. The general tone of their discussion is that while knowledge management is a major change effort, it can be planned and managed as with other organizational change activities.

Long-term versus short-term orientation. Cultural values associated with long-term orientation are thrift and perseverance. Values associated with short-term orientation are respect for tradition, fulfilling social obligations, and protecting one's "face." Although the values of this dimension are based on the teachings of Confucius, Hofstede believes that the dimension also applies to countries without a Confucian heritage. A long-term orientation is mostly found in East Asian countries, in China, Hong Kong, Taiwan, Japan, and South Korea.

Both Nonaka and Takeuchi and Davenport and Prusak recognize that knowledge creation and generation are closer to R&D activities than production activities. They require a long-term perspective in which appropriate kinds and levels of resources can be invested and nurtured. In today's business environment, where firms are pressured to deliver financial returns on a quarterly cycle, adopting a long-term orientation for activities whose value is intangible, or not easily measured, poses a huge challenge.

There is a danger of applying Hofstede's polarized cultural dimensions a little too rigidly. Cultural values that are regarded as opposites in one country may be perceived as complementary in another. Nonaka and Takeuchi argue that the two Japanese intellectual traditions of "the oneness of humanity and nature" and "the oneness of body and mind" have led the Japanese to value the interaction between self and other. It is within this context that "the Japanese emphasize subjective knowledge and intuitive intelligence."[31] They conclude that:

> Western management practice is still dominated by the Cartesian dualism between subject and object, mind and body, or mind and matter. Following the Japanese intellectual tradition, however, we do not see these distinctions as an either-or dichotomy, but as mutually complementary.[32]

Our attempts to relate knowledge management concepts and practices to national cultures remain largely speculative until we see more empirical studies of cultural effects on knowledge management. One recent study is by Yoo and Torrey[33] who explore the effects of national cultures on knowledge management practices in a global organization. In a field study at Accenture (then known as Andersen Consulting) in Korea and the U.S., interviews with 53 consultants provided critical incidents of how the consultants create, seek, and share knowledge. In knowledge creation, two common forms were observed in both countries: invention and integration. The Korean consultants emphasized integration: many respondents had difficulty finding an example of creating new knowledge. In contrast, the U.S. consultants believed more frequently that they were inventing new knowledge as a result of their activities. In knowledge seeking, the Korean consultants focused on finding best practices in the online knowledge repository. A primary motivation for using the repository was to affirm the authority and quality of their solutions. The U.S. consultants seldom mentioned the term "best practices" in their accounts, and some were, in fact, skeptical about the notion of best practices. There were also differences in evaluating results from searching the repository. Several Korean consultants developed a preferred list of authors and sorted search results by these authors first. None of the U.S. consultants said they paid attention to authors' names. Instead, they used the synopses accompanying search results to assess the usefulness of documents. Korean consultants also felt that posting contributions into the repository and contacting foreign "experts" were the responsibilities of their superiors. In knowledge sharing, few of the Korean consultants contributed to the repository system, whereas the U.S. consultants saw the repository as their primary vehicle for preserving and sharing knowledge. The authors offered explanations for these patterns based on differences in the national cultures of the two countries. They suggest that national cultural differences may be managed to enhance knowledge creation and sharing within multinational firms.

CONCLUSION

In the influential models developed by Nonaka and Takeuchi, and Davenport and Prusak, many of the theoretical concepts appeared to have grown naturally out of the cultural and intellectual traditions of the authors. Nonaka and Takeuchi made it clear that their notions of tacit knowledge, embracing opposites, and recognizing the oneness of body and mind, are all based on Japanese cultural and intellectual traditions. The ideas in Davenport and Prusak's book evolved from discussions with mainly U.S. corporate managers about how knowledge functions in organizations. The work grew out of a research program on new approaches in information management that brought together executives from about 25 client companies.

On the other hand, some of the principles and practices presented in the models appear initially to be incompatible with the expected national cultural dimensions. These exceptions may be an attempt to balance or compensate for tendencies in the national cultures that might impede knowledge creation and transfer. For example, in the Japanese culture that is generally thought to be averse to uncertainty, Nonaka and Takeuchi propose that organizations introduce a sense of chaos and crisis to inspire new knowledge creation.

Both models recognize that knowledge creation, sharing and use are inherently social activities that are embedded in a web of cultural norms and human relationships. The creation and utilization of knowledge takes place most effectively in groups and teams that share common purpose and beliefs. Thus, Davenport and Prusak write about the importance of "communities of practice," while Nonaka introduces the idea of "ba" or shared contexts for creating and sharing knowledge.

In today's global environment where knowledge has to cross national boundaries, there is an urgent need to understand the influence of cultures in different countries on the organizational processes of knowledge creation and transfer.

REFERENCES

1. Ikujiro Nonaka, and Hirotaka Takeuchi, *The Knowledge-Creating Company: How Japanese Companies Create the Dynamics of Innovation*. New York, NY: Oxford University Press, 1995.

2. Thomas H. Davenport and Lawrence Prusak, *Working Knowledge: How Organizations Manage What They Know*. Cambridge, MA: Harvard Business School Press, 1998.

3. as 1.

4. as 1, p. 58.

5. as 1, p. 8.

6. as 1, p. 59.

7. as 1.

8. as 2, p. 5.

9. as 2, p. 69.

10. as 2, p. 93.

11. as 1, p. 8.

12. Ikujiro Nonaka, Ryoko Toyama, and Philippe Boysiere, "A Theory of Organizational Knowledge Creation: Understanding the Dynamic Process of Creating Knowledge," in *Handbook of Organizational Learning and Knowledge*, edited by Meinolf Dierkes, Ariane Berthoin Antal, John Child and Ikujiro Nonaka. Oxford, UK: Oxford University Press, 2001: 512-513.

13. as in 1.

14. Geert Hofstede, *Cultures and Organizations: Software of the Mind*. New York: McGraw-Hill, 1997.

15. Geert Hofstede, *Culture's Consequences: Comparing Values, Behaviors, Institutions, and Organizations Across Nations*. 2nd ed. Thousand Oaks, CA: Sage Publications, 2001.
16. as in 14.
17. as in 15.
18. Geert Hofstede and Michael H. Bond, "The Confucius Connection: From Cultural Roots to Economic Growth," *Organizational Dynamics* 16: 4 (1988): 4-21.
19. as in 14, p. 28.
20. as in 2, p. 79.
21. Thomas H. Davenport, Robert G. Eccles, and Laurence Prusak, "Information Politics," *Sloan Management Review* 34:1 (1992): 53-63.
22. as in 14, p. 51.
23. as in 1.
24. Rabi S. Bhagat, Ben L Kedia, Paula D. Harveston and Harry C. Triandi, "Cultural Variations in the Cross-Border Transfer of Organizational Knowledge: An Integrative Framework," *Academy of Management Review* 27:2 (2002): 209-210.
25. Etienne Wenger, *Communities of Practice: Learning, Meaning and Identity* Cambridge, UK: Cambridge University Press, 1998.
26. as in 12.
27. as in 14, p. 82-83.
28. Georg von Krogh, Kazuo Ichijo, and Ikujiro Nonaka, *Enabling Knowledge Creation: How to Unlock the Mystery of Tacit Knowledge and Release the Power of Innovation*. New York: Oxford University Press, 2000: 47-48.
29. as in 2.
30. as in 14, p. 113.
31. as in 1, p. 31.
32. as in 1, p. 32.
33. Youngjin Yoo and Ben Torrey, "National Culture and Knowledge Sharing in a Global Learning Organization," in *Strategic Management of Intellectual Capital and Organizational Knowledge: A Collection of Readings*, edited by Chun Wei Choo and Nick Bontis. New York: Oxford University Press, 2002: 421-435.

Global Abstractions: The Classification of International Economic Data for Bibliographic and Statistical Purposes

D. Grant Campbell

SUMMARY. This paper compares the representation of national and international agricultural economic information in the North American Industry Classification System (NAICS) and the Library of Congress Classification (LCC). While LCC presents geographically-specific information within a larger context of agriculture as a field of study, NAICS presents agriculture as part of the overall depiction of economic activity in and between countries. To facilitate statistical aggregation and cross-comparison, NAICS has normalized economic activity by presenting it as a series of abstract activities that can be uniformly measured across different countries and regions. This rigorous standardization of economic data, while effective for statistical analysis, threatens to diminish the specific national, cultural and social contexts in which such data must be interpreted. *[Article copies available for a fee from The Haworth Document Delivery Service: 1-800-HAWORTH. E-mail address: <docdelivery@haworthpress.com> Website: <http://www.HaworthPress.com> © 2003 by The Haworth Press, Inc. All rights reserved.]*

D. Grant Campbell, MA, PhD, MIST, currently teaches in the Faculty of Information and Media Studies, University of Western Ontario (E-mail: gcampbel@uwo.ca).

[Haworth co-indexing entry note]: "Global Abstractions: The Classification of International Economic Data for Bibliographic and Statistical Purposes." Campbell, D. Grant. Co-published simultaneously in *Cataloging & Classification Quarterly* (The Haworth Information Press, an imprint of The Haworth Press, Inc.) Vol. 37, No. 1/2, 2003, pp. 221-234; and: *Knowledge Organization and Classification in International Information Retrieval* (ed: Nancy J. Williamson, and Clare Beghtol) The Haworth Information Press, an imprint of The Haworth Press, Inc., 2003, pp. 221-234. Single or multiple copies of this article are available for a fee from The Haworth Document Delivery Service [1-800-HAWORTH, 9:00 a.m. - 5:00 p.m. (EST). E-mail address: docdelivery@haworthpress.com].

http://www.haworthpress.com/store/product.asp?sku=J104
© 2003 by The Haworth Press, Inc. All rights reserved.
Digital Object Identifier: 10.1300/J104v37n01_15

KEYWORDS. North American Industry Classification, NAICS, statistical classification, international classification, Library of Congress Classification, LCC

INTRODUCTION

Classification systems have always been formed on complex conceptions of physical, political, geographic and cultural space. Indeed, current classification research is divided between those who study classification as a cultural construct that reflects specific information ecologies,[1] and those who study the elements of classification that transcend such cultural specifics.[2] Classification systems, particularly those purporting to be "international"–to be capable of collecting data and/or documents from different countries and integrating them within a common scheme–must balance these two perspectives. The designers of such systems must permit the collocation of information and navigation of information spaces in ways that are true to the cultural expectations of specific communities. At the same time, these cultural expectations must be created using classification principles of sufficient universality to allow for meaningful comparison and consistent arrangement.

Classification systems for the collection and use of economic statistics in an international context operate in an especially vexed space. Within a volatile political environment in which globalism and free trade are defended by some and decried by others, classifications such as the new North American Industry Classification System (NAICS) strive to order economic data to produce illustrations of economic life in North America that are true both to the individual countries and to the international community in which these countries exist. The present paper will compare NAICS to the Library of Congress Classification (LCC) to illustrate that industrial classifications for gathering economic statistics represent the international reality through using different techniques from those used in bibliographic classification: techniques which suggest significant differences in the underlying approaches to geographical and political boundaries.

BACKGROUND AND CONTEXT

NAICS was formulated in the wake of the North American Free Trade Agreement (NAFTA) between Canada, the United States and Mexico in 1994. It evolved, therefore, in a context of intense and volatile debate on the merits of Free Trade, one that continues today with recurring anti-globalism protests at G8 summits. The Council of Canadians argued in 1996 that free trade undermined Canada's capacity for self-government and self-determination: "Canadian capital has gone global. Having escaped beyond the borders of nation-state law, it has called off its partnership with Canadian citizens."[3] Globalism, such opponents posit, threatens the cultural sovereignty and social identity of individual countries. In this sense, NAICS, as a classification system for harmonizing economic data, could be taken as an embodiment of Benjamin Barber's gloomy forecast of a future world divided between the "Jihad" and "McWorld": part of a larger force that is corroding national boundaries.[4]

Despite this gloomy picture, consensus in the information studies community has been fairly unanimous: NAICS is a big improvement on its predecessor, the 1980 Standard Industrial Code (SIC), which was the latest revision of a code first developed in the 1930s.[5] Empirical economic research had arguably suffered seriously by the eclecticism and confusion of the SIC system: "there is no single consistent economic concept underlying the existing structure of the SIC . . . The lack of a well-identified and carefully applied conceptual framework for the SIC undoubtedly affects empirical economic research."[6]

The creators of NAICS set out to rectify this problem by formulating a classification scheme that used a production-oriented conceptual framework that gave special attention to emerging industries and was compatible with the United Nations International Standard Industrial Classification.[7] This production-oriented framework groups industries "according to similarity in the production processes used to produce goods and services."[8] The grouping principle, then, is activity rather than product: industries are collocated according to what they do, rather than according to what they produce. Because of this clearly articulated foundation, "NAICS is a vast improvement over the SIC codes; allowing for greater detail, logical groupings of industries, and international compatibility with NAFTA partners."[9] And, because the system will ultimately be adopted by all three NAFTA countries, all three countries will "share a common language for easier comparisons of international trade, industrial production, labor costs and other statistics."[10]

None of this is likely to appease the protesters who march at the gates of G8 summits. If, however, we are to assess international statistics-gathering classification schemes like NAICS, we have to understand how they work, and, in particular, how they differ from bibliographic classification systems. This paper, therefore, aims to enhance our understanding by taking an economic activity that is firmly based on geography–agriculture–and comparing its treatment in NAICS and in Class S of LCC.[11] It seeks to answer two questions:

- How does a statistical classification scheme like NAICS differ from a bibliographic classification scheme in its representation of different countries, and what mechanisms does each use to facilitate comparison and cross-analysis of common topics in different countries?
- How does the representation of specific geographical, regional or political space in a statistical international scheme differ from that of a "universal" bibliographic scheme?

LCC does not offer the sophisticated faceting capabilities for representing geographical subdivisions that are offered by other schemes such as the Universal Decimal Classification (UDC). Nonetheless, the system has been widely and effectively used across North America, and as a system explicitly designed to classify documents on shelves rather than knowledge in the abstract, LCC forms an effective contrast to NAICS.

AGRICULTURE IN NAICS AND LCC

NAICS[12] divides economic activity into twenty industry sectors and assigns each a two-digit notation. Subsectors are arranged with hierarchical notation to a maximum of six digits. The scheme divides roughly in half, with the first eight sectors given to manufacturing and production activities and the following eleven to service industries, with Public Administration at the end. Agriculture, which had been spread over three main classes in SIC, has been collapsed into one sector:

11 Agriculture, Forestry, Fishing, Hunting

111 Crop Production

112 Animal Production

113 Forestry, Logging

114 Fishing, Hunting, Trapping

Agriculture is therefore cast within a class order that is roughly evolutionary; it is a primary industry involved in resource extraction, together with Mining (21) and Utilities (22), and will be followed by the activities that mark the general progress of raw materials towards consumer goods: Construction (23), Manufacturing (31-33), Wholesale Trade (42), Retail Trade (44-45) and Transportation and Warehousing (48-49). This deliberate class order, which matches the processes of extraction, refinement and distribution, casts the switch to service industries with Information (51) on the same continuum. Clearly, service industries are seen to "grow from" the manufacturing sectors. They are activities that presuppose the active and thriving extraction of resources and manufacturing and distribution of physical goods.

Class 11 is divided into four subsectors, based on the primary activity, followed by a fifth subsector for support activities:

11 Agriculture, Forestry, Fishing and Hunting

111 Crop Production

112 Animal Production

113 Forestry and Logging

114 Fishing, Hunting and Trapping

115 Support Activities for Agriculture and Forestry

Each of these subclasses is further subdivided by the product that is being cultivated. Crop Production, for instance, divides into Oilseed and Grain (1111), Vegetable and Melon (1112), Fruit and Tree Nut (1113), Greenhouse, Nursery and Floriculture (1114) and Other (1119). Animal Production divides into Cattle Ranching and Farming (1121), Hog and Pig Farming (1122), Poultry and Egg Production (1123), Sheep and Goats (1124), Animal Aquaculture (1125) and Other (1129).

In keeping with the focus on economic activity, rather than on the end product, activities which might well be closely linked in practical ways are separated by the classification. Sheep farming (11241), for instance, is separated from sheep dipping and shearing, which is placed in Support Activities for Animal Production (11521). Other activities, arguably integral to the agricultural sector and vital to its survival, have been displaced still further. Veterinary services, soil and seed testing services, agricultural consultants and agricultural research and development, all formerly belonging to the Agricultural sector in SIC 1980, have been displaced into the Services section: Professional, Scientific and Technical Services (54). Sectors, as defined by NAICS, clearly do not group economic units that are related by a common objective, by the production of a common good or service, or by geographical proximity. Rather, the sector is defined strictly by the activity performed, and the technologies or skills required to perform that service.

LCC employs the same categories for Agriculture as those of NAICS, and collects them under a common class. The subclass order is slightly different. LCC divides agricultural topics into those dealing with plants and those dealing with animals:

S Agriculture (General)

SB Plant culture

SD Forestry

SF Animal culture

SH Aquaculture

SK Hunting sports

Each subclass has approximately the same structure: a preliminary section on history is followed by a section on methods, a section on the type of material or commodity being cultivated, and other related topics or activities at the end (see Table 1).

The purpose of Class S is not to group and differentiate different types of economic activity, but rather to provide a useful reflection of agriculture as a field of study: a form of semantic warrant[13] based on what Bliss would call "scientific and educational consensus"[14] on the nature of agriculture and the most meaningful categories and divisions that can be made. Class S of LCC, therefore, is far more heterogeneous in its content and principles of subdivision than is Class 11 of NAICS. LCC exists to support a wide range of research and educational activities. NAICS has the purity and consistency of a system designed for one purpose only: the

TABLE 1. General Breakdown of Subclasses in SB and SD

	Plant Culture (SB)	Animal Culture (SF)
History	SB 1-87, incl. Horticultural voyages, etc. History	SF 1-55, incl. History
Methods	SB 107-130, incl. Irrigation Seeds Nurseries Propagation Training/Pruning Artificial light Hydroponics Forcing Growth regulators Harvesting	SF 84-121, incl. Rangelands Acclimatization Transportation Housing and environmental control Equipment and supplies Feeds and feeding Brands and branding Cost, yield, profit. Accounting Exhibitions
Types	SB 169-450.87, inc. Tree crops Food crops Field crops Horticulture Vegetables Fruit Flowers	SF 170-561, incl. Cattle Horses Donkeys Sheep Goats Swine Fur-bearing animals Laboratory animals Zoo animals Small animal culture Pets Birds Poultry Reptiles Bee culture Lac-insects
Related topics and activities	SB 450.9-998, incl. Gardens Landscape gardening Parks Pests and diseases Economic/agricultural zoology	SF600-1100 Veterinary medicine

classification of enterprises for purposes of compiling production statistics within countries, and harmonizing those statistics between countries. Although industrial codes have traditionally been used for many purposes–market research, investment analysis, journalism and job hunting–the designers warn us that none of these uses have been considered in the system design: "NAICS Canada has been designed for statistical purposes. Government departments and agencies and other users that use it for administrative, legislative and other non-statistical purposes, are responsible for interpreting the classification for the purpose or purposes for which they use it."[15]

REPRESENTING COUNTRIES IN NAICS AND LCC

How, then, do these two schemes–one designed for statistical purposes and the other for bibliographic organization–represent internationalist perspectives? How do they represent specific, named geographical regions and political jurisdictions, and how do they facilitate cross-comparison between those regions?

NAICS has no visible mechanism for representing countries within the classification scheme, for the simple reason that countries, or geographic region, are the subject of the classification in the first place. Unlike LCC, which is representing a subject area in which geographical emphasis provides a means of subdivision where needed, NAICS is designed to represent specific regions in terms of economic activity. By its very refusal to name specific countries and regions in its scheme, NAICS is inherently incapable of treating one country differently from another. There are no "10-number countries," "5-number countries" and "1-number countries" in NAICS as there are in LCC; every country has the same subdivisions, the same amount of hospitality, and the same range of notation for its economic activities.

Countries and regions *do* appear in LCC, and Class S provides ample places for arranging materials according to geographic emphasis. Because the LCC was designed on the principle of literary warrant, with the primary purpose of representing the national library of the United States, the system makes no bones about favouring the United States in its schedules. Frequently, the United States appears first in a sequence, followed by the rest of the world (see Figure 1).

In general, LCC provides two ways of subdividing geographically. First, it frequently provides references to the "Regions and Countries in One Alphabet," signalled in the schedules by such notes as "By region or country, A-Z." The Regions and Countries table is of general application across the different schedules, and collocates documents according to the country of emphasis, which is represented by a Cutter number (see Figure 1).

Second, LCC frequently provides tables of limited application with the specific schedule being used. In such cases, a range of numbers has been assigned to

FIGURE 1. Class S and the Alphabetical Listing of Countries

SB	PLANT CULTURE
	Vegetables
	History
320.5	General
	By region or country
320.6	United States
320.7.A-Z	By region or state, A-Z
320.8.A-Z	Other regions or countries, A-Z

a topic with geographical emphasis, and each country has been assigned a certain range of numbers within this broader range. These tables arrange countries according to geographic adjacency rather than alphabetical order, and they often assign a greater range of numbers to those countries that are heavily represented in the LC collection.

Supplementing these tables of specific application, LCC frequently provides a table of internal subarrangement, which allows for sophisticated and highly detailed subdivision within a country area according to standard topical subdivisions. The tables of internal subarrangement are relatively modest in Class S, but in H-HJ, they are frequent and detailed, enabling the documents relating to every country to be arranged in the same fashion.

The NAICS system, then, resembles the Tables of internal subarrangement in LCC. In both cases, the classification scheme provides a range of subdivisions that apply equally across the countries, so that the same topic appears in the same relative position regardless of the country context. Tables of internal subarrangement, however, are only used in complex cases; in most cases, at least with Class S, geographical treatments appear alphabetically by the name of the country.

COMPARING BIBLIOGRAPHIC AND STATISTICAL CLASSIFICATION SCHEMES: I

Let us return, then, to our first question: how does a statistical classification scheme differ from a bibliographic classification scheme in its representation of different countries, and what mechanism does each use to facilitate comparison and cross-analysis of common topics in different countries?

To answer the second part of the question first, bibliographic classification schemes like LCC traditionally use geographical locations as subdivisions of broader topics. Other schemes with more expressive notation, such as DDC and

UDC, use geographical location as a facet to be added on to a base number. Either way, the end user encounters international perspectives in bibliographic classification schemes as visible subdivisions of broader topical classes, and the schedules and tables ensure that documents with geographical emphasis are collocated in an intuitive and mnemonic fashion. Statistical schemes, like NAICS, incorporate the international perspective into their base assumptions: NAICS is essentially a statistical template that can be uniformly applied across numerous different countries and regions, for purposes of comparison and cross-analysis. As such, they resemble LCC's tables of internal subarrangement, in the way they ensure that each country's data will be arranged in the same fashion.

The primary difference in the two schemes can be found in their underlying assumptions of how the scheme is to be used. As Figure 2 illustrates, the bibliographic classification scheme envisions a universe of documents with information-bearing properties; the user assembles the necessary data from a variety of documents and puts the information to use.

Because the human being is navigating the information store and aggregating the information acquired, the classification scheme is structured in a way that is humanly comprehensible and useful: it reflects some degree of consensus on the shape and dimensions of the field, and, despite its nationalist bias, it presents an international coverage through some easily-understood order, either alphabetical or geographical.

A statistical classification scheme, as illustrated by Figure 3, envisions a universe of data rather than documents: data that can be sorted by country or region. Comparable data can be gathered from any or all of these countries or

FIGURE 2. Model of Use in a Bibliographic Classification System

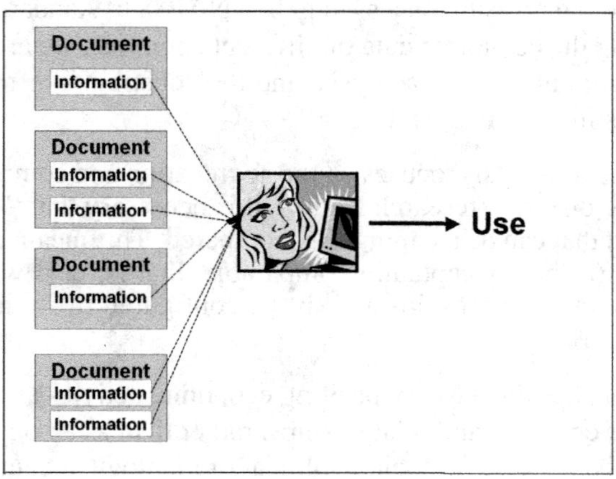

FIGURE 3. Model of Use in a Statistical Classification System

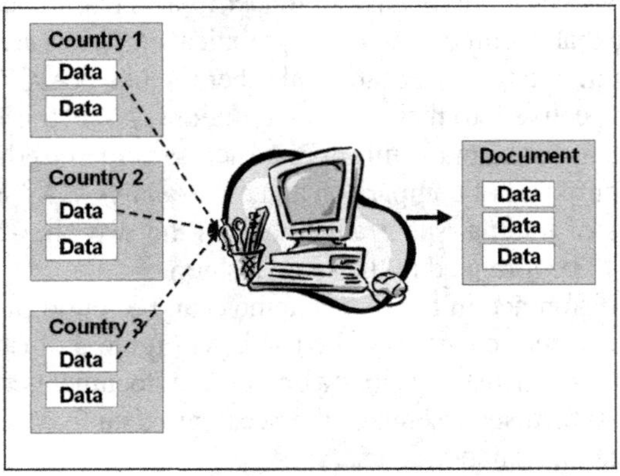

regions. However, the gathering is done by a system, rather than by the individual user, according to criteria, filters and limits that the user has specified. The appropriate data is then aggregated into a human-readable document.

COMPARING BIBLIOGRAPHIC AND STATISTICAL CLASSIFICATION SCHEMES: II

The difference between information aggregated by a human being and data collocated and presented automatically provides the key to understanding how the representation of geographical areas differs between bibliographic and statistical classification schemes. Because the actual system is doing the work, there is considerable pressure on a system like NAICS to standardize the data. When comparing the economic data of different countries, we are performing an action very similar to meta-analysis, and the constraints of meta-analysis hold for systems like NAICS as well:

> because meta-analysis focuses on the aggregation and comparison of the findings of different research studies, it is necessary that those findings be of a sort that can be meaningfully compared. This means that the findings must (a) be conceptually comparable, that is, deal with the same constructs and relationships and (b) be configured in similar statistical forms.[16]

NAICS accomplishes this task by positing economic activity as a universally applicable set of concepts and relationships, rather than as a body of data that has been shaped by a specific social, political or ideological context.

The difference between LCC and NAICS, therefore, can be partly defined as a difference in the choice of entities being subjected to data normalization. LCC seeks to represent the field of agriculture, both in its general characteristics and in geographical specificity. Schedule S is therefore patterned on a loose structure of History-Methods-Types-Other, with plenty of hospitality to ensure that the classification can do justice to scientific and educational consensus on the natural "shape" of agriculture as a field of study. Within this shape of agriculture, geographical emphasis is normalized in two separate fashions: through alphabetical order, and through geographical adjacency. The underlying picture is one of agriculture, and the international dimensions of this field are presented in a rigorously standardized fashion.

NAICS, on the other hand, is designed to represent the economic life of a particular country or region. Agriculture, as one sector of economic life, is subjected to the normalizing activity that, in LCC, placed countries in geographical or alphabetical order. In order to provide a coherent picture of a country that can be compared to pictures of other countries, each sector of the economy is standardized and abstracted from its specific geographical or political context.

This abstraction process in statistical classification gives rise to potential problems. To begin with, the regulation of economic data for purposes of harmonization and cross-country analysis opens NAICS to the same charges of "Procrusteanism" that have been levelled at the Dewey Decimal Classification (DDC). Dewey responded to charges that he was bending and breaking disciplines to fit his decimal scheme by arguing that such a process was necessary for efficiency: "A railroad also has the fault that it is Procrustean in its path and in its times. It cannot come to your door nor wait your convenience, as did the stage-coach or carriage; it cannot go to the fields for its loads of produce; it cannot turn out for obstacles; and it is simply because it is Procrustean that it can do its work so much better and quicker and cheaper."[17] NAICS has likewise enforced a consistent pattern upon economic sectors in the interests of consistency and efficiency.

This Procrustean efficiency carries costs. As others have noted, purity of classification concept does not translate into purity of results. By basing the classification on the economic activity of a single establishment, NAICS runs into problems with companies that operate multiple establishments engaged in many different activities, such as a bank that engages in both credit card issuing and insurance underwriting.[18] The real world is complicated, even at the level of statistical aggregation, and as quantitative researchers know through bitter experience, neat results are not always correct results.

Another potential cost lies in the economic activities that have been left out, or are relegated to "other" categories. Bowker and Star have characterized classifications as "universal master narratives,"[19] and the connection is apt in many ways. Chatman tells us that narratives make the world coherent by eliminating details, leaving the reader to fill in the gaps.[20] Bakhtin points out that many narratives set in the real world have characters that stand outside that world.[21] Like any classification scheme, NAICS has missed some activities entirely: illegal commerce, underground economies, housework.[22] Others lie in the "other" categories as testaments to human economic activity that no one knows what to do with: the cultivation of pregnant mares' urine (11292), or the manufacture of mouse pads (314990), cigarette papers (322299), drink powder mixes (31199) or toothpicks (321999). Every activity that a system discounts, or classifies as peripheral, has the potential to become important, and may have connections to other activities that belie its insignificant place in the scheme.

A third consequence lies in the differences between the abstract connections formed by the statistical data and the real connections formed in economic life. In the SIC 1980 code that preceded NAICS, the category for agriculture contained activities that, while not strictly agricultural, are deeply relevant to the agricultural community, such as agricultural research and veterinary services. The displacement of such activities into service sectors serves to separate establishments in the classification that are deeply related by geographic proximity, common interests and economic interdependence.[23]

NAICS, then, establishes an industrial classification that fosters inter-country comparison by enforcing standardized data collection. The classification, by its nature, implies that the economic activities of different countries can be extracted from their context, normalized by universal categories, and aggregated together to form meaningful pictures of economic life and accurate depictions of international economic relationships. But the abstraction required for harmonized data diminishes the context that makes the figures meaningful. Bibliographic classification systems provide an international perspective by allowing for visible national variations in broader fields: a transcendent area of inquiry is "dotted" throughout with documents that treat of regional and national variations. Statistical classification systems, on the other hand, provide an international perspective by effectively effacing the national perspective altogether, abstracting its categories from local contexts, and forcing its member countries to display their activities in a context-free, normalized world of data.

REFERENCES

1. Albrechtsen, Hanne and Jacob, Elin K. "Classification Systems as Boundary Objects in Diverse Information Ecologies." In *Advances in Classification Research. Vol. 8. Proceedings of the 8th ASIS SIG/CR Classification Research Workshop. Nov. 1-6, 1997. Washington, D.C.* edited by Efthimis N. Efthimiadis, Medford, N.J.: Information Today, 1998. pp 1-13.

2. Beghtol, Clare. "A Whole, Its Kinds, and Its Parts." In: *Dynamism and Stability in Knowledge Organization: Proceedings of the Sixth International ISKO Conference, 10-13 July 2000, Toronto, Canada.* edited by Clare Beghtol, Lynne C. Howarth, and Nancy J. Williamson. Wurzburg: Ergon, 2000. pp 313-319.

3. Barlow, Maude. "Globalization and the Dismantling of Canadian Democracy, Values and Society." *PCDForum* [Online]. March 10, 1996. [cited 20 June 2002]; available from http://iisd.ca/pcdf/1996/17barlow.htm.

4. Barber, Benjamin R. "Jihad vs. McWorld." *Atlantic Monthly* [Online]. March,1992. [cited 20 June 2002]; available from http://www.nancho.net/newchau/mcjihad.html.

5. O'Connor, Lisa. "Approaching the Challenges and Costs of the North American Industrial Classification System (NAICS)." *The Bottom Line: Managing Library Finance* 13(2) 2000: 83-90.

6. Triplett, Jack E., Kennet, D. Mark and Gollop, Frank M. "Do Industrial Classifications Need Re-Inventing? An Analysis of the Relevance of the U.S. SIC System for Productivity Research." *Advances in Classification Research. Vol. 6: Proceedings of the 6th ASIS SIG/CR Classification Research Workshop. Chicago, Ill., October 8, 1995.* ed. Raymond P. Schwartz, pp 127-138. Medford, N.J.: Information Today, 1998, p. 138.

7. Boettcher, Jennifer. "Challenges and Opportunities Presented by NAICS." *Journal of Business & Finance Librarianship* 5(2) 1999: 4.

8. Statistics Canada. *NAICS Canada Manual.* 1998 [Online]. [cited 25 March 2002]; available from http://www.statcan.ca/english/Subjects/Standard/.

9. as in 7.

10. Boettcher, Jennifer. "NAFTA Prompts a New Code System for Industry–the Death of SIC and Birth of NAICS." *Database* 19(2) 1996: 42-45.

11. Library of Congress. *Library of Congress Classification. S. Agriculture.* Washington, D.C.: Library of Congress, Cataloguing Distribution Service, 1996.

12. Statistics Canada. North American Industry Classification System (Canada). [Online]. [cited 29 November 2002]; available from http://www.statcan.ca/english/Subjects/Standard/1997/naics97-menu.htm.

13. Beghtol, Clare. "Semantic Validity: Concepts of Warrant in Bibliographic Classification Systems." *Library Resources & Technical Services*, 30(2) 1986: 109-125.

14. Bliss, Henry Evelyn. *The Organization of Knowledge in Libraries and the Subject Approach to Books.* New York: Wilson, 1936. p. 36.

15. Statistics Canada. *NAICS Canada Manual.* 1998. [Online]. [cited 25 March 2002]; available from http://www.statcan.ca/english/Subjects/Standard/.

16. Lipsey, Mark W. and Wilson, David B. *Practical Meta-Analysis.* London: Sage Publications, 2001. p. 2.

17. Dewey, Melvil. "Decimal Classification and Relativ Index: Introduction." In *Theory of Subject Analysis: A Sourcebook.* ed. Lois Mai Chan, Phyllis A. Richmond, and Elaine Svenonius. Littleton, Colo.: Libraries Unlimited, 1985: 23-34. p. 28.

18. Boettcher, Jennifer. "Challenges and Opportunities Presented by NAICS." *Journal of Business & Finance Librarianship* 5(2) 1999: 3-13. p. 7.

19. Bowker, Geoffrey C. and Star, Susan Leigh. *Sorting Things Out: Classification and Its Consequences.* Cambridge: MIT Press, 1999. p. 317.

20. Chatman, Seymour. *Story and Discourse: Narrative Structure in Fiction and Film.* Ithaca: Cornell University Press, 1978. p. 28.

21. Bakhtin, Mikhail. "Forms of Time and Chronotope in the Novel." *The Dialogic Imagination: Four Essays*. pp. 84-158. edited by Michael Holquist, trans. Caryl Emerson and Michael Holquist. Austin: University of Texas Press, 1981. p. 158.

22. Boettcher, Jennifer. "Challenges and Opportunities Presented by NAICS." *Journal of Business & Finance Librarianship* 5(2) 1999: 3-13. p. 6.

23. Campbell, D. Grant. "Chronotope and Classification: How Space-Time Configurations Affect the Gathering of Industrial Statistical Data." *Proceedings of the 2002 ISKO Conference. July 10-13. Granada, Spain.* edited by Maria Lopes Huertas. Wurzburg: Ergon, 2002.

Index

Numbers followed by *fig.* indicate figures; those followed by *n.* or *nn.* indicate note(s).

9780789023551